Multi-Core Programming

Increasing Performance through Software
Multi-threading

Shameem Akhter
Jason Roberts

Intel
PRESS

ISBN 0-9764832-4-6

Publisher: Richard Bowles
Editor: David J. Clark
Managing Editor: David B. Spencer
Content Architect: Stuart Goldstein
Text Design & Composition: Interactive Composition Corporation
Graphic Art: Kirsten Foote (illustrations), Ted Cyrek (cover)

Library of Congress Cataloging in Publication Data:

Printed in the United States of America

10 9 8 7 6 5 4 3 2 1

First printing, April 2006

To my beloved wife Munny and my parents.

—S.A.

To my mother.

—J.R.

Contents

Preface

By now, most technology professionals have heard of the radical transformation taking place in the way that modern computing platforms are being designed. Intel, IBM, Sun, and AMD have all introduced microprocessors that have multiple execution cores on a single chip. In 2005, consumers had the opportunity to purchase desktop platforms, servers, and game consoles that were powered by CPUs that had multiple execution cores. Future product roadmaps show that this is only the beginning; rather than racing towards being the first to 10 gigahertz, semiconductor manufacturers are now working towards the goal of leading the industry in the number of execution cores integrated onto a single die. In the future, computing platforms, whether they are desktop, mobile, server, or specialized embedded platforms are most likely to be multi-core in nature.

The fact that the hardware industry is moving in this direction presents new opportunities for software developers. Previous hardware platforms presented a sequential programming model to the programmer. Operating systems and other system software simulated multitasking environments by exploiting the speed, or lack thereof, of human perception. As a result, multi-threading was an effective illusion. With modern multi-core architectures, developers are now presented with a truly parallel computing platform. This affords software developers a great deal more power in terms of the ways that they design and implement their software. In this book, we'll take a look at a variety of topics that are relevant to writing software for multi-core platforms.

Intended Audience

Our primary objective is to provide the material software developers need to implement software effectively and efficiently on parallel hardware platforms. These platforms include multi-core processors and processors that use simultaneous multi-threading techniques, such as Hyper-Threading Technology (HT Technology). This book will focus on programming techniques that allow the developer to exploit the capabilities provided by the underlying hardware platform. We hope to reach as broad an audience as possible. In an effort to accomplish this, we've included introductory material on basic threading concepts for those new to multi-threaded programming. However, parallel programming is a complex subject, one with many different approaches and philosophies. Our intent, and challenge, is to provide a comprehensive discussion of the hardware capabilities provided by multi-core processors and platforms using simultaneous multi-threading techniques without getting lost in the different academic arguments about whether or not a particular approach is the optimal solution to the problem of writing reliable, easy to maintain, parallel programs. References to the definitive works on these topics, as they are introduced in the text, are included for readers who want to explore these topics in more detail.

We assume that the reader is an experienced programmer with little to no background in multi-threaded programming techniques. This may be an overly cautious assumption; many developers reading this text have probably used threads when writing applications designed to run on a single-core platform, are familiar with the basic principles of multi-threaded programming, and have knowledge of at least one threading API. However, it's important to remember the key differences when writing applications targeting single-core, multi-core, and platforms with simultaneous multi-threading technology. These differences are discussed in this book. For this reason, we have chosen to start from the beginning, highlighting these differences in the appropriate sections. The authors do assume that the reader is familiar with at least one high-level language, preferably C/C++. However, many of the suggestions made in this book apply equally to languages such as Java and Perl. We hope this approach accomplishes our goal of making this book relevant to as wide an audience as possible.

About This Book

This book is organized into three major sections. The first section (Chapters 1–4) presents an introduction to software threading. This section includes background material on why chipmakers have shifted to multi-core architectures, how threads work, how to measure the performance improvements achieved by a particular threading implementation, programming paradigms for parallel hardware platforms, and abstract data types used when working with threads. After completing these chapters, the reader should have a sense of the reasons why hardware platforms are evolving in the way that they are and understand the basic principles required to write parallel programs.

The next section of the book (Chapters 5 and 6) discusses common programming APIs for writing parallel programs. We look at three programming interfaces: Microsoft's APIs for Win32, MFC, and .NET; POSIX Threads; and OpenMP. We recognize that a large number of different APIs and programming models are available to developers. However, given the constraints of time and space, we have chosen a representative sample of the most commonly used APIs today.

The third and final section is a collection of topics related to multi-core programming. Chapter 7 discusses common parallel programming problems and how to solve them. Chapter 8 examines the topic of debugging multi-threaded implementations. Chapter 9 provides an introduction or review of hardware fundamentals, and Chapter 10 follows this up with an in-depth discussion of multi-core processors at the hardware level. In Chapter 11, we talk about the software tools developed by Intel that help software developers write, debug, and profile multi-threaded applications.

Finally, it should be noted that all of the Windows[†] based samples provided with this book were compiled and built with Microsoft's Visual Studio[†] 2005. These applications were tested using Microsoft XP with Service Pack 2 installed. For Linux[†], the gcc compiler was used and the examples were tested on Linux 2.6. All OpenMP examples were compiled using the latest Intel[®] C++ Compiler. For the code samples, updates, errata, and additional material, please visit the book's Web site: http://www.intel.com/intelpress/mcp.

Intel[®] Software Development Products

As you'll see throughout the text, and especially in Chapter 11, Intel provides more than just multi-core processors. In addition to the hardware platform, Intel has a number of resources for software developers, including a comprehensive tool suite for threading that includes:

■ Intel C++ and Fortran compilers, which support multi-threading by providing OpenMP and automatic parallelization support

- Intel Math Kernel Library and Intel Integrated Performance Primitives that are threaded via OpenMP

- Intel VTune™ Performance Analyzer, which can be used to monitor processor events related to multi-threaded performance

- Intel Thread Checker and the Intel Debugger, which help debug common multi-threaded problems like deadlocks

- Intel Thread Profiler, which helps developers optimize OpenMP, Microsoft Windows, and POSIX-based multi-threaded applications

In addition to tools, the Intel Software Network is focused on working with software vendors around the world to help develop and deploy production applications. The Intel Software Network consists of a number of different resources. One of these resources is a detailed knowledge base of whitepapers and articles written by Intel architects that share key insights on technology, including optimal threading techniques. The Intel Software Network also includes user discussion forums where you can interact with Intel engineers to discuss all things related to technology. The Intel Software College provides training courses in a variety of formats, including Webcasts, online training, and classroom-based training. These classes discuss a wide variety of topics including multi-threaded programming. Intel Solution Services provides consulting services for companies looking to get expert advice on a challenging technical issue.

To start exploring the online resources available to developers targeting multi-core platforms, visit Intel's multi-core homepage at: http://www.intel.com/multi-core/.

Acknowledgements

This book is the culmination of the efforts of a number of talented individuals. There are many people that need to be recognized. We'd like to start off with the list of contributors that developed content for this book. Chapter 6, "OpenMP[†]: A Portable Solution for Threading" was written by Xinmin Tian. Chapter 7, "Solutions to Common Parallel Programming Problems," was written by Arch Robison. Finally, James Reinders, with contributions by Eric Moore and Gordon Saladino, developed Chapter 11, "Intel Software Development Products." Other contributors who developed material for this book include: Sergey Zheltov, Stanislav Bratanov, Eugene Gorbatov, and Cameron McNairy.

No Intel Press book is published without peer review. We'd like to thank all the reviewers for identifying errors and for providing valuable insight and encouragement along the way. Without their help, this book would not have been a success. From Intel, these individuals participated, at one time or another, in the review of this project: Andy Anderson, Jeff Austin, Ernie Brickell, Daniel Brown, Doris Burrill, Stephen Chao, Brad Corrion, Jim Cownie, David Grawrock, Gerard Hartnett, William Holt, James Howard, Bob Kuhn, Tim Mattson, My-Hanh Nguyen, Paul Petersen, James Reinders, Arch Robison, Thom Sawicki, Sanjiv Shah, Xinmin Tian, Kimberly Turner, Richard Uhlig, Greg Welch, Paul Work, and Sergey Zheltov. Other reviewers included Andrew Binstock of Pacific Data Works, LLC, Thomas Kinsman of Eastman Kodak, and Hari Kalva, Assistant Professor at Florida Atlantic University.

Finally, we'd like to thank the team from Intel Press. Stuart Goldstein was the content architect for this project—his steady guidance and ability to find resources as we needed them kept this book on track. David Clark was the editor on the project, and helped take our engineering prose and turn it into a real book. David Spencer was involved in the early stages of this project, getting us started on the right foot.

For anyone that we may have missed, please accept our apologies.

Chapter 1

Introduction to Multi-Core Architecture

In 1945, mathematician John von Neumann, with the aid of J. Presper Eckert and John Mauchly, wrote a memo proposing the creation of an Electronic Discrete Variable Automatic Computer, more famously known as the EDVAC. In this paper, von Neumann suggested the stored-program model of computing. In the von Neumann architecture, a program is a sequence of instructions stored sequentially in the computer's memory. The program's instructions are executed one after the other in a linear, single-threaded fashion.

As time went on, advancements in mainframe technology expanded upon the ideas presented by von Neumann. The 1960s saw the advent of time-sharing operating systems. Run on large mainframe computers, these operating systems first introduced the concept of concurrent program execution. Multiple users could access a single mainframe computer simultaneously and submit jobs for processing. From the program's perspective, it was the only process in the system. The operating system handled the details of allocating CPU time for each individual program. At this time, concurrency existed at the process level, and the job of task switching was left to the systems programmer.

In the early days of personal computing, personal computers, or PCs, were standalone devices with simple, single-user operating systems. Only one program would run at a time. User interaction occurred via simple text based interfaces. Programs followed the standard model of straight-line instruction execution proposed by the von Neumann architecture. Over time, however, the exponential growth in computing performance quickly led to more sophisticated computing platforms. Operating system vendors used the advance in CPU and graphics performance to develop more sophisticated user environments. Graphical User Interfaces, or GUIs, became standard and enabled users to start and run multiple programs in the same user environment. Networking on PCs became pervasive.

This rapid growth came at a price: increased user expectations. Users expected to be able to send e-mail while listening to streaming audio that was being delivered via an Internet radio station. Users expected their computing platform to be quick and responsive. Users expected applications to start quickly and handle inconvenient background tasks, such as automatically saving a file with minimal disruption. These challenges are the problems that face software developers today.

Motivation for Concurrency in Software

Most end users have a simplistic view of complex computer systems. Consider the following scenario: A traveling businessman has just come back to his hotel after a long day of presentations. Too exhausted to go out, he decides to order room service and stay in his room to watch his favorite baseball team play. Given that he's on the road, and doesn't have access to the game on his TV, he decides to check out the broadcast via the Internet. His view of the system might be similar to the one shown in Figure 1.1.

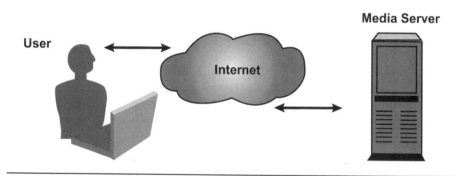

Figure 1.1   End User View of Streaming Multimedia Content via the Internet

The user's expectations are based on conventional broadcast delivery systems which provide continuous, uninterrupted delivery of content. The user does not differentiate between streaming the content over the Internet and delivering the data via a broadcast network. To the user, watching a baseball game on a laptop seems like a simple, straightforward task.

The reality is that the implementation of such a system is far more difficult. From the client side, the PC must be able to download the streaming video data, decompress/decode it, and draw it on the video display. In addition, it must handle any streaming audio that accompanies the video stream and send it to the soundcard. Meanwhile, given the general purpose nature of the computer, the operating system might be configured to run a virus scan or some other system tasks periodically. On the server side, the provider must be able to receive the original broadcast, encode/compress it in near real-time, and then send it over the network to potentially hundreds of thousands of clients. A system designer who is looking to build a computer system capable of streaming a Web broadcast might look at the system as it's shown in Figure 1.2.

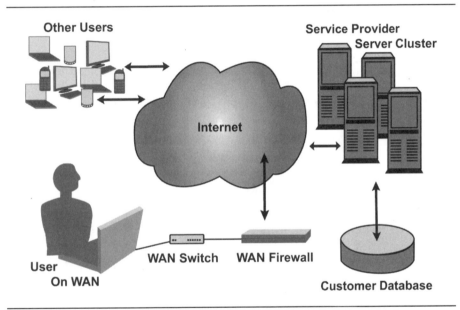

Figure 1.2 End-to-End Architecture View of Streaming Multimedia Content over the Internet

Contrast this view of a streaming multimedia delivery service with the end user's perspective of the system shown in Figure 1.1. In order to provide an acceptable end-user experience, system designers must be able to effectively manage many independent subsystems that operate in parallel.

Careful inspection of Figure 1.2 shows that the problem of streaming media content may be broken into a number of disparate parts; each acting independently[1] from one another. This decomposition allows us to break down each task into a single isolated problem, making the problem much more manageable.

Concurrency in software is a way to manage the sharing of resources used at the same time. Concurrency in software is important for several reasons:

- Concurrency allows for the most efficient use of system resources. Efficient resource utilization is the key to maximizing performance of computing systems. Unnecessarily creating dependencies on different components in the system drastically lowers overall system performance. In the aforementioned streaming media example, one might naively take this, serial, approach on the client side:

  1. Wait for data to arrive on the network

  2. Uncompress the data

  3. Decode the data

  4. Send the decoded data to the video/audio hardware

  This approach is highly inefficient. The system is completely idle while waiting for data to come in from the network. A better approach would be to stage the work so that while the system is waiting for the next video frame to come in from the network, the previous frame is being decoded by the CPU, thereby improving overall resource utilization.

- Many software problems lend themselves to simple concurrent implementations. Concurrency provides an abstraction for implementing software algorithms or applications that are naturally parallel. Consider the implementation of a simple FTP server. Multiple clients may connect and request different files. A single-threaded solution would require the application to keep track of all the different state information for each connection. A more intuitive implementation would create a separate thread for each connection. The connection state would be managed by this separate entity. This multi-threaded approach provides a solution that is much simpler and easier to maintain.

It's worth noting here that the terms *concurrent* and *parallel* are not interchangeable in the world of parallel programming. When multiple

---

[1] The term "independently" is used loosely here. Later chapters discuss the managing of interdependencies that is inherent in multi-threaded programming.

software threads of execution are running in parallel, it means that the active threads are running simultaneously on different hardware resources, or processing elements. Multiple threads may make progress simultaneously. When multiple software threads of execution are running concurrently, the execution of the threads is interleaved onto a single hardware resource. The active threads are ready to execute, but only one thread may make progress at a given point in time. In order to have parallelism, you must have concurrency exploiting multiple hardware resources.

Parallel Computing Platforms

In order to achieve parallel execution in software, hardware must provide a platform that supports the simultaneous execution of multiple threads. Generally speaking, computer architectures can be classified by two different dimensions. The first dimension is the number of *instruction streams* that a particular computer architecture may be able to process at a single point in time. The second dimension is the number of *data streams* that can be processed at a single point in time. In this way, any given computing system can be described in terms of how instructions and data are processed. This classification system is known as Flynn's taxonomy (Flynn, 1972), and is graphically depicted in Figure 1.3.

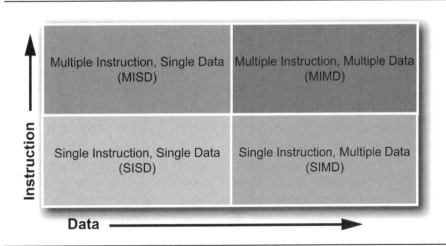

Figure 1.3 Flynn's Taxonomy

Flynn's taxonomy places computing platforms in one of four categories:

- A single instruction, single data (SISD) machine is a traditional sequential computer that provides no parallelism in hardware. Instructions are executed in a serial fashion. Only one data stream is processed by the CPU during a given clock cycle. Examples of these platforms include older computers such as the original IBM PC, older mainframe computers, or many of the 8-bit home computers such as the Commodore 64 that were popular in the early 1980s.

- A multiple instruction, single data (MISD) machine is capable of processing a single data stream using multiple instruction streams simultaneously. In most cases, multiple instruction streams need multiple data streams to be useful, so this class of parallel computer is generally used more as a theoretical model than a practical, mass-produced computing platform.

- A single instruction, multiple data (SIMD) machine is one in which a single instruction stream has the ability to process multiple data streams simultaneously. These machines are useful in applications such as general digital signal processing, image processing, and multimedia applications such as audio and video. Originally, supercomputers known as array processors or vector processors such as the Cray-1 provided SIMD processing capabilities. Almost all computers today implement some form of SIMD instruction set. Intel processors implement the MMX™, Streaming SIMD Extensions (SSE), Streaming SIMD Extensions 2 (SSE2), and Streaming SIMD Extensions 3 (SSE3) instructions that are capable of processing multiple data elements in a single clock. The multiple data elements are stored in the floating point registers. PowerPC[†] processors have implemented the AltiVec instruction set to provide SIMD support.

- A multiple instruction, multiple data (MIMD) machine is capable of is executing multiple instruction streams, while working on a separate and independent data stream. This is the most common parallel computing platform today. New multi-core platforms such as the Intel® Core™ Duo processor fall into this category.

Given that modern computing machines are either the SIMD or MIMD machines, software developers have the ability to exploit data-level and task level parallelism in software.

Parallel Computing in Microprocessors

In 1965, Gordon Moore observed that the number of transistors available to semiconductor manufacturers would double approximately every 18 to 24 months. Now known as Moore's law, this observation has guided computer designers for the past 40 years. Many people mistakenly think of Moore's law as a predictor of CPU clock frequency, and it's not really hard to understand why. The most commonly used metric in measuring computing performance is CPU clock frequency. Over the past 40 years, CPU clock speed has tended to follow Moore's law. It's an important distinction to make, however, as taking this view of Moore's law imposes unnecessary limits on a silicon designer. While improving straight-line instruction throughput and clock speeds are goals worth striving for, computer architects can take advantage of these extra transistors in less obvious ways.

For example, in an effort to make the most efficient use of processor resources, computer architects have used instruction-level parallelization techniques to improve processor performance. Instruction-level parallelism (ILP), also known as dynamic, or out-of-order execution, gives the CPU the ability to reorder instructions in an optimal way to eliminate pipeline stalls. The goal of ILP is to increase the number of instructions that are executed by the processor on a single clock cycle[2]. In order for this technique to be effective, multiple, independent instructions must execute. In the case of in-order program execution, dependencies between instructions may limit the number of instructions available for execution, reducing the amount of parallel execution that may take place. An alternative approach that attempts to keep the processor's execution units full is to reorder the instructions so that independent instructions execute simultaneously. In this case, instructions are executed out of program order. This dynamic instruction scheduling is done by the processor itself. You will learn much more about these techniques in a later chapter, but for now what is important to understand is that this parallelism occurs at the hardware level and is transparent to the software developer.

As software has evolved, applications have become increasingly capable of running multiple tasks simultaneously. Server applications today often consist of multiple threads or processes. In order to support this thread-level parallelism, several approaches, both in software and hardware, have been adopted.

---

[2] A processor that is capable of executing multiple instructions in a single clock cycle is known as a super-scalar processor.

One approach to address the increasingly concurrent nature of modern software involves using a preemptive, or time-sliced, multitasking operating system. Time-slice multi-threading allows developers to hide latencies associated with I/O by interleaving the execution of multiple threads. This model does not allow for parallel execution. Only one instruction stream can run on a processor at a single point in time.

Another approach to address thread-level parallelism is to increase the number of physical processors in the computer. Multiprocessor systems allow true parallel execution; multiple threads or processes run simultaneously on multiple processors. The tradeoff made in this case is increasing the overall system cost.

As computer architects looked at ways that processor architectures could adapt to thread-level parallelism, they realized that in many cases, the resources of a modern processor were underutilized. In order to consider this solution, you must first more formally consider what a thread of execution in a program is. A thread can be defined as a basic unit of CPU utilization. It contains a program counter that points to the current instruction in the stream. It contains CPU state information for the current thread. It also contains other resources such as a stack.

A physical processor is made up of a number of different resources, including the architecture state—the general purpose CPU registers and interrupt controller registers, caches, buses, execution units, and branch prediction logic. However, in order to define a thread, only the architecture state is required. A logical processor can thus be created by duplicating this architecture space. The execution resources are then shared among the different logical processors. This technique is known as *simultaneous multi-threading,* or SMT. Intel's implementation of SMT is known as Hyper-Threading Technology, or HT Technology. HT Technology makes a single processor appear, from software's perspective, as multiple logical processors. This allows operating systems and applications to schedule multiple threads to logical processors as they would on multiprocessor systems. From a microarchitecture perspective, instructions from logical processors are persistent and execute simultaneously on shared execution resources. In other words, multiple threads can be scheduled, but since the execution resources are shared, it's up to the microarchitecture to determine how and when to interleave the execution of the two threads. When one thread stalls, another thread is allowed to make progress. These stall events include handling cache misses and branch mispredictions.

The next logical step from simultaneous multi-threading is the multi-core processor. Multi-core processors use chip multiprocessing (CMP). Rather than just reuse select processor resources in a single-core processor, processor manufacturers take advantage of improvements in manufacturing technology to implement two or more "execution cores" within a single processor. These cores are essentially two individual processors on a single die. Execution cores have their own set of execution and architectural resources. Depending on design, these processors may or may not share a large on-chip cache. In addition, these individual cores may be combined with SMT; effectively increasing the number of logical processors by twice the number of execution cores. The different processor architectures are highlighted in Figure 1.4.

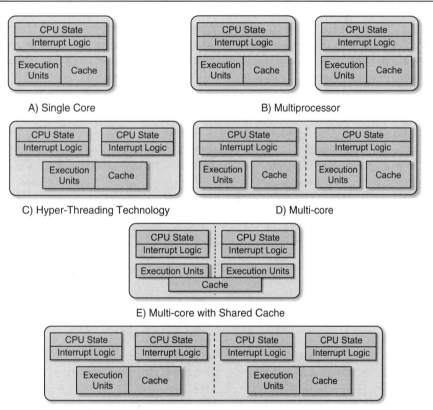

Figure 1.4   Simple Comparison of Single-core, Multi-processor, and Multi-Core Architectures

Differentiating Multi-Core Architectures from Hyper-Threading Technology

With HT Technology, parts of the one processor are shared between threads, while other parts are duplicated between them. One of the most important shared resources is the actual execution engine. This engine works on both threads at the same time by executing instructions for one thread on resources that the other thread is not using. When both threads are running, HT Technology literally interleaves the instructions in the execution pipeline. Which instructions are inserted when depends wholly on what execution resources of the processor are available at execution time. Moreover, if one thread is tied up reading a large data file from disk or waiting for the user to type on the keyboard, the other thread takes over all the processor resources—without the operating system switching tasks—until the first thread is ready to resume processing. In this way, each thread receives the maximum available resources and the processor is kept as busy as possible. An example of a thread running on a HT Technology enabled CPU is shown in Figure 1.5.

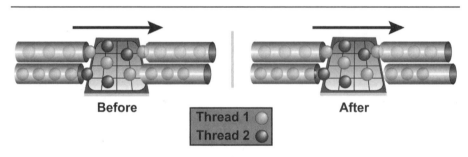

Before   Thread 1   **After**
             Thread 2

Figure 1.5   Two Threads Executing on a Processor with Hyper-Threading Technology

HT Technology achieves performance gains through latency hiding. Fundamentally, a single execution core is shared among multiple threads. Therefore, thread execution is not parallel. As a result, performance results vary based on application and hardware platform. With HT Technology, in certain applications, it is possible to attain, on average, a 30-percent increase in processor throughput. In other words, in certain cases, the processor can perform 1.3 times the number of executed instructions that it could if it were running only one thread. To see a performance improvement, applications must make good use of threaded programming models and of the capabilities of Hyper-Threading Technology.

The performance benefits of HT Technology depend on how much latency hiding can occur in your application. In some applications, developers may have minimized or effectively eliminated memory latencies through cache optimizations. In this case, optimizing for HT Technology may not yield any performance gains.

On the other hand, multi-core processors embed two or more independent execution cores into a single processor package. By providing multiple execution cores, each sequence of instructions, or thread, has a hardware execution environment entirely to itself. This enables each thread run in a truly parallel manner. An example of two threads running on a dual-core processor is shown in Figure 1.6. Compare this with the HT Technology example provided in Figure 1.5, and note that a dual-core processor provides true parallel execution of each thread.

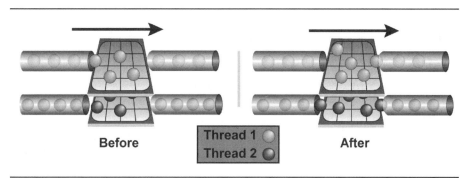

Figure 1.6   Two Threads on a Dual-Core Processor with each Thread Running Independently

It should be noted that HT Technology does not attempt to deliver multi-core performance, which can theoretically be close to a 100-percent, or 2x improvement in performance for a dual-core system. HT Technology is more of a facility in which the programmer may be able to use idle CPU resources in order to accomplish more work. When combined with multi-core technology, HT Technology can provide powerful optimization opportunities, increasing system throughput substantially.

Multi-threading on Single-Core versus Multi-Core Platforms

At this point, many readers may be asking themselves what all the commotion is about. The concept of multiple threads in a single process space has been around for decades. Most modern applications use threads in one fashion or another today. As a result, many developers are already familiar with the concept of threading, and have probably worked on applications that have multiple threads. There are however, certain important considerations developers should be aware of when writing applications targeting multi-core processors:

■ *Optimal application performance on multi-core architectures will be achieved by effectively using threads to partition software workloads.* Many applications today use threads as a tool to improve user responsiveness on single-core platforms. Rather than blocking the user interface (UI) on a time consuming database query or disk access, an application will spawn a thread to process the user's request. This allows the scheduler to individually schedule the main control loop task that receives UI events as well as the data processing task that is running the database query. In this model, developers rely on straight-line instruction throughput improvements to improve application performance.

This is the significant limitation of multi-threading on single-core processors. Since single-core processors are really only able to interleave instruction streams, but not execute them simultaneously, the overall performance gains of a multi-threaded application on single-core architectures are limited. On these platforms, threads are generally seen as a useful programming abstraction for hiding latency.

This performance restriction is removed on multi-core architectures. On multi-core platforms, threads do not have to wait for any one resource. Instead, threads run independently on separate cores. As an example, consider two threads that both wanted to execute a shift operation. If a core only had one "shifter unit" they could not run in parallel. On two cores, there would be two "shifter units," and each thread could run without contending for the same resource.

Multi-core platforms allow developers to optimize applications by intelligently partitioning different workloads on different processor cores. Application code can be optimized to use multiple processor resources, resulting in faster application performance.

■ *Multi-threaded applications running on multi-core platforms have different design considerations than do multi-threaded applications running on single-core platforms.* On single-core platforms, assumptions may be made by the developer to simplify writing and debugging a multi-threaded application. These assumptions may not be valid on multi-core platforms. Two areas that highlight these differences are *memory caching* and *thread priority*.

In the case of memory caching, each processor core may have its own cache.[3] At any point in time, the cache on one processor core may be out of sync with the cache on the other processor core. To help illustrate the types of problems that may occur, consider the following example. Assume two threads are running on a dual-core processor. Thread 1 runs on core 1 and thread 2 runs on core 2. The threads are reading and writing to neighboring memory locations. Since cache memory works on the principle of locality, the data values, while independent, may be stored in the same cache line. As a result, the memory system may mark the cache line as invalid, even though the data that the thread is interested in hasn't changed. This problem is known as *false sharing*. On a single-core platform, there is only one cache shared between threads; therefore, cache synchronization is not an issue.

Thread priorities can also result in different behavior on single-core versus multi-core platforms. For example, consider an application that has two threads of differing priorities. In an attempt to improve performance, the developer assumes that the higher priority thread will always run without interference from the lower priority thread. On a single-core platform, this may be valid, as the operating system's scheduler will not yield the CPU to the lower priority thread. However, on multi-core platforms, the scheduler may schedule both threads on separate cores. Therefore, both threads may run simultaneously. If the developer had optimized the code to assume that the higher priority thread would always run without interference from the lower priority thread, the code would be unstable on multi-core and multi-processor systems.

One goal of this book is to help developers correctly utilize the number of processor cores they have available.

Understanding Performance

At this point one may wonder—how do I measure the performance benefit of parallel programming? Intuition tells us that if we can subdivide disparate tasks and process them simultaneously, we're likely

---

[3] Multi-core CPU architectures can be designed in a variety of ways: some multi-core CPUs will share the on-chip cache between execution units; some will provide a dedicated cache for each execution core; and others will take a hybrid approach, where the cache is subdivided into layers that are dedicated to a particular execution core and other layers that are shared by all execution cores. For the purposes of this section, we assume a multi-core architecture with a dedicated cache for each core.

to see significant performance improvements. In the case where the tasks are completely independent, the performance benefit is obvious, but most cases are not so simple. How does one quantitatively determine the performance benefit of parallel programming? One metric is to compare the elapsed run time of the best sequential algorithm versus the elapsed run time of the parallel program. This ratio is known as the speedup and characterizes how much faster a program runs when parallelized.

$$\text{Speedup}(n_t) = \frac{Time_{best\_sequential\_algorithm}}{Time_{parallel\_implementation}(n_t)}$$

Speedup is defined in terms of the number of physical threads (n_t) used in the parallel implementation.

Amdahl's Law

Given the previous definition of speedup, is there a way to determine the theoretical limit on the performance benefit of increasing the number of processor cores, and hence physical threads, in an application? When examining this question, one generally starts with the work done by Gene Amdahl in 1967. His rule, known as Amdahl's Law, examines the maximum theoretical performance benefit of a parallel solution relative to the best case performance of a serial solution.

Amdahl started with the intuitively clear statement that program speedup is a function of the fraction of a program that is accelerated and by how much that fraction is accelerated.

$$\text{Speedup} = \frac{1}{(1 - Fraction_{Enhanced}) + (Fraction_{Enhanced}/Speedup_{Enhanced})}$$

So, if you could speed up half the program by 15 percent, you'd get:

$$\text{Speedup} = 1/((1 - .50) + (.50/1.15)) = 1/(.50 + .43) = 1.08$$

This result is a speed increase of 8 percent, which is what you'd expect. If half of the program is improved 15 percent, then the whole program is improved by half that amount.

Amdahl then went on to explain how this equation works out if you make substitutions for fractions that are parallelized and those that are run serially, as shown in Equation 1.1.

Equation 1.1   Amdahl's Law

$$\text{Speedup} = \frac{1}{S + (1 - S)/n}$$

In this equation, S is the time spent executing the serial portion of the parallelized version and n is the number of processor cores. Note that the numerator in the equation assumes that the program takes 1 unit of time to execute the best sequential algorithm.

If you substitute 1 for the number of processor cores, you see that no speedup is realized. If you have a dual-core platform doing half the work, the result is:

$$1 / (0.5S + 0.5S/2) = 1/0.75S = 1.33$$

or a 33-percent speed-up, because the run time, as given by the denominator, is 75 percent of the original run time. For an 8-core processor, the speedup is:

$$1 / (0.5S + 0.5S/8) = 1/0.75S = 1.78$$

Setting n = ∞ in Equation 1.1, and assuming that the best sequential algorithm takes 1 unit of time yields Equation 1.2.

Equation 1.2   Upper Bound of an Application with S Time Spent in Sequential Code

$$\text{Speedup} = \frac{1}{S}$$

As stated in this manner, Amdahl assumes that the addition of processor cores is perfectly scalable. As such, this statement of the law shows the maximum benefit a program can expect from parallelizing some portion of the code is limited by the serial portion of the code. For example, according Amdahl's law, if 10 percent of your application is spent in serial code, the maximum speedup that can be obtained is 10x, regardless of the number of processor cores.

It is important to note that endlessly increasing the processor cores only affects the parallel portion of the denominator. So, if a program is only 10-percent parallelized, the maximum theoretical benefit is that the program can run in 90 percent of the sequential time.

Given this outcome, you can see the first corollary of Amdahl's law: decreasing the serialized portion by increasing the parallelized portion is of greater importance than adding more processor cores. For example, if you have a program that is 30-percent parallelized running on a dual-core system, doubling the number of processor cores reduces run time from 85 percent of the serial time to 77.5 percent, whereas doubling the amount of parallelized code reduces run time from 85 percent to 70 percent. This is illustrated in Figure 1.7. Only when a program is mostly parallelized does adding more processors help more than parallelizing the remaining code. And, as you saw previously, you have hard limits on how much code can be serialized and on how many additional processor cores actually make a difference in performance.

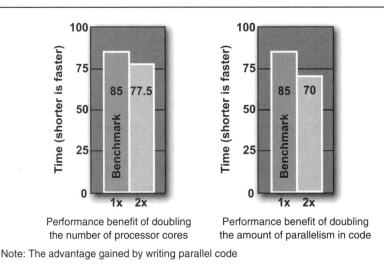

Performance benefit of doubling the number of processor cores

Performance benefit of doubling the amount of parallelism in code

Note: The advantage gained by writing parallel code

Figure 1.7   Theoretical Performance Comparison between Increasing Number of CPU Cores versus Increasing Concurrency in Implementation

To make Amdahl's Law reflect the reality of multi-core systems, rather than the theoretical maximum, system overhead from adding threads should be included:

$$\text{Speedup} = \frac{1}{S + (1-S)/n + H(n)}$$

where H(n) = overhead, and again, we assume that the best serial algorithm runs in one time unit. Note that this overhead is not linear on a good parallel machine.

This overhead consists of two portions: the actual operating system overhead and inter-thread activities, such as synchronization and other forms of communication between threads. Notice that if the overhead is big enough, it offsets the benefits of the parallelized portion. In fact, if the overhead is large enough, the speedup ration can ultimately have a value of less than 1, implying that threading has actually slowed performance when compared to the single-threaded solution. This is very common in poorly architected multi-threaded applications. The important implication is that the overhead introduced by threading must be kept to a minimum. For this reason, most of this book is dedicated to keeping the cost of threading as low as possible.

Amdahl's Law Applied to Hyper-Threading Technology

The previous section demonstrated Amdahl's law as it applies to multi-processor and multi-core systems. Hyper-Threading Technology imposes an additional factor on how you apply Amdahl's Law to your code. On processors enabled with HT Technology, the fact that certain processor resources are shared between the different threads of execution has a direct effect on the maximum performance benefit of threading an application.

Given the interleaved execution environment provided by HT Technology, it's important to develop a form of Amdahl's law that works for HT Technology. Assume that your application experiences a performance gain of around 30 percent when run on a processor with HT Technology enabled. That is, performance improves by 30 percent over the time required for a single processor to run both threads. If you were using a quad-core platform, with each processor completely dedicated to the thread it was running, the number could, in theory, be up to 4x. That is, the second, third, and fourth processor core could give a 300-percent boost to program throughput. In practice it's not quite 300 percent, due to overhead and code that cannot be parallelized, and the performance benefits will vary based on the application.

Inside the processor enabled with HT Technology, each thread is running more slowly than it would if it had the whole processor to itself. HT Technology is not a replacement for multi-core processing since many processing resources, such as the execution units, are shared. The slowdown varies from application to application. As example, assume each thread runs approximately one-third slower than it would if it owned the entire processor. Amending Amdahl's Law to fit HT Technology, then, you get:

$$\text{Speedup}_{\text{HTT}} = \frac{1}{S + 0.67((1-S)/n) + H(n)}$$

where n = number of logical processors.

This equation represents the typical speed-up for programs running on processor cores with HT Technology performance. The value of H(n) is determined empirically and varies from application to application.

Growing Returns: Gustafson's Law

Based on Amdahl's work, the viability of massive parallelism was questioned for a number of years. Then, in the late 1980s, at the Sandia National Lab, impressive linear speedups in three practical applications were observed on a 1,024-processor hypercube. The results (Gustafson 1988) demonstrated that near linear speedup was possible in many practical cases, even when Amdahl's Law predicted otherwise.

Built into Amdahl's Law are several assumptions that may not hold true in real-world implementations. First, Amdahl's Law assumes that the best performing serial algorithm is strictly limited by the availability of CPU cycles. This may not be the case. A multi-core processor may implement a separate cache on each core. Thus, more of the problem's data set may be stored in cache, reducing memory latency. The second flaw is that Amdahl's Law assumes that the serial algorithm is the best possible solution for a given problem. However, some problems lend themselves to a more efficient parallel solution. The number of computational steps may be significantly less in the parallel implementation.

Perhaps the biggest weakness, however, is the assumption that Amdahl's Law makes about the problem size. Amdahl's Law assumes that as the number of processor cores increases, the problem size stays the same. In most cases, this is not valid. Generally speaking, when given more computing resources, the problem generally grows to meet the resources available. In fact, it is more often the case that the run time of the application is constant.

Based on the work at Sandia, an alternative formulation for speedup, referred to as scaled speedup was developed by E. Barsis.

$$\text{Scaled speedup} = N + (1-N)^* s$$

where N = is the number of processor cores and s is the ratio of the time spent in the serial port of the program versus the total execution time.

Scaled speedup is commonly referred to as Gustafson's Law. From this equation, one can see that the speedup in this case is linear.

Gustafson's Law has been shown to be equivalent to Amdahl's Law (Shi 1996). However, Gustafson's Law offers a much more realistic look at the potential of parallel computing on multi-core processors.

Key Points

This chapter demonstrated the inherent concurrent nature of many software applications and introduced the basic need for parallelism in hardware. An overview of the different techniques for achieving parallel execution was discussed. Finally, the chapter examined techniques for estimating the performance benefits of using proper multi-threading techniques. The key points to keep in mind are:

- Concurrency refers to the notion of multiple threads in progress at the same time. This is often achieved on sequential processors through interleaving.

- Parallelism refers to the concept of multiple threads executing simultaneously.

- Modern software applications often consist of multiple processes or threads that can be executed in parallel.

- Most modern computing platforms are multiple instruction, multiple data (MIMD) machines. These machines allow programmers to process multiple instruction and data streams simultaneously.

- In practice, Amdahl's Law does not accurately reflect the benefit of increasing the number of processor cores on a given platform. Linear speedup is achievable by expanding the problem size with the number of processor cores.

Chapter 2

System Overview
of Threading

W hen implemented properly, threading can enhance performance by making better use of hardware resources. However, the improper use of threading can lead to degraded performance, unpredictable behavior, and error conditions that are difficult to resolve. Fortunately, if you are equipped with a proper understanding of how threads operate, you can avoid most problems and derive the full performance benefits that threads offer. This chapter presents the concepts of threading starting from hardware and works its way up through the operating system and to the application level.

To understand threading for your application you need to understand the following items:

- The design approach and structure of your application
- The threading application programming interface (API)
- The compiler or runtime environment for your application
- The target platforms on which your application will run

From these elements, a threading strategy can be formulated for use in specific parts of your application.

Since the introduction of instruction-level parallelism, continuous advances in the development of microprocessors have resulted in processors with multiple cores. To take advantage of these multi-core processors you must understand the details of the software threading model as well as the capabilities of the platform hardware.

You might be concerned that threading is difficult and that you might have to learn specialized concepts. While it's true in general, in reality threading can be simple, once you grasp the basic principles.

Defining Threads

A *thread* is a discrete sequence of related instructions that is executed independently of other instruction sequences. Every program has at least one thread—the main thread—that initializes the program and begins executing the initial instructions. That thread can then create other threads that perform various tasks, or it can create no new threads and simply do all the work itself. In either case, every program has at least one thread. Each thread maintains its current machine state.

At the hardware level, a thread is an execution path that remains independent of other hardware thread execution paths. The operating system maps software threads to hardware execution resources as described later in this chapter

The decision to thread your application should reflect the needs of the program and the basic execution capabilities of the deployment platform. Not everything should be threaded. Too much threading can hurt performance. As with many aspects of programming, thoughtful design and proper testing determine the right balance.

System View of Threads

The thread computational model is represented in Figure 2.1. As illustrated, there are three layers for threading:

- *User-level threads*. Threads created and manipulated in the application software.
- *Kernel-level threads*. The way the operating system implements most threads.
- *Hardware threads*. How threads appear to the execution resources in the hardware.

A single program thread frequently involves all three levels: a program thread is implemented by the operating system as a kernel-level thread, and executed as a hardware thread.

Between these layers are interfaces, which are frequently handled automatically by the executing system. However, to make good use of threading resources, it's important to know how these interfaces work.

They are touched on in this chapter and treated in greater detail in Chapters 3, 4, and 5.

Figure 2.1   Computation Model of Threading

Threading above the Operating System

Developers can best understand the problems they face using threads if they know what actually takes place when threads are used in an application. In applications that do not rely on a runtime framework, the thread creation code is made as a call to system APIs. These calls are then executed at runtime as calls to the operating system kernel to create a thread. The instructions for the thread's activity are then passed to the processor for execution. Figure 2.2 shows the thread flow in a typical system for traditional applications. In the Defining and Preparing stage, threads are specified by the programming environment and encoded by the compiler. During the Operating stage, threads are created and managed by the operating system. Finally, in the Executing stage, the processor executes the sequence of thread instructions.

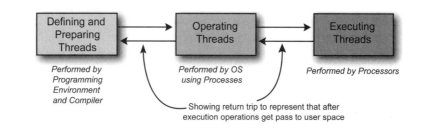

Figure 2.2   Flow of Threads in an Execution Environment

The application code might rely on a runtime environment. Such code, known as *managed code* runs in an environment that performs some application functions and makes calls the underlying operating system. Managed environments include both Java Virtual Machine (JVM) and Microsoft's Common Language Runtime (CLR). These environments do not provide any scheduling capability, relying instead on the operating system for scheduling. Threading is passed to the operating system scheduler, which handles the remaining downstream thread activity.

In general, application threads can be implemented at the application level using established APIs. The most common APIs are OpenMP[†] and explicit low-level threading libraries such as Pthreads and Windows threads. The choice of API depends on the requirements and the system platform. In general, low-level threading requires significantly more code than solutions such as OpenMP; the benefit they deliver, however, is fine-grained control over the program's use of threads. OpenMP, in contrast, offers ease of use and a more developer-friendly threading implementation. OpenMP requires a compiler that supports the OpenMP API. Today, these are limited to C/C++ and Fortran compilers. Coding low-level threads requires only access to the operating system's multi-threading libraries. For further details on OpenMP, Pthreads, and Windows threads, see Chapters 5 and 6.

To show how threading is used in a program, Listing 2.1 and Listing 2.2 are simple "Hello World" programs that use the OpenMP and Pthreads libraries, respectively.

```
#include <stdio.h>
// Have to include 'omp.h' to get OpenMP definitons
#include <omp.h>
void main()
{
    int threadID, totalThreads;
 /* OpenMP pragma specifies that following block is
    going to be parallel and the threadID variable is
    private in this openmp block. */

    #pragma omp parallel private(threadID)
    {
        threadID = omp_get_thread_num();
        printf("\nHello World is from thread %d\n",
            (int)threadID);
          /* Master thread has threadID = 0 */
        if (threadID == 0) {
            printf("\nMaster thread being called\n");
            totalThreads = omp_get_num_threads();
```

```
        printf("Total number of threads are %d\n",
               totalThreads);
        }
    }
}
```

Listing 2.1   "Hello World" Program Using OpenMP

```
#include <pthread.h>
#include <stdio.h>
#include <stdlib.h>
#define NUM_THREADS      5

void *PrintHello(void *threadid)
{
   printf("\n%d: Hello World!\n", threadid);
   pthread_exit(NULL);
}

int main(int argc, char *argv[])
{
   pthread_t threads[NUM_THREADS];
   int rc, t;
   for (t=0; t < NUM_THREADS; t++) {
      printf("Creating thread %d\n", t);
      rc = pthread_create( &threads[t], NULL,
                           PrintHello,(void *)t);
      if (rc) {
        printf("ERROR return code from pthread_create(): %d\n",
               rc);
        exit(-1);
      }
   }
   pthread_exit(NULL);
}
```

Listing 2.2   "Hello World" Program Using Pthreads

As can be seen, the OpenMP code in Listing 2.1 has no function that corresponds to thread creation. This is because OpenMP creates threads automatically in the background. Explicit low-level coding of threads is more evident in Pthreads, shown in Listing 2.2, where a call to pthread_create() actually creates a single thread and points it at the work to be done in PrintHello().

Threads inside the OS

The key to viewing threads from the perspective of a modern operating system is to recognize that operating systems are partitioned into two distinct layers: the user-level partition (where applications are run) and the kernel-level partition (where system oriented activities occur). Figure 2.3 shows these partitions along with other components. This figure shows the interface between application layer and the kernel-level operating system, referred to as system libraries. These contain the necessary operating-system components that can be run with user-level privilege. As illustrated, the interface between the operating system and the processor is the hardware abstraction layer (HAL).

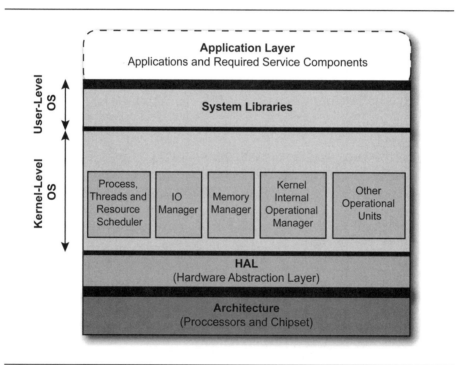

Figure 2.3   Different Layers of the Operating System

The *kernel* is the nucleus of the operating system and maintains tables to keep track of processes and threads. The vast majority of thread-level activity relies on kernel-level threads. Threading libraries such as OpenMP and Pthreads (POSIX standard threads) use kernel-level threads. Windows supports both kernel-level and user-level threads. User-level threads, which are called *fibers* on the Windows platform, require the programmer to create the entire management infrastructure for the threads and to manually schedule their execution. Their benefit is that the developer can manipulate certain details that are obscured in kernel-level threads. However, because of this manual overhead and some additional limitations, fibers might not add much value for well designed multi-threaded applications.

Kernel-level threads provide better performance, and multiple kernel threads from the same process can execute on different processors or cores. The overhead associated with kernel-level threading is higher than user-level threading and so kernel-level threads are frequently reused once they have finished their original work.

Processes are discrete program tasks that have their own address space. They are the coarse-level execution unit maintained as an independent entity inside an operating system. There is a direct correlation between processes and threads. Multiple threads can reside in a process. All threads in a process share the same address space and so they benefit from simple inter-thread communication. Instead of maintaining an individual process-based thread list, the kernel maintains a thread table to keep track of all threads. The operating system assigns a process control block (PCB) to each process; it contains data on the process's unique identity, current machine state, the priority of the process, and the address of the virtual memory where the process resides.

Figure 2.4 shows the relationship between processors, processes, and threads in modern operating systems. A processor runs threads from one or more processes, each of which contains one or more threads.

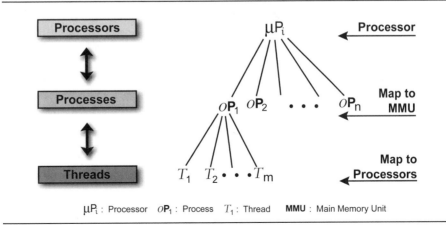

μP_i : Processor oP_1 : Process T_1 : Thread   **MMU** : Main Memory Unit

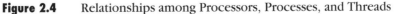

Figure 2.4   Relationships among Processors, Processes, and Threads

A program has one or more processes, each of which contains one or more threads, each of which is mapped to a processor by the scheduler in the operating system. A concept known as *processor affinity* enables the programmer to request mapping of a specific thread to a specific processor. Most operating systems today attempt to obey these requests, but they do not guarantee fulfillment.

Various mapping models are used between threads and processors: one to one (1:1), many to one (M:1), and many to many (M:N), as shown in Figure 2.5. The 1:1 model requires no thread-library scheduler overhead and the operating system handles the thread scheduling responsibility. This is also referred to as *preemptive multi-threading*. Linux, Windows 2000, and Windows XP use this preemptive multi-threading model. In the M:1 model, the library scheduler decides which thread gets the priority. This is called *cooperative multi-threading*. In the case of M:N, the mapping is flexible.

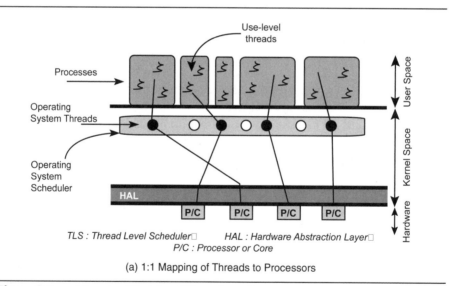

TLS : Thread Level Scheduler   HAL : Hardware Abstraction Layer
P/C : Processor or Core

(a) 1:1 Mapping of Threads to Processors

Figure 2.5   Mapping Models of Threads to Processors

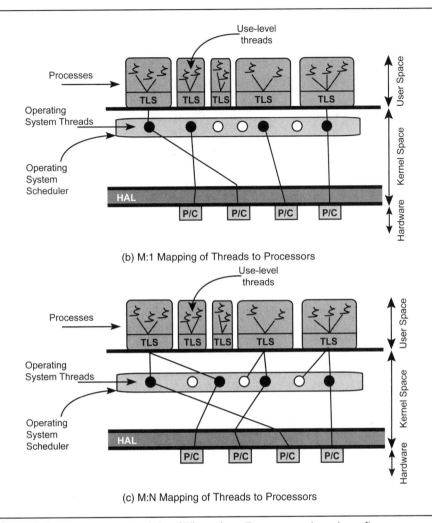

(b) M:1 Mapping of Threads to Processors

(c) M:N Mapping of Threads to Processors

Figure 2.5   Mapping Models of Threads to Processors (continued)

User-level threads such as those in Windows are mapped to kernel threads; and so, when they are executing, the processor knows them only as kernel-level threads.

In general, a preemptive or 1:1 model enables stronger handling of the threads by the operating system. This book focuses only on Windows and Linux and so it emphasizes this mode. For other operating systems, see the References section.

Threads inside the Hardware

The hardware executes the instructions from the software levels. Instructions of your application threads are mapped to resources and flow down through the intermediate components—the operating system, runtime environment, and virtual layer—to the hardware.

Threading on hardware once required multiple CPUs to implement parallelism: each thread ran on its own separate processor. Today, processors with Hyper-Threading Technology (HT Technology) and multiple cores provide multi-threading on a single processor. These multi-threaded processors allow two or more threads of execution to run on a single CPU at the same time. This CPU might have only one execution engine or core but share the pipeline and other hardware resources among the executing threads. Such processing would be considered *concurrent* but not parallel; Figure 2.6 illustrates this difference.

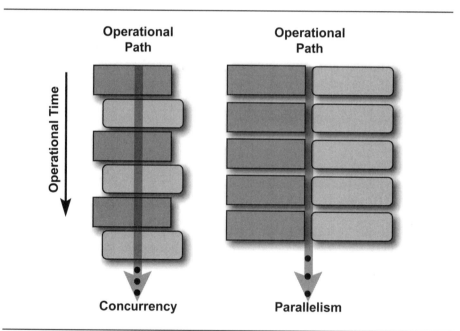

Figure 2.6   Concurrency versus Parallelism

Multi-core CPUs, however, provide two or more execution cores, and so they deliver true hardware-based multi-threading. Because both threads execute on the same processor, this design is sometimes referred to as *chip multi-threading* (CMT). By contrast, HT Technology uses a single core in which two threads share most of the execution resources. This approach is called *simultaneous multi-threading* (SMT). SMT uses a hardware scheduler to manage different hardware threads that are in need of resources. The number of hardware threads that can execute simultaneously is an important consideration in the design of software; to achieve true parallelism, the number of active program threads should always equal the number of available hardware threads. In most cases, program threads will exceed the available hardware threads. However, too many software threads can slow performance. So, keeping a balance of software and hardware threads delivers good results.

What Happens When a Thread Is Created

As discussed earlier, there can be more than one thread in a process; and each of those threads operates independently, even though they share the same address space and certain resources, such as file descriptors. In addition, each thread needs to have its own stack space. These stacks are usually managed by the operating system. Figure 2.7 shows a typical stack representation of a multi-threaded process. As an application developer, you should not have to worry about the details of stack management, such as thread stack sizes or thread stack allocation. On the other hand, system-level developers must understand the underlying details. If you want to use threading in your application, you must be aware of the operating system's limits. For some applications, these limitations might be restrictive, and in other cases, you might have to bypass the default stack manager and manage stacks on your own. The default stack size for a thread varies from system to system. That is why creating many threads on some systems can slow performance dramatically.

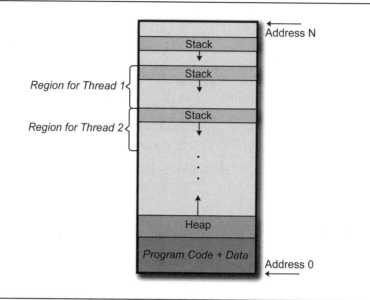

Figure 2.7 Stack Layout in a Multi-threaded Process

Once created, a thread is always in one of four states: ready, running, waiting (blocked), or terminated. There are additional *sub*-states that reflect various reasons for entering one of the four basic states. These finer sub-states can be valuable in debugging or analyzing a threaded application.

Every process has at least one thread. This *initial thread* is created as part of the process initialization. Application threads you create will run while the initial thread continues to execute. As indicated in the state diagram in Figure 2.8, each thread you create starts in a ready state. Afterwards, when the new thread is attempting to execute instructions, it is either in the running state or blocked. It is blocked if it is waiting for a resource or for another thread. When a thread has completed its work, it is either terminated or put back by the program into the ready state. At program termination, the main thread and subsidiary threads are terminated.

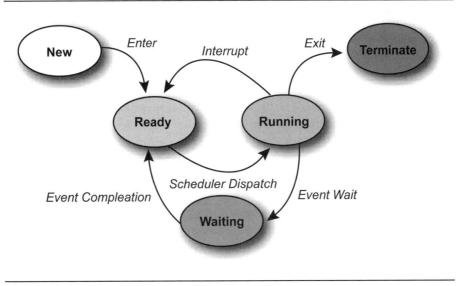

Figure 2.8   State Diagram for a Thread

Application Programming Models and Threading

Threads are used liberally by the operating system for its own internal activities so even if you write a single-threaded application, your runtime setup will be heavily threaded. All major programming languages today support the use of threads, whether those languages are imperative (C, Fortran, Pascal, Ada), object-oriented (C++, Java, C#), functional (Lisp, Miranda, SML), or logical (Prolog).

Virtual Environment: VMs and Platforms

One of the most important trends in computing today is virtualization. Virtualization is the process of using computing resources to create the appearance of a different set of resources. Runtime virtualization, such as found in the Java JVM, creates the appearance to a Java application that it is running in its own private environment or machine. System virtualization creates the appearance of a different kind of virtual machine, in which there exists a complete and independent instance of the operating system. Both forms of virtual environments make effective use of threads internally.

Runtime Virtualization

The operation of runtime virtualization is being provided by runtime virtual machine. These virtual machines (VMs) can be considered as a container and executor application on top of an operating system. There are two mainstream VMs in use today: the Java VM and Microsoft's Common Language Runtime (CLR) that were discussed previously. These VMs, for example, create at least three threads: the executing thread, a garbage-collection thread that frees memory blocks that are no longer in use, and a thread for just-in-time (JIT) compilation of bytecodes into executable binary code. The VMs generally create other threads for internal tasks. The VM and the operating system work in tandem to map these threads to the available execution resources in a way that will benefit performance as much as possible.

System Virtualization

System virtualization creates a different type of virtual machine. These VMs recreate a complete execution context for software: they use virtualized network adapters and disks and run their own instance of the operating system. Several such VMs can run on the same hardware platform, each with its separate operating system. The virtualization layer that sits between the host system and these VMs is called the *virtual machine monitor* (VMM). The VMM is also known as the hypervisor. Figure 2.9 compares systems running a VMM with one that does not.

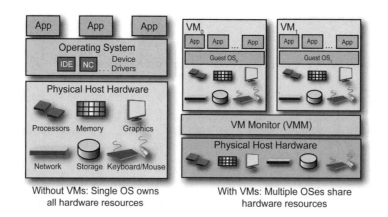

Figure 2.9   Comparison of Systems without and with a VMM

A VMM delivers the necessary virtualization of the underlying platform such that the operating system in each VM runs under the illusion that it owns the entire hardware platform.

When virtualizing the underlying hardware, VM software makes use of a concept called virtual processors. It presents as many virtual processors to the guest operating system as there are cores on the actual host hardware. HT Technology does not change the number of virtual processors, only cores count. One of the important benefits of processor virtualization is that it can create isolation of the instruction-set architecture (ISA). Certain processor instructions can be executed only by the operating system because they are privileged instructions. On today's Intel processors, only one piece of software—the host operating system—has this level of privilege. The VMM and the entire VM run as applications. So, what happens when one of the guest operating systems needs to run a privileged instruction? This instruction is trapped by the virtual processor in the VM and a call is made to the VMM. In some cases, the VMM can handle the call itself, in others it must pass the call on to the host operating system, wait for the response and emulate that response in the virtual processor. By this means, the VMM manages to sidestep the execution of privileged instructions.

However, this process has a distinct performance cost associated with it. As a result, Intel has developed a series of extensions to the ISA that provide efficient ways for VMMs to execute the privileged instructions of guest operating systems. These extensions are part of Intel® Virtualization Technology, and are designed to improve the performance of VMMs.

Mapping Application Threads

VMMs do very little unusual to handle application threads. When an application running in a VM creates a thread, the thread creation and subsequent scheduling is all handled by the guest operating system. The VMM does not need to know about it. When the guest operating system schedules the thread, the virtual processor executes the instructions using the same methods it executes any other sequence instructions. The VMM makes no attempt to match application threads to specific processor cores or to second-guess the guest operating system's scheduler. So, on a system with a dual-core processor, for example, the VMM presents two virtual processors to the guest operating system. That OS then schedules threads on those processors as it would if it were running on the actual hardware. The VMM executes the instructions but pays little notice to what application threads are running.

The only time the VMM interrupts this process is when it needs to swap out a VM or perform internal tasks. In such a case, several issues can arise. For example, when a VMM is running multiple guest VMs, it has to time-slice between them. Suppose a thread is locked and waiting for a thread running on a different virtual processor when that other processor is swapped out. The original VM will encounter a substantial delay that would not occur if both VMs had been running on their own dedicated hardware systems. This problem, known as *lock-holder preemption*, is one of several that arise from the fact that guest VM resources must be swapped out at times and the exact state of all threads might not expect this situation. However, as virtualization becomes more widely adopted, it's likely that operating systems will offer features that assist VMMs to coordinate this kind of activity.

Key Points

The concepts of threading depend on an understanding of the interaction of various system components.

■ To properly comprehend the impact of threading, it is important to understand the impact of threads on system components.

■ Software threads are different than hardware threads, but maintain a direct relationship.

■ Application threading can be implemented using APIs or multi-threading libraries.

■ Processes, threads, and fibers are different levels of the execution mechanism within a system.

■ The thread life cycle has four stages: ready, running, waiting (blocked), and terminated.

■ There are two types of virtualization on a system: runtime virtualization and system virtualization.

■ A virtual machine monitor (VMM) typically makes no attempt to match application threads to specific processor cores or to second-guess the guest operating system's scheduler.

Chapter 3

Fundamental Concepts of Parallel Programming

As discussed in previous chapters, parallel programming uses threads to enable multiple operations to proceed simultaneously. The entire concept of parallel programming centers on the design, development, and deployment of threads within an application and the coordination between threads and their respective operations. This chapter examines how to break up programming tasks into chunks that are suitable for threading. It then applies these techniques to the apparently serial problem of error diffusion.

Designing for Threads

Developers who are unacquainted with parallel programming generally feel comfortable with traditional programming models, such as object-oriented programming (OOP). In this case, a program begins at a defined point, such as the `main()` function, and works through a series of tasks in succession. If the program relies on user interaction, the main processing instrument is a loop in which user events are handled. From each allowed event—a button click, for example, the program performs an established sequence of actions that ultimately ends with a wait for the next user action.

When designing such programs, developers enjoy a relatively simple programming world because only one thing is happening at any given moment. If program tasks must be scheduled in a specific way, it's because the developer imposes a certain order on the activities. At any point in the process, one step generally flows into the next, leading up to a predictable conclusion, based on predetermined parameters.

To move from this linear model to a parallel programming model, designers must rethink the idea of process flow. Rather than being constrained by a sequential execution sequence, programmers should identify those activities that can be executed in parallel. To do so, they must see their programs as a set of tasks with dependencies between them. Breaking programs down into these individual tasks and identifying dependencies is known as *decomposition*. A problem may be decomposed in several ways: by task, by data, or by data flow. Table 3.1 summarizes these forms of decomposition. As you shall see shortly, these different forms of decomposition mirror different types of programming activities.

Table 3.1   Summary of the Major Forms of Decomposition

Decomposition	Design	Comments
Task	Different activities assigned to different threads	Common in GUI apps
Data	Multiple threads performing the same operation but on different blocks of data	Common in audio processing, imaging, and in scientific programming
Data Flow	One thread's output is the input to a second thread	Special care is needed to eliminate startup and shutdown latencies

Task Decomposition

Decomposing a program by the functions that it performs is called *task decomposition*. It is one of the simplest ways to achieve parallel execution. Using this approach, individual tasks are catalogued. If two of them can run concurrently, they are scheduled to do so by the developer. Running tasks in parallel this way usually requires slight modifications to the individual functions to avoid conflicts and to indicate that these tasks are no longer sequential.

If we were discussing gardening, task decomposition would suggest that gardeners be assigned tasks based on the nature of the activity: if two gardeners arrived at a client's home, one might mow the lawn while the other weeded. Mowing and weeding are separate functions broken out as such. To accomplish them, the gardeners would make sure to have some coordination between them, so that the weeder is not sitting in the middle of a lawn that needs to be mowed.

In programming terms, a good example of task decomposition is word processing software, such as Microsoft Word[†]. When the user opens a very long document, he or she can begin entering text right away. While the user enters text, document pagination occurs in the background, as one can readily see by the quickly increasing page count that appears in the status bar. Text entry and pagination are two separate tasks that its programmers broke out by function to run in parallel. Had programmers not designed it this way, the user would be obliged to wait for the entire document to be paginated before being able to enter any text. Many of you probably recall that this wait was common on early PC word processors.

Data Decomposition

Data decomposition, also known as *data-level parallelism*, breaks down tasks by the data they work on rather than by the nature of the task. Programs that are broken down via data decomposition generally have many threads performing the same work, just on different data items. For example, consider recalculating the values in a large spreadsheet. Rather than have one thread perform all the calculations, data decomposition would suggest having two threads, each performing half the calculations, or n threads performing $1/n^{th}$ the work.

If the gardeners used the principle of data decomposition to divide their work, they would both mow half the property and then both weed half the flower beds. As in computing, determining which form of decomposition is more effective depends a lot on the constraints of the system. For example, if the area to mow is so small that it does not need two mowers, that task would be better done by just one gardener—that is, task decomposition is the best choice—and data decomposition could be applied to other task sequences, such as when the mowing is done and both gardeners begin weeding in parallel.

As the number of processor cores increases, data decomposition allows the problem size to be increased. This allows for more work to be done in the same amount of time. To illustrate, consider the gardening example. Two more gardeners are added to the work crew. Rather than assigning all four gardeners to one yard, we can we can assign the two new gardeners to another yard, effectively increasing our total problem size. Assuming that the two new gardeners can perform the same amount of work as the original two, and that the two yard sizes are the same, we've doubled the amount of work done in the same amount of time.

Data Flow Decomposition

Many times, when decomposing a problem, the critical issue isn't what tasks should do the work, but how the data flows between the different tasks. In these cases, data flow decomposition breaks up a problem by how data flows between tasks.

The *producer/consumer* problem is a well known example of how data flow impacts a programs ability to execute in parallel. Here, the output of one task, the producer, becomes the input to another, the consumer. The two tasks are performed by different threads, and the second one, the consumer, cannot start until the producer finishes some portion of its work.

Using the gardening example, one gardener prepares the tools—that is, he puts gas in the mower, cleans the shears, and other similar tasks— for both gardeners to use. No gardening can occur until this step is mostly finished, at which point the true gardening work can begin. The delay caused by the first task creates a pause for the second task, after which both tasks can continue in parallel. In computer terms, this particular model occurs frequently.

In common programming tasks, the producer/consumer problem occurs in several typical scenarios. For example, programs that must rely on the reading of a file fit this scenario: the results of the file I/O become the input to the next step, which might be threaded. However, that step cannot begin until the reading is either complete or has progressed sufficiently for other processing to kick off. Another common programming example is parsing: an input file must be parsed, or analyzed semantically, before the back-end activities, such as code generation in a compiler, can begin.

The producer/consumer problem has several interesting dimensions:

■ The dependence created between consumer and producer can cause significant delays if this model is not implemented correctly. A performance-sensitive design seeks to understand the exact nature of the dependence and diminish the delay it imposes. It also aims to avoid situations in which consumer threads are idling while waiting for producer threads.

■ In the ideal scenario, the hand-off between producer and consumer is completely clean, as in the example of the file parser. The output is context-independent and the consumer has no need to know anything about the producer. Many times, however, the producer and consumer components do not enjoy such a clean division of labor, and scheduling their interaction requires careful planning.

■ If the consumer is finishing up while the producer is completely done, one thread remains idle while other threads are busy working away. This issue violates an important objective of parallel processing, which is to balance loads so that all available threads are kept busy. Because of the logical relationship between these threads, it can be very difficult to keep threads equally occupied.

In the next section, we'll take a look at the pipeline pattern that allows developers to solve the producer/consumer problem in a scalable fashion.

Implications of Different Decompositions

Different decompositions provide different benefits. If the goal, for example, is ease of programming and tasks can be neatly partitioned by functionality, then task decomposition is more often than not the winner. Data decomposition adds some additional code-level complexity to tasks, so it is reserved for cases where the data is easily divided and performance is important.

The most common reason for threading an application is performance. And in this case, the choice of decompositions is more difficult. In many instances, the choice is dictated by the problem domain: some tasks are much better suited to one type of decomposition. But some tasks have no clear bias. Consider for example, processing images in a video stream. In formats with no dependency between frames, you'll have a choice of decompositions. Should they choose task decomposition, in which one thread does decoding, another color balancing, and so on, or data decomposition, in which each thread does all the work on one frame and then moves on to the next? To return to the analogy of the gardeners, the decision would take this form: If two gardeners need to mow two lawns and weed two flower beds, how should they proceed? Should one gardener only mow—that is, they choose task based decomposition—or should both gardeners mow together then weed together?

In some cases, the answer emerges quickly—for instance when a resource constraint exists, such as only one mower. In others where each gardener has a mower, the answer comes only through careful analysis of the constituent activities. In the case of the gardeners, task decomposition looks better because the start-up time for mowing is saved if only one mower is in use. Ultimately, you determine the right answer for your application's use of parallel programming by careful planning and testing. The empirical timing and evaluation plays a more significant role in the design choices you make in parallel programming than it does in standard single-threaded programming.

Challenges You'll Face

The use of threads enables you to improve performance significantly by allowing two or more activities to occur simultaneously. However, developers cannot fail to recognize that threads add a measure of complexity that requires thoughtful consideration to navigate correctly. This complexity arises from the inherent fact that more than one activity is occurring in the program. Managing simultaneous activities and their possible interaction leads you to confronting four types of problems:

- *Synchronization* is the process by which two or more threads coordinate their activities. For example, one thread waits for another to finish a task before continuing.

- *Communication* refers to the bandwidth and latency issues associated with exchanging data between threads.

- *Load balancing* refers to the distribution of work across multiple threads so that they all perform roughly the same amount of work.

- *Scalability* is the challenge of making efficient use of a larger number of threads when software is run on more-capable systems. For example, if a program is written to make good use of four processor cores, will it scale properly when run on a system with eight processor cores?

Each of these issues must be handled carefully to maximize application performance. Subsequent chapters describe many aspects of these problems and how best to address them on multi-core systems.

Parallel Programming Patterns

For years object-oriented programmers have been using design patterns to logically design their applications. Parallel programming is no different than object-oriented programming—parallel programming problems generally fall into one of several well known patterns. A few of the more common parallel programming patterns and their relationship to the aforementioned decompositions are shown in Table 3.2.

Table 3.2   Common Parallel Programming Patterns

Pattern	Decomposition
Task-level parallelism	Task
Divide and Conquer	Task/Data
Geometric Decomposition	Data
Pipeline	Data Flow
Wavefront	Data Flow

In this section, we'll provide a brief overview of each pattern and the types of problems that each pattern may be applied to.

- *Task-level Parallelism Pattern*. In many cases, the best way to achieve parallel execution is to focus directly on the tasks themselves. In this case, the task-level parallelism pattern makes the most sense. In this pattern, the problem is decomposed into a set of tasks that operate independently. It is often necessary remove dependencies between tasks or separate dependencies using replication. Problems that fit into this pattern include the so-called *embarrassingly parallel* problems, those where there are no dependencies between threads, and *replicated data* problems, those where the dependencies between threads may be removed from the individual threads.

- *Divide and Conquer Pattern*. In the divide and conquer pattern, the problem is divided into a number of parallel sub-problems. Each sub-problem is solved independently. Once each sub-problem is solved, the results are aggregated into the final solution. Since each sub-problem can be independently solved, these sub-problems may be executed in a parallel fashion.

- The divide and conquer approach is widely used on sequential algorithms such as merge sort. These algorithms are very easy to parallelize. This pattern typically does a good job of load balancing and exhibits good locality; which is important for effective cache usage.

- *Geometric Decomposition Pattern*. The geometric decomposition pattern is based on the parallelization of the data structures used in the problem being solved. In geometric decomposition, each thread is responsible for operating on data 'chunks'. This pattern may be applied to problems such as heat flow and wave propagation.

■ *Pipeline Pattern*. The idea behind the pipeline pattern is identical to that of an assembly line. The way to find concurrency here is to break down the computation into a series of stages and have each thread work on a different stage simultaneously.

■ *Wavefront Pattern*. The wavefront pattern is useful when processing data elements along a diagonal in a two-dimensional grid. This is shown in Figure 3.1

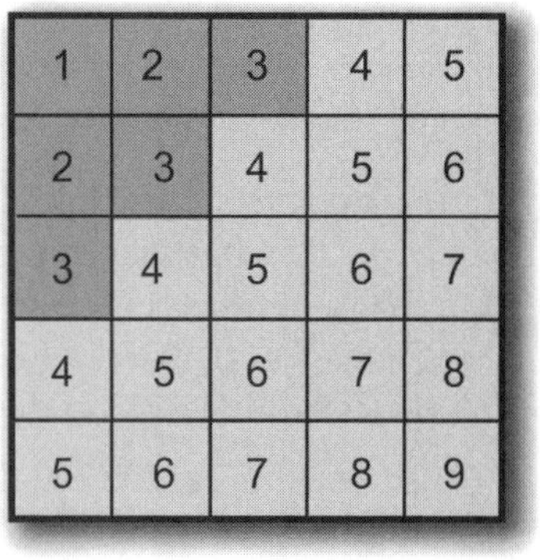

Figure 3.1   Wavefront Data Access Pattern

The numbers in Figure 3.1 illustrate the order in which the data elements are processed. For example, elements in the diagonal that contains the number "3" are dependent on data elements "1" and "2" being processed previously. The shaded data elements in Figure 3.1 indicate data that has already been processed. In this pattern, it is critical to minimize the idle time spent by each thread. Load balancing is the key to success with this pattern.

For a more extensive and thorough look at parallel programming design patterns, refer to the book *Patterns for Parallel Programming* (Mattson 2004).

A Motivating Problem: Error Diffusion

To see how you might apply the aforementioned methods to a practical computing problem, consider the error diffusion algorithm that is used in many computer graphics and image processing programs. Originally proposed by Floyd and Steinberg (Floyd 1975), *error diffusion* is a technique for displaying continuous-tone digital images on devices that have limited color (tone) range. Printing an 8-bit grayscale image to a black-and-white printer is problematic. The printer, being a bi-level device, cannot print the 8-bit image natively. It must simulate multiple shades of gray by using an approximation technique. An example of an image before and after the error diffusion process is shown in Figure 3.2. The original image, composed of 8-bit grayscale pixels, is shown on the left, and the result of the image that has been processed using the error diffusion algorithm is shown on the right. The output image is composed of pixels of only two colors: black and white.

Original 8-bit image on the left, resultant 2-bit image on the right. At the resolution of this printing, they look similar.

The same images as above but zoomed to 400 percent and cropped to 25 percent to show pixel detail. Now you can clearly see the 2-bit black-white rendering on the right and 8-bit gray-scale on the left.

Figure 3.2   Error Diffusion Algorithm Output

The basic error diffusion algorithm does its work in a simple three-step process:

1. Determine the output value given the input value of the current pixel. This step often uses quantization, or in the binary case, thresholding. For an 8-bit grayscale image that is displayed on a 1-bit output device, all input values in the range [0, 127] are to be displayed as a 0 and all input values between [128, 255] are to be displayed as a 1 on the output device.

2. Once the output value is determined, the code computes the error between what should be displayed on the output device and what is actually displayed. As an example, assume that the current input pixel value is 168. Given that it is greater than our threshold value (128), we determine that the output value will be a 1. This value is stored in the output array. To compute the error, the program must normalize output first, so it is in the same scale as the input value. That is, for the purposes of computing the display error, the output pixel must be 0 if the output pixel is 0 or 255 if the output pixel is 1. In this case, the display error is the difference between the actual value that should have been displayed (168) and the output value (255), which is –87.

3. Finally, the error value is distributed on a fractional basis to the neighboring pixels in the region, as shown in Figure 3.3.

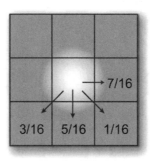

Figure 3.3   Distributing Error Values to Neighboring Pixels

This example uses the Floyd-Steinberg error weights to propagate errors to neighboring pixels. 7/16ths of the error is computed and added to the pixel to the right of the current pixel that is being processed. 5/16ths of the error is added to the pixel in the next row, directly below the current pixel. The remaining errors propagate in a similar fashion. While you can use other error weighting schemes, all error diffusion algorithms follow this general method.

The three-step process is applied to all pixels in the image. Listing 3.1 shows a simple C implementation of the error diffusion algorithm, using Floyd-Steinberg error weights.

```
/*****************************************
 * Initial implementation of the error diffusion algorithm.
 *****************************************/
void error_diffusion(unsigned int width,
                     unsigned int height,
                     unsigned short **InputImage,
                     unsigned short **OutputImage)
{
    for (unsigned int i = 0; i < height; i++)
    {
        for (unsigned int j = 0; j < width; j++)
        {
            /* 1. Compute the value of the output pixel*/
            if (InputImage[i][j] < 128)
                OutputImage[i][j] = 0;
            else
                OutputImage[i][j] = 1;

            /* 2. Compute the error value */
            int err = InputImage[i][j] - 255*OutputImage[i][j];

            /* 3. Distribute the error */
            InputImage[i][j+1]   += err * 7/16;
            InputImage[i+1][j-1] += err * 3/16;
            InputImage[i+1][j]   += err * 5/16;
            InputImage[i+1][j+1] += err * 1/16;
        }
    }
}
```

Listing 3.1   C-language Implementation of the Error Diffusion Algorithm

Analysis of the Error Diffusion Algorithm

At first glance, one might think that the error diffusion algorithm is an inherently serial process. The conventional approach distributes errors to neighboring pixels as they are computed. As a result, the previous pixel's error must be known in order to compute the value of the next pixel. This interdependency implies that the code can only process one pixel at a time. It's not that difficult, however, to approach this problem in a way that is more suitable to a multithreaded approach.

An Alternate Approach: Parallel Error Diffusion

To transform the conventional error diffusion algorithm into an approach that is more conducive to a parallel solution, consider the different decomposition that were covered previously in this chapter. Which would be appropriate in this case? As a hint, consider Figure 3.4, which revisits the error distribution illustrated in Figure 3.3, from a slightly different perspective.

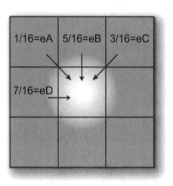

In this case, we look at the error propagation from the perspective of the receiving pixel.

Figure 3.4   Error-Diffusion Error Computation from the Receiving Pixel's Perspective

Given that a pixel may not be processed until its spatial predecessors have been processed, the problem appears to lend itself to an approach where we have a producer—or in this case, multiple producers—producing data (error values) which a consumer (the current pixel) will use to compute the proper output pixel. The flow of error data to the current pixel is critical. Therefore, the problem seems to break down into a data-flow decomposition.

Now that we identified the approach, the next step is to determine the best pattern that can be applied to this particular problem. Each independent thread of execution should process an equal amount of work (load balancing). How should the work be partitioned? One way, based on the algorithm presented in the previous section, would be to have a thread that processed the even pixels in a given row, and another thread that processed the odd pixels in the same row. This approach is ineffective however; each thread will be blocked waiting for the other to complete, and the performance could be worse than in the sequential case.

To effectively subdivide the work among threads, we need a way to reduce (or ideally eliminate) the dependency between pixels. Figure 3.4 illustrates an important point that's not obvious in Figure 3.3—that in order for a pixel to be able to be processed, it must have three error values (labeled eA, eB, and eC[1] in Figure 3.3) from the previous row, and one error value from the pixel immediately to the left on the current row. Thus, once these pixels are processed, the current pixel may complete its processing. This ordering suggests an implementation where each thread processes a row of data. Once a row has completed processing of the first few pixels, the thread responsible for the next row may begin its processing. Figure 3.5 shows this sequence.

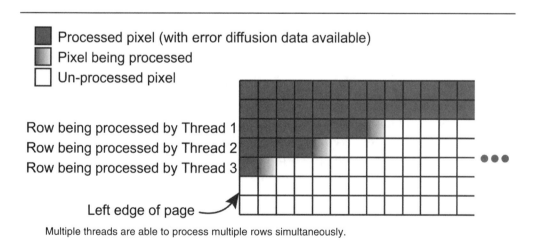

Multiple threads are able to process multiple rows simultaneously.

Figure 3.5   Parallel Error Diffusion for Multi-thread, Multi-row Situation

---

[1] We assume eA = eD = 0 at the left edge of the page (for pixels in column 0); and that eC = 0 at the right edge of the page (for pixels in column W-1, where W = the number of pixels in the image).

Notice that a small latency occurs at the start of each row. This latency is due to the fact that the previous row's error data must be calculated before the current row can be processed. These types of latency are generally unavoidable in producer-consumer implementations; however, you can minimize the impact of the latency as illustrated here. The trick is to derive the proper workload partitioning so that each thread of execution works as efficiently as possible. In this case, you incur a two-pixel latency before processing of the next thread can begin. An 8.5" X 11" page, assuming 1,200 dots per inch (dpi), would have 10,200 pixels per row. The two-pixel latency is insignificant here.

The sequence in Figure 3.5 illustrates the data flow common to the wavefront pattern.

Other Alternatives

In the previous section, we proposed a method of error diffusion where each thread processed a row of data at a time. However, one might consider subdividing the work at a higher level of granularity. Instinctively, when partitioning work between threads, one tends to look for independent tasks. The simplest way of parallelizing this problem would be to process each page separately. Generally speaking, each page would be an independent data set, and thus, it would not have any interdependencies. So why did we propose a row-based solution instead of processing individual pages? The three key reasons are:

- *An image may span multiple pages.* This implementation would impose a restriction of one image per page, which might or might not be suitable for the given application.

- *Increased memory usage.* An 8.5 x 11-inch page at 1,200 dpi consumes 131 megabytes of RAM. Intermediate results must be saved; therefore, this approach would be less memory efficient.

- *An application might, in a common use-case, print only a single page at a time.* Subdividing the problem at the page level would offer no performance improvement from the sequential case.

A hybrid approach would be to subdivide the pages and process regions of a page in a thread, as illustrated in Figure 3.6.

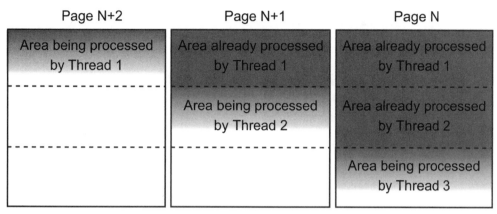

Page N+2	Page N+1	Page N
Area being processed by Thread 1	Area already processed by Thread 1	Area already processed by Thread 1
	Area being processed by Thread 2	Area already processed by Thread 2
		Area being processed by Thread 3

Multiple threads processing multiple page sections

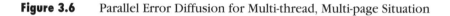

Figure 3.6   Parallel Error Diffusion for Multi-thread, Multi-page Situation

Note that each thread must work on sections from different page. This increases the startup latency involved before the threads can begin work. In Figure 3.6, Thread 2 incurs a 1/3 page startup latency before it can begin to process data, while Thread 3 incurs a 2/3 page startup latency. While somewhat improved, the hybrid approach suffers from similar limitations as the page-based partitioning scheme described above. To avoid these limitations, you should focus on the row-based error diffusion implementation illustrated in Figure 3.5.

Key Points

This chapter explored different types of computer architectures and how they enable parallel software development. The key points to keep in mind when developing solutions for parallel computing architectures are:

- Decompositions fall into one of three categories: task, data, and data flow.

- Task-level parallelism partitions the work between threads based on tasks.

- Data decomposition breaks down tasks based on the data that the threads work on.

■ Data flow decomposition breaks down the problem in terms of how data flows between the tasks.

■ Most parallel programming problems fall into one of several well known patterns.

■ The constraints of synchronization, communication, load balancing, and scalability must be dealt with to get the most benefit out of a parallel program.

Many problems that appear to be serial may, through a simple transformation, be adapted to a parallel implementation.

Chapter 4

Threading and Parallel Programming Constructs

T his chapter describes the theory and practice of the principal parallel programming constructs that focus on threading and begins with the fundamental concepts of synchronization, critical section, and deadlock. The following chapters cover implementation details and related issues.

Synchronization

Synchronization is an enforcing mechanism used to impose constraints on the order of execution of threads. The synchronization controls the relative order of thread execution and resolves any conflict among threads that might produce unwanted behavior. In simple terms, synchronization is used to coordinate thread execution and manage shared data.

In an environment where messages are used for communicating between a sender and a receiver, synchronization is implicit, as a message must be sent before the message can be received. On the other hand, for a shared-memory based environment, threads have no implicit interdependency unless some constraints are imposed.

Two types of synchronization operations are widely used: mutual exclusion and condition synchronization. In the case of *mutual exclusion*, one thread blocks a critical section—a section of code that contains shared data—and one or more threads wait to get their turn to enter into the section. This helps when two or more threads share the same memory space and run simultaneously. The mutual exclusion is controlled by a scheduler and depends on the granularity of the scheduler. *Condition synchronization*, on the other hand, blocks a thread until the system state specifies some specific conditions. The condition synchronization allows a thread to wait until a specific condition is reached. Figure 4.1 shows the generic representation of synchronization.

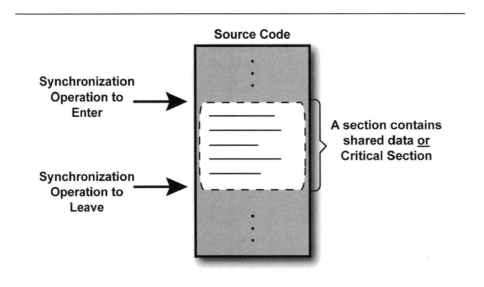

Figure 4.1   Generic Representation of Synchronization Block inside Source Code

While a number of techniques are available for synchronization, only a few methods are used by developers on a regular basis. The techniques used are also to some extent determined by the programming environment.

The scope of synchronization is broad. Proper synchronization orders the updates to data and provides an expected outcome. In Figure 4.2, shared data d can get access by threads T_i and T_j at time t_i, t_j, t_k, t_l, where $t_i \neq t_j \neq t_k \neq t_l$ and a proper synchronization maintains the order to update d at these instances and considers the state of d as a synchronization function of time. This synchronization function, s, represents the behavior of a synchronized construct with respect to the execution time of a thread.

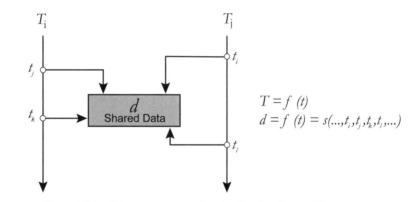

Shared data d depends on synchronization functions of time

Figure 4.2   Shared Data Synchronization, Where Data d Is Protected by a Synchronization Operation

Figure 4.3 represents how synchronization operations are performed in an actual multi-threaded implementation in a generic form, and demonstrates the flow of threads. When $m>=1$, the creation timing for initial threads $T_1...T_m$ might not be the same. After block B_i as well as B_j, the number of threads could be different, which means m is not necessarily equal to n and n is not necessarily equal to p. For all operational environments, the values of m, n, and p are at least 1.

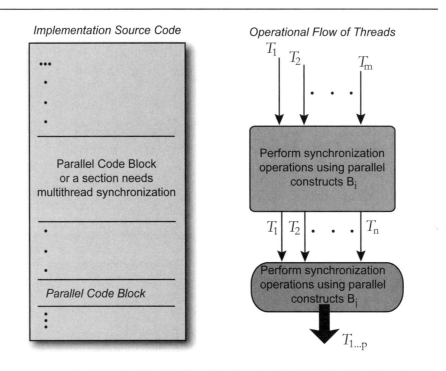

Figure 4.3   Operational Flow of Threads for an Application

Critical Sections

A section of a code block called a *critical section* is where shared dependency variables reside and those shared variables have dependency among multiple threads. Different synchronization primitives are used to keep critical sections safe. With the use of proper synchronization techniques, only one thread is allowed access to a critical section at any one instance. The major challenge of threaded programming is to implement critical sections in such a way that multiple threads perform mutually exclusive operations for critical sections and do not use critical sections simultaneously.

Critical sections can also be referred to as *synchronization blocks*. Depending upon the way critical sections are being used, the size of a critical section is important. Minimize the size of critical sections when practical. Larger critical sections-based code blocks should split into multiple code blocks. This is especially important in code that is likely to experience significant thread contention. Each critical section has an entry and an exit point. A critical section can be represented as shown in Figure 4.4.

```
<Critical Section Entry,
  to keep other threads in waiting status>
  ...
Critical Section
  ...
<Critical Section Exit,
  allow other threads to enter critical section>
```

Figure 4.4   Implement Critical Section in Source Code

Deadlock

Deadlock occurs whenever a thread is blocked waiting on a resource of another thread that will never become available. According to the circumstances, different deadlocks can occur: self-deadlock, recursive deadlock, and lock-ordering deadlock. In most instances, deadlock means lock-ordering deadlock.

The self-deadlock is the instance or condition when a thread, T_i, wants to acquire a lock that is already owned by thread T_i. In Figure 4.5 (a), at time t_a thread T_i owns lock l_i, where l_i is going to get released at t_c. However, there is a call at t_b from T_i, which requires l_i. The release time of l_i is t_d, where t_d can be either before or after t_c. In this scenario, thread T_i is in self-deadlock condition at t_b. When the wakeup path of thread T_i, resides in another thread, T_j, that condition is referred to as *recursive deadlock*, as shown in Figure 4.5 (b). Figure 4.5 (c) illustrates a lock-ordering thread, where thread T_i locks resource r_j and waits for resource r_i, which is being locked by thread T_j. Also, thread T_j locks resource r_i and waits for resource r_j, which is being locked by thread T_i. Here, both threads T_i and T_j are in deadlock at t_a, and w is the *wait-function* for a lock.

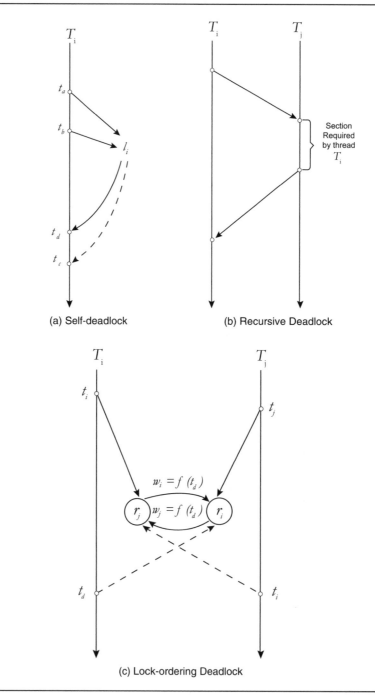

(a) Self-deadlock

(b) Recursive Deadlock

(c) Lock-ordering Deadlock

Figure 4.5   Deadlock Scenarios

To represent the transition model of deadlock of an environment, consider representing atomic states by s_i and each thread of the system by T_i. Each thread can transition from one state to another by requesting a resource, acquiring a resource, or freeing the current resource. So, the transition can be represented as shown in Figure 4.6, where, $r_i \equiv$ requesting a resource, $a_i \equiv$ acquiring a resource, and $f_i \equiv$ freeing current resource.

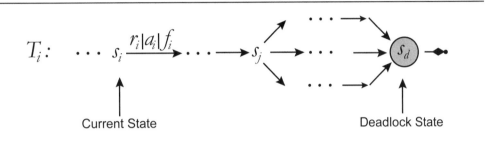

Figure 4.6   Deadlock Scenario in a State Transition for a Thread

For any thread T_i, if the state transition of T_i becomes s_d for all possible scenarios and remains blocked at s_d, thread T_i would not have any way to transition from s_d to any other state. That is why state s_d is called the deadlock state for thread T_i.

Avoiding deadlock is one of the challenges of multi-threaded programming. There must not be any possibility of deadlock in an application. A lock-holding prevention mechanism or the creation of lock hierarchy can remove a deadlock scenario. One recommendation is to use only the appropriate number of locks when implementing synchronization. Chapter 7 has a more detailed description of deadlock and how to avoid it.

Synchronization Primitives

Synchronization is typically performed by three types of primitives: semaphores, locks, and condition variables. The use of these primitives depends on the application requirements. These synchronization primitives are implemented by atomic operations and use appropriate memory fences. A *memory fence*, sometimes called a memory barrier, is a processor dependent operation that guarantees that threads see other threads' memory operations by maintaining reasonable order. To hide the granularity of these synchronization primitives, higher level synchronizations are used. That way application developers have to concern themselves less about internal details.

Semaphores

Semaphores, the first set of software-oriented primitives to accomplish mutual exclusion of parallel process synchronization, were introduced by the well known mathematician Edsger Dijkstra in his 1968 paper, "The Structure of the "THE"-Multiprogramming System" (Dijkstra 1968). Dijkstra illustrated that synchronization can be achieved by using only traditional machine instructions or hierarchical structure. He proposed that a semaphore can be represented by an integer, *sem,* and showed that a semaphore can be bounded by two basic atomic operations, *P* (proberen, which means test) and *V* (verhogen, which means increment). These atomic operations are also referred as synchronizing primitives. Even though the details of Dijkstra's semaphore representation have evolved, the fundamental principle remains same. Where, P represents the "potential delay" or "wait" and V represents the "barrier removal" or "release" of a thread. These two synchronizing primitives can be represented for a semaphore s as follows:

```
Thread "T" performs operation "P":
    P(s) → atomic {sem = sem-1; temp = sem}
          if (temp < 0)
              {Thread T blocked and enlists on a
               waiting list for s}
Thread "T" performs operation "V":
    V(s) → atomic {sem = sem +1; temp = sem}
          if (temp <=0)
              {Release one thread from the waiting
               list for s}
```

where semaphore value sem is initialized with the value 0 or 1 before the parallel processes get started. In Dijkstra's representation, T referred to processes. Threads are used here instead to be more precise and to remain consistent about the differences between threads and processes. The P operation blocks the calling thread if the value remains 0, whereas the V operation, independent of P operation, signals a blocked thread to allow it to resume operation. These P and V operations are "indivisible actions" and perform simultaneously. The positive value of sem represents the number of threads that can proceed without blocking, and the negative number refers to the number of blocked threads. When the sem value becomes zero, no thread is waiting, and if a thread needs to decrement, the thread gets blocked and keeps itself in a waiting list. When the value of sem gets restricted to only 0 and 1, the semaphore is a *binary semaphore*.

To use semaphore, you can consider semaphore as a counter, which supports two atomic operations. Implementation of semaphores varies. From a usability perspective, two kinds of semaphores exist: strong and weak. These represent the success of individual calls on P. A strong semaphore maintains First-Come-First-Serve (FCFS) model and provides guarantee to threads to calls on P and avoid starvation. And a weak semaphore is the one which does not provide any guarantee of service to a particular thread and the thread might starve. For example, in POSIX, the semaphores can get into starvation status and implemented differently than what Dijkstra defined and considered as a weak semaphore (Reek 2002).

According to Dijkstra, the mutual exclusion of parallel threads using P and V atomic operations represented as follows:

```
semaphore s
s.sem = 1
begin
    T: <non-critical section>
        P(s)
        <critical section>
        V(s)
        Goto T
end
```

Semaphores are largely of historical interest. They are the unstructured "goto" statements of multi-threaded programming. Most programming environments provide higher-level structured synchronization primitives. However, like the goto, semaphores are occasionally the best primitive to use. A typical use of a semaphore is protecting a shared resource of which at most n instances are allowed to exist simultaneously. The semaphore starts out with value n. A thread that needs to acquire an instance of the resource performs operation P. It releases the resource using operation V.

Let's examine how semaphores might be used for the producer-consumer problem and whether the problem can be resolved using semaphores or not. Producer-consumer is a classic synchronization problem, also known as the bounded-buffer problem. Here a producer function generates data to be placed in a shared buffer and a consumer function receives the data out of the buffer and operates on it, where both producer and consumer functions execute concurrently.

Pseudo-code using a semaphore for the producer-consumer problem is shown in Figure 4.7.

```
semaphore s

void producer () {
    while (1) {
        <produce the next data>
        s->release()
    }
}

void consumer() {
    while (1) {
        s->wait()
        <consume the next data>
    }
}
```

Figure 4.7   Pseudo-code of Producer-Consumer Problem

Here neither producer nor consumer maintains any order. If the producer function operates forever prior to the consumer function then the system would require an infinite capacity and that is not possible. That is why the buffer size needs to be within a boundary to handle this type of scenario and make sure that if the producer gets ahead of the consumer then the time allocated for the producer must be restricted. The problem of synchronization can be removed by adding one more semaphores in the previous solution shown in Figure 4.7. Adding the semaphore would maintain the boundary of buffer as shown in Figure 4.8, where sEmpty and sFull retain the constraints of buffer capacity for operating threads.

```
semaphore sEmpty, sFull

void producer() {
    while (1) {
        sEmpty->wait()
        <produce the next data>
        sFull->release()
    }
}

void consumer() {
    while (1) {
        sFull->release()
        <consume the next data>
        sEmpty->wait()
    }
}
```

Figure 4.8   Dual Semaphores Solution for Producer-Consumer Problem

Instead of using two independent semaphores and having a constraint-based solution, the solution in Figure 4.8 can be implemented using other synchronization primitives as well. The following sections discuss how to solve the producer-consumer problem using locks and conditional variables primitives.

Locks

Locks are similar to semaphores except that a single thread handles a lock at one instance. Two basic atomic operations get performed on a lock:

- acquire(): Atomically waits for the lock state to be unlocked and sets the lock state to lock.

- release(): Atomically changes the lock state from locked to unlocked.

At most one thread acquires the lock. A thread has to acquire a lock before using a shared resource; otherwise it waits until the lock becomes available. When one thread wants to access shared data, it first acquires the lock, exclusively performs operations on the shared data and later releases the lock for other threads to use. The level of granularity can be either coarse or fine depending on the type of shared data that needs to be protected from threads. The coarse granular locks have higher lock contention than finer granular ones. To remove issues with lock granularity, most of the processors support the Compare and Swap (CAS) operation, which provides a way to implement lock-free synchronization. The atomic CAS operations guarantee that the shared data remains synchronized among threads. If you require the use of locks, it is recommended that you use the lock inside a critical section with a single entry and single exit, as shown in Figure 4.9.

```
{define all necessary locks}
<Start multithreading blocks>
...
<critical section start>

<acquire lock L>

.. operate on shared memory protected by lock L ..


<release lock L>
<critical section end>
...
<End multithreading blocks>
```

Figure 4.9   A Lock Used Inside a Critical Section

From an implementation perspective, it is always safe to use explicit locks rather than relying on implicit locks. In general a lock must not be held for a long periods of time. The explicit locks are defined by the developer, whereas implicit locks come from the underlying framework used, such as database engines provides lock the maintain data consistency.

In the produce-consumer problem, if the consumer wants to consume a shared data before the producer produces, it must wait. To use locks for the producer-consumer problem, the consumer must loop until the data is ready from the producer. The reason for looping is that the lock does not support any wait operation, whereas Condition Variables does.

Lock Types

An application can have different types of locks according to the constructs required to accomplish the task. You must avoid mixing lock types within a given task. For this reason, special attention is required when using any third party library. If your application has some third party dependency for a resource $\mathcal{R}$ and the third party uses lock type $\mathcal{L}$ for $\mathcal{R}$, then if you need to use a lock mechanism for $\mathcal{R}$, you must use lock type $\mathcal{L}$ rather any other lock type. The following sections cover these locks and define their purposes.

Mutexes. The mutex is the simplest lock an implementation can use. Some texts use the mutex as the basis to describe locks in general. The release of a mutex does not depend on the release() operation only. A timer attribute can be added with a mutex. If the timer expires before a release operation, the mutex releases the code block or shared memory to other threads. A try-finally clause can be used to make sure that the mutex gets released when an exception occurs. The use of a timer or try-finally clause helps to prevent a deadlock scenario.

Recursive Locks. Recursive locks are locks that may be repeatedly acquired by the thread that currently owns the lock without causing the thread to deadlock. No other thread may acquire a recursive lock until the owner releases it once for each time the owner acquired it. Thus when using a recursive lock, be sure to balance acquire operations with release operations. The best way to do this is to lexically balance the operations around single-entry single-exit blocks, as was shown for ordinary locks. The recursive lock is most useful inside a recursive function. In general, the recursive locks are slower than nonrecursive locks. An example of recursive locks use is shown in Figure 4.10.

```
Recursive_Lock L
void recursiveFunction (int count) {
   L->acquire()
   if (count > 0) {
      count = count - 1;
      recursiveFunction(count);
   }
   L->release();
}
```

Figure 4.10   An Example of Recursive Lock Use

Read-Write Locks. Read-Write locks are also called shared-exclusive or multiple-read/single-write locks or non-mutual exclusion semaphores. Read-write locks allow simultaneous read access to multiple threads but limit the write access to only one thread. This type of lock can be used efficiently for those instances where multiple threads need to read shared data simultaneously but do not necessarily need to perform a write operation. For lengthy shared data, it is sometimes better to break the data into smaller segments and operate multiple read-write locks on the dataset rather than having a data lock for a longer period of time.

Spin Locks. Spin locks are non-blocking locks owned by a thread. Waiting threads must "spin," that is, poll the state of a lock rather than get blocked. Spin locks are used mostly on multiprocessor systems. This is because while the thread spins in a single-core processor system, no process resources are available to run the other thread that will release the lock. The appropriate condition for using spin locks is whenever the hold time of a lock is less than the time of blocking and waking up a thread. The change of control for threads involves context switching of threads and updating thread data structures, which could require more instruction cycles than spin locks. The spin time of spin locks should be limited to about 50 to 100 percent of a thread context switch (Kleiman 1996) and should not be held during calls to other subsystems. Improper use of spin locks might cause thread starvation. Think carefully before using this locking mechanism. The thread starvation problem of spin locks can be alleviated by using a queuing technique, where every waiting thread to spin on a separate local flag in memory using First-In, First-Out (FIFO) or queue construct.

Condition Variables

Condition variables are also based on Dijkstra's semaphore semantics, with the exception that no stored value is associated with the operation. This means condition variables do not contain the actual condition to test; a shared data state is used instead to maintain the condition for threads. A thread waits or wakes up other cooperative threads until a condition is satisfied. The condition variables are preferable to locks when pooling requires and needs some scheduling behavior among threads. To operate on shared data, condition variable C, uses a lock, L. Three basic atomic operations are performed on a condition variable C:

- wait(L): Atomically releases the lock and waits, where *wait* returns the lock been acquired again

- signal(L): Enables one of the waiting threads to run, where *signal* returns the lock is still acquired

- broadcast(L): Enables all of the waiting threads to run, where *broadcast* returns the lock is still acquired

To control a pool of threads, use of a signal function is recommended. The penalty for using a broadcast-based signaling function could be severe and extra caution needs to be undertaken before waking up all waiting threads. For some instances, however, broadcast signaling can be effective. As an example, a "write" lock might allow all "readers" to proceed at the same time by using a broadcast mechanism.

To show the use of a condition variable for a synchronization problem, the pseudocode in Figure 4.11 solves the producer-consumer problem discussed earlier. A variable LC is used to maintain the association between condition variable C and an associated lock L.

```
Condition C;
Lock L;
Bool LC = false;

void producer() {
   while (1) {
      L ->acquire();
      // start critical section
      while (LC  == true) {
         C ->wait(L);
      }
      // produce the next data
      LC  = true;
      C ->signal(L);
      // end critical section
      L ->release();
   }
}

void consumer() {
   while (1) {
      L ->acquire();
      // start critical section
      while (LC  == false) {
         C ->wait(L);
      }
      // consume the next data
      LC = false;
      // end critical section
      L ->release();
   }
}
```

Figure 4.11   Use of a Condition Variable for the Producer-Consumer Problem

Monitors

For structured synchronization, a higher level construct is introduced for simplifying the use of condition variables and locks, known as a *monitor*. The purpose of the monitor is to simplify the complexity of primitive synchronization operations and remove the implementation details from application developers. The compiler for the language that supports monitors automatically inserts lock operations at the beginning and the end of each synchronization-aware routine. Most recent programming languages do not support monitor explicitly, rather they expose lock and unlock operations to the developers. The Java language supports explicit monitor objects along with synchronized blocks inside a method. In Java, the monitor is maintained by the "synchronized" constructs, such as

```
synchronized (object) {

    <Critical Section>
}
```

where the "condition" primitives are used by `wait()`, `notify()`, or `notifyAll()` methods. Do not confuse this with the Monitor object in the Java SDK though. The Java Monitor object is used to perform resource management in Java Management Extension (JMX). Similarly, the monitor object in C# is used as lock construct.

Messages

The *message* is a special method of communication to transfer information or a signal from one domain to another. The definition of domain is different for different scenarios. For multi-threading environments, the domain is referred to as the *boundary* of a thread. The three M's of message passing are multi-granularity, multithreading, and multitasking (Ang 1996). In general, the conceptual representations of messages get associated with processes rather than threads. From a message-sharing perspective, messages get shared using an intra-process, inter-process, or process-process approach, as shown in Figure 4.12.

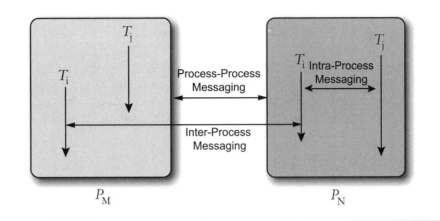

Figure 4.12   Message Passing Model

Two threads that communicate with messages and reside in the same process use *intra-process messaging*. Two threads that communicate and reside in different processes use *inter-process messaging*. From the developer's perspective, the most common form of messaging is the *process-process* approach, when two processes communicate with each other rather than depending on the thread.

In general, the messaging could be devised according to the memory model of the environment where the messaging operation takes place. Messaging for the shared memory model must be synchronous, whereas for the distributed model messaging can be asynchronous. These operations can be viewed at a somewhat different angle. When there is nothing to do after sending the message and the sender has to wait for the reply to come, the operations need to be synchronous, whereas if the sender does not need to wait for the reply to arrive and in order to proceed then the operation can be asynchronous.

The generic form of message communication can be represented as follows:

```
Sender:
        <sender sends message to one or more recipients
         through structure>
        \\ Here, structure can be either queue or port
        <if shared environment>
              {wait for the acknowledgement>
        <else>
              {sender does the next possible operation>
```

```
Receiver:
      <might wait to get message from sender from
       appropriate structure>
      <receive message from appropriate structure and
       process>
```

The generic form of message passing gives the impression to developers that there must be some interface used to perform message passing. The most common interface is the Message Passing Interface (MPI). MPI is used as the medium of communication, as illustrated in Figure 4.13.

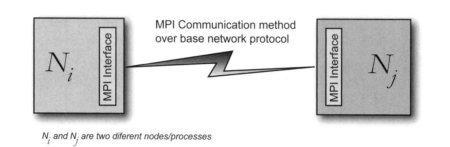

N_i and N_j are two diferent nodes/processes

Figure 4.13 Basic MPI Communication Environment

To synchronize operations of threads, semaphores, locks, and condition variables are used. These synchronization primitives convey status and access information. To communicate data, they use *thread messaging*. In thread messaging, synchronization remains explicit, as there is acknowledgement after receiving messages. The acknowledgement avoids primitive synchronization errors, such as deadlocks or race conditions. The basic operational concepts of messaging remain the same for all operational models. From an implementation point of view, the generic client-server model can be used for all messaging models.

Inside hardware, message processing occurs in relationship with the size of the message. Small messages are transferred between processor registers and if a message is too large for processor registers, caches get used. Larger messages require main memory. In the case of the largest messages, the system might use processor-external DMA, as shown in Figure 4.14.

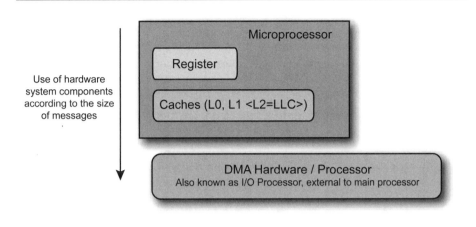

Figure 4.14 System Components Associated with Size of Messages

Flow Control-based Concepts

In the parallel computing domain, some restraining mechanisms allow synchronization among multiple attributes or actions in a system. These are mainly applicable for shared-memory multiprocessor or multi-core environments. The following section covers only two of these concepts, fence and barrier.

Fence

The *fence* mechanism is implemented using instructions and in fact, most of the languages and systems refer to this mechanism as a fence *instruction*. On a shared memory multiprocessor or multi-core environment, a fence instruction ensures consistent memory operations. At execution time, the fence instruction guarantees completeness of all pre-fence memory operations and halts all post-fence memory operations until the completion of fence instruction cycles. This fence mechanism ensures proper memory mapping from software to hardware memory models, as shown in Figure 4.15. The semantics of the fence instruction depend on the architecture. The software memory model implicitly supports fence instructions. Using fence instructions explicitly could be error-prone and it is better to rely on compiler technologies. Due to the performance penalty of fence instructions, the number of memory fences needs to be optimized.

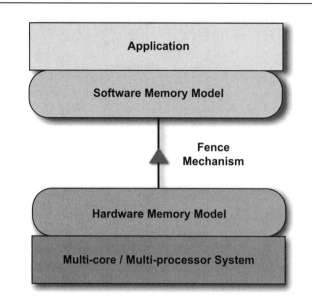

Figure 4.15   Fence Mechanism

Barrier

The *barrier* mechanism is a synchronization method by which threads in the same set keep collaborating with respect to a logical computational point in the control flow of operations. Through this method, a thread from an operational set has to wait for all other threads in that set to complete in order to be able to proceed to the next execution step. This method guarantees that no threads proceed beyond an execution logical point until all threads have arrived at that logical point. Barrier synchronization is one of the common operations for shared memory multiprocessor and multi-core environments. Due to the aspect of waiting for a barrier control point in the execution flow, the barrier synchronization wait function for *i*th thread can be represented as

$$(W_{barrier})_i = f\,((T_{barrier})_i, (R_{thread})_i)$$

where $W_{barrier}$ is the wait time for a thread, $T_{barrier}$ is the number of threads has arrived, and R_{thread} is the arrival rate of threads.

For performance consideration and to keep the wait time within a reasonable timing window before hitting a performance penalty, special consideration must be given to the granularity of tasks. Otherwise, the implementation might suffer significantly.

Implementation-dependent Threading Features

The functionalities and features of threads in different environments are very similar; however the semantics could be different. That is why the conceptual representations of threads in Windows and Linux remain the same, even though the way some concepts are implemented could be different. Also, with the threading APIs of Win32, Win64, and POSIX threads (Pthreads), the semantics are different as well. Windows threading APIs are implemented and maintained by Microsoft and work on Windows only, whereas the implementation of Pthreads APIs allows developers to implement threads on multiple platforms. The IEEE only defined the Pthreads APIs and let the implementation be done by OS developers. Due to the implementation issues of Pthreads, not all features exist in Pthreads APIs. Developers use Pthreads as a wrapper of their own thread implementations. There exists a native Linux Pthreads library similar to Windows native threads, known as Native POSIX Thread Library (NPTL).

Consider the different mechanisms used to signal threads in Windows and in POSIX threads. Windows uses an event model to signal one or more threads that an event has occurred. However, no counterpart to Windows events is implemented in POSIX threads. Instead, condition variables are used for this purpose.

These differences are not necessarily limited to cross-library boundaries. There may be variations within a single library as well. For example, in the Windows Win32 API, Microsoft has implemented two versions of a mutex. The first version, simply referred to as a mutex, provides one method for providing synchronized access to a critical section of the code. The other mechanism, referred to as a *CriticalSection,* essentially does the same thing, with a completely different API. What's the difference?

The conventional mutex object in Windows is a kernel mechanism. As a result, it requires a user-mode to kernel-mode transition to work. This is an expensive operation, but provides a more powerful synchronization mechanism that can be used across process boundaries. However, in many applications, synchronization is only needed within a single process. Therefore, the ability for a mutex to work across process boundaries is unnecessary, and leads to wasted overhead. To remove overhead associated with the standard mutex Microsoft implemented the CriticalSection, which provides a user-level locking mechanism. This eliminates any need to make a system call, resulting in much faster locking.

Even though different threading libraries will have different ways of implementing the features described in this chapter, the key to being able to successfully develop multithreaded applications is to understand the fundamental concepts behind these features.

Key Points

This chapter presented parallel programming constructs and later chapters provide details about the implementation of the constructs. To become proficient in threading techniques and face fewer issues during design and development of a threaded solution, an understanding of the theory behind different threading techniques is helpful. Here are some of the points you should remember:

- For synchronization, an understanding of the atomic actions of operations will help avoid deadlock and eliminate race conditions.

- Use a proper synchronization construct-based framework for threaded applications.

- Use higher-level synchronization constructs over primitive types.

- An application cannot contain any possibility of a deadlock scenario.

- Threads can perform message passing using three different approaches: intra-process, inter-process, and process-process.

- Understand the way threading features of third-party libraries are implemented. Different implementations may cause applications to fail in unexpected ways.

Chapter 5

Threading APIs

Previous chapters introduced the basic principles behind writing concurrent applications. While describing every thread package available today is beyond the scope of this book, it is important to illustrate the aforementioned principles with practical examples. This chapter will provide an overview of several popular thread packages used by developers today.

Threading APIs for Microsoft Windows

Since the advent of Windows NT, Microsoft has enabled application developers to write multi-threaded software applications. Advances in processor technology have allowed Microsoft to add additional capabilities, evolving its programming interface to support more and more advanced threading operations. As a result, the Microsoft threading APIs have become a powerful tool for writing multi-threaded applications running on Windows.

Historically, native Windows applications have been written in C/C++ using Microsoft's Win32 or MFC APIs. However, many new applications are being developed using Microsoft's .NET platform and associated common language runtime (CLR). This chapter examines writing multi-threaded applications using both programming techniques.

Win32/MFC Thread APIs

The Win32/MFC API provides developers with a C/C++ interface for developing Windows applications. While there are a large number of developers moving to a managed code development environment, understanding the Win32/MFC model is important for several reasons:

■ *Performance.* Applications that run in a managed runtime environment run on a software virtual machine. Managed code is compiled to virtual machine op-codes. These op-codes are then translated, at runtime, to native processor instructions. A number of optimizations minimize this overhead. However, native applications run directly on the processor; the overhead of translating virtual machine op-codes is eliminated. In some applications, the overhead of the virtual machine may not be acceptable.

■ *Legacy Application Support.* There are a number of existing applications where it is not reasonable to port to a managed runtime environment. In order to maximize the performance of these applications for multi-core processors, the existing code must be multi-threaded.

Creating Threads

All processes start with a single thread of execution: the main thread. In order to write multi-threaded code, one must have the ability to create new threads. The most basic thread creation mechanism provided by Microsoft is CreateThread():

```
HANDLE CreateThread(
    LPSECURITY_ATTRIBUTES lpThreadAttributes,
    SIZE_T dwStackSize,
    LPTHREAD_START_ROUTINE lpStartAddress,
    LPVOID lpParameter,
    DWORD dwCreationFlags,
    LPDWORD lpThreadId );
```

The first parameter, lpThreadAttributes, is a data structure that specifies several different security parameters. It also defines whether or not processes created from the current process (child processes) inherit this handle. In other words, this parameter gives advanced control over how the thread handle may be used in the system. If the programmer does not need control over these attributes, the programmer may specify NULL for this field.

The second parameter, dwStackSize, specifies the stack size of the thread. The size is specified in bytes, and the value is rounded up to the nearest page size.

The third parameter, `lpStartAddress`, specifies a function pointer to the actual code that the thread runs. The function pointer that has the following signature:

```
DWORD WINAPI ThreadFunc(LPVOID data)
```

From the thread function's signature, one can see that a thread will return a status value on exit and will take a void pointer to some data value or structure. This provides the basic communication mechanism between the thread and the outside world.

The fourth parameter in `CreateThread()`, `lpParameter`, is the data value to pass into the thread function. In other words, considering the aforementioned `ThreadFunc()`, the value specified in this argument to `CreateThread()` will be passed in as the data value in `ThreadFunc()`.

The fifth parameter, `dwCreationFlags`, specifies various configuration options. For example, using this flag, the programmer may specify that the thread be created in the suspended state, thus giving the programmer control of when the thread is started.

The final parameter, `lpThreadId`, points to where the function should store a value that uniquely identifies a thread in the system. This identifier is global and is useful in debugging.

On success, `CreateThread()` returns a HANDLE to the new thread. An observant reader may at this point ask what the difference is between the HANDLE returned by `CreateThread()` and the Thread ID. There are actually a number of differences; for our purposes it's only important to note that there are two different return values for `CreateThread()` and that different Thread API calls will expect one value or the other. The HANDLE value is the most frequently used of the two.

Once a thread is created, the programmer will at some point want to terminate the thread. This is accomplished by calling the `ExitThread()` function:

```
VOID ExitThread(DWORD dwExitCode);
```

`ExitThread()` is called at the end of `ThreadFunc()` to indicate that the thread should terminate. Note that an explicit call to `ExitThread()` is not mandatory; simply returning the exit code will result in this function being called implicitly:

```
DWORD WINAPI ThreadFunc( LPVOID data )
{
```

```
    // do something
    ...
    // ready to exit thread
    return 0; // will implicitly call ExitThread(0);
}
```

Note that in C++, calling `ExitThread()` will exit the thread before any constructors/automatic variables are cleaned up. Thus, Microsoft recommends that the program simply return from the `ThreadFunc()` rather than call `ExitThread()` explicitly.

The `CreateThread()` and `ExitThread()` functions provide a flexible, easy to use mechanism for creating threads in Windows applications. There's just one problem. `CreateThread()` does not perform per-thread initialization of C runtime datablocks and variables. Hence, you cannot use `CreateThread()` and `ExitThread()`, in any application that uses the C runtime library. Instead, Microsoft provides two other methods, `_beginthreadex()` and `_endthreadex()` that perform the necessary initialization prior to calling `CreateThread()`. `CreateThread()` and `ExitThread()` are adequate for writing applications that just use the Win32 API; however, for most cases, it is recommended that developers use `_beginthreadex()` and `_endthreadex()` to create threads.

The definition of `_beginthreadex()` is similar to that of `CreateThread()`; the only difference being one of semantics.

```
unsigned long _beginthreadex(  // unsigned long
                               //   instead of HANDLE,
                               //   but technically the
                               //   same
void *security,                // same as CreateThread()
unsigned stack_size,           // same as CreateThread()
unsigned (__stdcall func) (void),  // ptr to func
                               // returning unsigned
                               // instead of void
void *arglist,                 // same as CreateThread()
unsigned initflag,             // same as CreateThread()
unsigned* threadID);           // same as CreateThread()
```

Similarly, the definition of `_endthreadex()` follows that of `ExitThread()`:

```
void _endthreadex( unsigned retval );
```

For applications written in C++ using MFC, Microsoft provides yet another function to create a thread—`AfxBeginThread()`:[1]

```
CWinThread* AfxBeginThread(
    AFX_THREADPROC pfnThreadProc,
    LPVOID pParam,
    int nPriority = THREAD_PRIORITY_NORMAL,
    UINT nStackSize = 0,
    DWORD dwCreateFlags = 0,
    LPSECURITY_ATTRIBUTES lpSecurityAttrs = NULL );
```

`AfxBeginThread()` differs from `CreateThread()` in several ways:

- `AfxBeginThread()` returns a pointer to a `CWinThread` object rather than a HANDLE to a thread.
- `AfxBeginThread()` re-orders the parameters and replaces the `threadId` parameter with *nPriority*, which allows the programmer to specify the thread's priority.
- `AfxBeginThread()` expects the following definition for `ThreadFunc()`:

  `UINT ThreadFunc (LPVOID pParam);`

- `AfxBeginThread()` calls `_beginthreadex()`; thus it is safe to use with the C runtime library.

For all intent and purpose, `AfxBeginThread` is conceptually identical to `CreateThread`. MFC provides a complimentary function to `ExitThread` as well:

```
void AFXAPI AfxEndThread( UINT nExitCode,
                          BOOL bDelete = TRUE );
```

The `bDelete` parameter specifies whether or not the framework should automatically delete the associated thread object upon termination. It should be set to FALSE if a program wishes to check the exit code of the thread; however, it then becomes the program's responsibility to destroy the CWinThread object.

Managing Threads

Now that you know how to create a thread, let's examine the process of controlling or manipulating the execution of threads. It was previously demonstrated that Windows allows developers to create threads in one of two initial states: suspended or running. For the remainder of the

---

[1] There are two types of threads that can be created using `AfxBeginThread()`: worker threads and user-interface threads. This text only considers worker threads.

chapter, we'll use Win32 definitions to illustrate the concepts of programming in Windows. Most MFC calls will be identical to Win32; the only difference is that the MFC calls will be methods called on MFC-based classes, such as CWinThread, rather than C function calls.

The following functions allow the programmer to control the execution of a thread:

```
DWORD SuspendThread( HANDLE hThread );
DWORD ResumeThread( HANDLE hThread );
BOOL TerminateThread( HANDLE hThread, DWORD dwExitCode );
```

SuspendThread() allows the developer to suspend execution of the thread specified by the HANDLE parameter. The kernel keeps track of the current suspend count for a given thread in the thread's data structure. A suspend count of 0 indicates that the thread is ready to run. A suspend count greater than 0 indicates that the thread is suspended. SuspendThread(), when called, will increment this field and return the previous value of suspend count. ResumeThread() will decrement the suspend count for the thread specified by the HANDLE value. It will return the previous suspend count. This implies that if a thread is transitioning from the suspended state to the run state, its suspend count will be 1. Calling ResumeThread() on a currently running thread will return 0. This does not indicate an error condition, as calling ResumeThread() on a thread with a suspend count of 0 has no effect.

The TerminateThread() function forces the thread specified by the HANDLE parameter to terminate. No user code executes; the thread is immediately terminated. If the function is successful, a non-zero value is returned.

Developers must be very careful when calling SuspendThread(), as the thread may be in a state in which it is dangerous to suspend. For example, if the thread is holding a semaphore and is suspended, it will not release the semaphore prior to being suspended. As a result, other threads will not be able to access critical sections until the suspended thread is resumed and releases the resource. This may cause significant performance problems or even deadlock.

TerminateThread() is even more dangerous. The thread that is being terminated will not be given a chance to do any clean-up; therefore, a number of particularly nasty side-effects may occur. For example, if a thread is holding on to a synchronization object such as a mutex, and is abruptly terminated by this call, the synchronization object will remain locked; hence, a deadlock will occur as the thread no longer exists and will be unable to release this resource. It is strongly recommended that you avoid using this function.

In order to safely suspend/terminate threads, we need a signaling mechanism that allows one thread, say the main thread, to notify the targeted thread that it must suspend/terminate itself. Fortunately, Windows provides developers with a way to do such an operation by using Windows events.

Thread Communication using Windows Events

As previously demonstrated, multiple threads within an application need a mechanism that can be used for inter-thread communication. Microsoft has provided Event objects that may be used for this purpose. The code sample provided in Listing 5.1 illustrates the use of Windows Events to communicate between threads.

```
1    // This example illustrates the use of
2    // Windows Events as a inter-thread communication
3    // mechanism.
4    #define NUM_THREADS  10
5    #include <windows.h>
6    #include <stdio.h>
7    #include <process.h>
8
9    typedef struct
10   {
11       int Id;
12       HANDLE hTerminate;
13   } ThreadArgs;
14
15   unsigned __stdcall ThreadFunc( void *pArgs )
16   {
17       HANDLE hTerminate = ((ThreadArgs *)pArgs)->hTerminate;
18       int id = ((ThreadArgs *)pArgs)->Id;
19
20       // run until we are told to terminate
21       while (1)
22       {
23           // Check to see if we should terminate
24           if (WaitForSingleObject(hTerminate, 0) ==
25                               WAIT_OBJECT_0)
26           {
27               // Terminate Thread - we call ResetEvent to
28               // return the terminate thread to its non-
29               // signaled state, then exit the while() loop
30               printf("Terminating Thread %d\n", id);
```

```
31                  ResetEvent(hTerminate);
32                  break;
33              }
34              // we can do our work now...
35              // simulate the case that it takes 1 s
36              // to do the work the thread has to do
37              Sleep(1000);
38          }
39          _endthreadex(0);
40          return 0;
41      }
42
43
44      int main( int argc, char* argv[] )
45      {
46          unsigned int threadID[NUM_THREADS];
47          HANDLE hThread[NUM_THREADS];
48          ThreadArgs threadArgs[NUM_THREADS];
49
50          // Create 10 threads
51          for (int i = 0; i < NUM_THREADS; i++)
52          {
53              threadArgs[i].Id = i;
54              threadArgs[i].hTerminate = CreateEvent(NULL, TRUE,
55                                              FALSE, NULL);
56              hThread[i] = (HANDLE)_beginthreadex(NULL, 0,
57                  &ThreadFunc, &threadArgs[i], 0, &threadID[i]);
58          }
59
60          printf("To kill a thread (gracefully), press 0-9, " \
61                  "then <Enter>.\n");
62          printf("Press any other key to exit.\n");
63
64          while (1)
65          {
66              int c = getc(stdin);
67              if (c == '\n') continue;
68              if (c < '0' || c > '9') break;
69              SetEvent(threadArgs[c - '0'].hTerminate);
70          }
71
72          return 0;
73      }
```

Listing 5.1   A Thread Application that uses Windows Events

The application in Listing 5.1 is very simple. When loaded, the application creates multiple threads to process different tasks. It uses `_beginthreadex()` as discussed in the previous section. The application notifies the user that the application is started and gives the user an interface in which a thread may be terminated. If the user enters a thread ID, the application, using Windows Events, terminates the thread gracefully. Otherwise, the different threads in the system continue to run until the user indicates that the program should be terminated.

In order to use events, a programmer must first create an event. We do this in line 54 using the `CreateEvent()` method:

```
HANDLE CreateEvent(
            LPSECURITY_ATTRIBUTES lpEventAttributes,
            BOOL bManualReset,
            BOOL bInitialState,
            LPCTSTR lpName );
```

The first parameter, `lpEventAttributes`, should look familiar. It's the same security attributes data structure defined in the `CreateThread()` function call. The default attributes are valid for this case, so we simply pass in NULL. The second parameter, `bManualReset`, allows the programmer to specify whether or not the event being created should be explicitly reset by the programmer using the `ResetEvent` function call. This parameter gives the programmer the option to determine whether or not more than one thread will respond to a given event. If `bManualReset` is FALSE, then Windows will create an auto-reset event and return the event to the non-signaled state after a single thread has been run. If `bManualReset` is TRUE, Windows will create a manual reset event and it is up to the program to return the event object to the non-signaled state. In the example given in Listing 5.1, it was a moot point, as each thread had its own event that it was monitoring. Therefore, the event could have just as easily been set to FALSE. The third parameter, `bInitialState`, determines the initial state of the Event. The programmer may specify that the event is in either the signaled or non-signaled state. In the example application, the event was initialized to the non-signaled state, indicating that the user is not yet ready to terminate the thread. Finally, the programmer may specify a name for the event in the fourth parameter, `lpName`. Providing a name creates a system-wide event. Upon successful completion, a handle to the event is returned. This handle is used in the other API calls to operate on the event.

Once the event is created, it is ready to use. The event handle is stored locally from the main thread, and is also passed to each individual thread. This defines an interface between the threads that contain a reference to this object. In this example, the main thread and individual worker threads now have a communication channel. How do the threads communicate? They communicate by using the messages described in Chapter 4. In this case, our messages are Windows Events. By using `SetEvent()`, `ResetEvent()`, and the Wait routines, `WaitForSingleObject()` and `WaitForMultipleObjects()`, we can send messages between threads.

The Wait routines wait on a specific handle—or multiple handles in the case of `WaitForMultipleObjects()`—for a specified timeout period. Since a handle in Windows is a generic concept used to reference objects of multiple types, the Wait routines provided by Microsoft wait on multiple object types.[2] In this aforementioned example, the handle used references that an event object created specifically to terminate the thread. The timeout period is 0, which indicates that the programmer is only interested in checking to see if the event has been signaled, or a numeric value that specifies a timeout. If the programmer specifies a timeout of 0, and the event hasn't been signaled, `WaitForSingleObject()` will return immediately and indicate to the programmer that the event has not yet occurred. In other situations, it may make sense to specify a non-zero timeout value. In that case, `WaitForSingleObject()` will wait for the period of time specified by the timeout value for the event to occur. Microsoft defines a special constant, INFINITE, to indicate that the thread of control wants to wait indefinitely for the event to occur. In this way, the programmer can notify the OS that the thread has no other work to do until this particular event occurs, and hence can be moved off the run queue to the wait queue. The OS can then switch to a thread that is in the ready-to-run state.

The function prototype for the `WaitForSingleObject()` function has the following syntax:

```
DWORD WaitForSingleObject( HANDLE hHandle,
                           DWORD dwMilliseconds );
```

`WaitForSingleObject()` will return one of four values:

- *WAIT_OBJECT_0*. This value is returned when the object that is being waited on enters the signaled[3] state.

- *WAIT_TIMEOUT*. This value is returned when the specified timeout value occurs prior to the object entering the signaled state.

---

[2] `WaitForXXX()` may wait on events, jobs, mutexes, processes, semaphores, threads, and timers, among other objects.

[3] The meaning of a signaled state varies based on the type of object being waited on. In the example in Figure 5.1, we wait on an Event object, hence, WAIT_OBJECT_0 is returned once `SetEvent()` sets the event's state to signaled.

- *WAIT_ABANDONED*. In the case that the handle refers to a Mutex object, this return code indicates that the thread that owned the mutex did not release the mutex prior to termination.

- *WAIT_FAILED*. This value indicates that an error occurred. `GetLastError()` should be used to get extended error information regarding the cause of failure.

The function `WaitForMultipleObjects()` has the following prototype:

```
DWORD WaitForMultipleObjects( DWORD nCount,
                              const HANDLE* lpHandles,
                              BOOL bWaitAll,
                              DWORD dwMilliseconds );
```

Note that the `WaitForMultipleObjects()` call takes in a different parameter set than `WaitForSingleObject()`. The parameter `nCount` specifies the number of handles to wait on. This value cannot exceed the maximum number of object handles specified by the MAXIMUM_WAIT_OBJECTS constant. The parameter `lpHandles` specifies an array of object handles to wait on. Parameter `bWaitAll` indicates whether or not the programmer wants to wait on all handles to be signaled before returning, or wait on any one or more of the handles to be signaled before returning. In the case of the former, the developer should set `bWaitAll` to TRUE; for the latter case, the developer should set `bWaitAll` to FALSE. The timeout value is the same for both `WaitForSingleObject()` and `WaitForMultipleObjects()`.

The return value for `WaitForMultipleObjects()` is identical in the case of WAIT_TIMEOUT or WAIT_FAILED. In the case that an event is signaled, or a handle is abandoned, the return value is slightly different. In that case, `WaitForMultipleObjects()` returns WAIT_OBJECT_I or WAIT_ABANDONED_I, where I is the index position in the array of object handles where the signaled event was found.[4] For example, assuming that the programmer wanted to be notified when any object was signaled, the code excerpt illustrated in Listing 5.2 can be used to determine which object handle has been signaled.

---

[4] If `bWaitAll` is set to FALSE, and if the number of objects in the signaled state happens to be greater than 1, the array index of the first signaled or abandoned value in the array—starting at array index 0—is returned.

```
1    DWORD event, arrayIndex = 0;
2
3    // Assume eventArray and count are initialized elsewhere
4    // Wait for any of the events in eventArray to occur
5
6    event = WaitForMultipleObjects(
7                                    count,
8                                    eventArray,
9                                    FALSE,
10                                   INFINITE );
11   switch (event)
12   {
13       case WAIT_OBJECT_0 + 0:
14       // eventArray[0] signaled
15       case WAIT_OBJECT_0 + 1:
16       // eventArray[1] signaled
17       ...
```

Listing 5.2   Computing the Index of the Event that Has Been Signaled while Waiting on Multiple Objects

Now that the thread has a mechanism for waiting for a particular event to occur, we need a mechanism to signal the thread when it is time to terminate. Microsoft provides the SetEvent() call for this purpose. SetEvent() sets an event object to the signaled state. This allows a thread to notify another thread that the event has occurred. SetEvent() has the following signature:

```
BOOL SetEvent( HANDLE hEvent );
```

SetEvent() takes a single parameter which is the HANDLE value of the specific event object, and returns TRUE if the event was signaled successfully. The handle to the event object must be modifiable; in other words, the access rights for the handle must have the EVENT_MODIFY_STATE field set.

In the case of a manual reset event, the programmer must return the event object the non-signaled state. To do this, a programmer uses the ResetEvent() function. The ResetEvent() function has the following prototype:

```
BOOL ResetEvent( HANDLE hEvent );
```

ResetEvent() accepts as a parameter the handle to reset and returns TRUE upon success. Like SetEvent(), the handle to the event object must have the appropriate access rights set, otherwise the call to ResetEvent() will fail.[5]

It is important to contrast the example program in Listing 5.1 to the case where the TerminateThread() function is used to terminate a thread. TerminateThread() fails to give the thread any chance of graceful exit; the thread is terminated immediately and without any chance to properly free any resources it may have acquired. It recommended that you use a notification mechanism such as the one defined above to give the thread a chance to do proper cleanup.

Thread Synchronization

Generally speaking, creating a thread is a relatively simple task, and one that does not consume the bulk of the development time when writing a multi-threaded application. The challenge in writing a multi-threaded application lies in making sure that in a chaotic, unpredictable, real-world runtime environment threads act in an orderly, well-known manner, avoiding such nasty conditions as deadlock and data corruption caused by race conditions. The example in Figure 5.1 showed one Windows mechanism for coordinating the actions of multiple threads—events. This section will look at the different object types Microsoft provides for sharing data among threads.

Microsoft defines several different types of synchronization objects as part of the Win32 API. These include events, semaphores, mutexes, and critical sections. In addition, the Wait methods allow the developer to wait on thread and process handles, which may be used to wait for thread and process termination. Finally, atomic access to variables and linked lists can be achieved through the use of interlocked functions.

Before we discuss the different data structures provided by Windows, let's review a few of the basic concepts that are used to synchronize concurrent access requests to shared resources. The *critical section* is the block of code that can only be accessed by a certain number of threads at a single time. In most cases, only one thread may be executing in a critical section at one time. A *semaphore* is a data structure that limits access of a particular critical section to a certain number of threads. A *mutex* is a special case of a semaphore that grants exclusive access of the critical section to only one thread. With these basic

---

[5] Microsoft defines an additional function for signaling events: PulseEvent(). PulseEvent() combines the functionality of SetEvent() with ResetEvent(). It is not covered in this text, other than in this footnote, as Microsoft's documentation indicates that the function is unreliable and should not be used.

definitions in hand, we are now in a position to examine how Microsoft implements these constructs. Generally speaking, the implementation of these concepts is straightforward in Windows.

A semaphore object is created using the Windows CreateSemaphore() call:

```
HANDLE CreateSemaphore(
        LPSECURITY_ATTRIBUTES lpSemaphoreAttributes,
        LONG lInitialCount,
        LONG lMaximumCount,
        LPCTSTR lpName );
```

Like the previous thread functions, CreateSemaphore() allows the programmer to set certain security attributes that determine whether or not the handle will be inherited by child processes. The maximum number of threads that may be accessing the critical section protected by the semaphore is specified by the lMaximumCount parameter. A name, as pointed to by the lpName parameter, can be given to the semaphore. This name can then be used by the OpenSemaphore() function to get a handle to an already created semaphore:

```
HANDLE OpenSemaphore( DWORD dwDesiredAccess,
                BOOL bInheritHandle,
                LPCTSTR lpName );
```

It should be noted that by specifying a name in the lpName parameter, the program will create a system-wide semaphore that is available and visible to all processes. Specifying NULL for this parameter creates a local semaphore. Unless inter-process communication is needed, it is recommended that programs use local semaphores.

Once a semaphore is created, the developer can wait on the semaphore using WaitForSingleObject(). WaitForSingleObject() will wait on the semaphore handle until the thread is able to acquire the semaphore, the specified timeout has expired, or an error occurred with the call to WaitForSingleObject(). In the case that the thread is allowed to enter the critical section, the semaphore count is decreased by 1 until it reaches 0. At that point, the semaphore enters the non-signaled state and no other threads are allowed into the critical section until one of the threads exits the critical section by calling ReleaseSemaphore():

```
BOOL ReleaseSemaphore( HANDLE hSemaphore,
                LONG lReleaseCount,
                LPLONG lpPreviousCount );
```

ReleaseSemaphore() will increment the semaphore's object count by the increment value specified in lReleaseCount.[6] An example of using semaphore objects to protect a critical section of code is shown in Listing 5.3:

```
1   HANDLE hSemaphore;
2   DWORD status;
3
4   // Create a binary semaphore that is unlocked
5   // We don't care about the name in this case
6   hSemaphore = CreateSemaphore(NULL, 1, 1, NULL);
7
8   // verify semaphore is valid
9   if (NULL == hSemaphore)
10  {
11      // Handle error
12      ;
13  }
14
15  ...
16
17  // We are now testing our critical section
18  status = WaitForSingleObject(hSemaphore, 0);
19
20  if (status != WAIT_OBJECT_0)
21  {
22    // cannot enter critical section - handle appropriately
23  }
24  else
25  {
26    // enter critical section
27    // time to exit critical section
28    status = ReleaseSemaphore(hSemaphore, 1, NULL);
29    if (!status)
30    {
31      // release failed, recover from error here
32    }
33  }
```

Listing 5.3   Using a Semaphore Object to Protect a Critical Section of Code

---

[6] If the increment value were to cause the semaphore's count to exceed the maximum count, the count will remain unchanged, and the function will return FALSE, indicating an error condition. Always check return values for error conditions!

A mutex in Windows works in much the same way as the semaphore object does. The programmer makes a call to `CreateMutex()`, which returns a handle which may be used by `WaitForSingleObject()` to determine whether or not a thread may access a critical section. When a thread is about to leave a critical section, it makes a call to `ReleaseMutex()`, which indicates that the thread is exiting the critical section. A mutex may be named, and may be opened by calling `OpenMutex()`. As in the case of semaphores, associating a name to a mutex will create a system wide mutex. Listing 5.4 shows how to use a mutex object:

```
1    HANDLE hMutex;
2    DWORD status;
3
4    // Create a mutex
5    // Note that there aren't count parameters
6    // A mutex only allows a single thread to be executing
7    // in the critical section
8    // The second parameter indicates whether or not
9    // the thread that creates the mutex will automatically
10   // acquire the mutex. In our case it won't
11   // We don't care about the name in this case
12   hMutex = CreateMutex(NULL, FALSE, NULL);
13   if (NULL == hMutex) // verify mutex is valid
14   {
15       // handle error here
16   }
17
18   ...
19
20   // We are now testing our critical section
21   status = WaitForSingleObject(hMutex, 0);
22
23   if (status != WAIT_OBJECT_0)
24   {
25     // cannot enter critical section - handle appropriately
26   }
27   else
28   {
29     // enter critical section
30     // do some work
31
32     ...
33
34     // time to exit critical section
35     status = ReleaseMutex(hMutex);
36     if (!status)
```

```
37     {
38        // release failed, recover from error here
39     }
40  }
```

Listing 5.4   Using a Mutex Object to Protect a Critical Section of Code

There's one important point to note with regards to both the mutex and semaphore objects. These objects are kernel objects, and can be used to synchronize access between process boundaries. This ability comes at a price; in order to acquire a semaphore, a call to the kernel must be made. As a result, acquiring a semaphore or mutex incurs overhead, which may hurt the performance of certain applications. In the case that the programmer wants to synchronize access to a group of threads in a single process, the programmer may use the CRITICAL_SECTION data structure. This object will run in user space, and does not incur the performance penalty of transferring control to the kernel to acquire a lock.

The semantics of using CRITICAL_SECTION objects are different from those of mutex and semaphore objects. The CRITICAL_SECTION API defines a number of functions that operation on CRITICAL_SECTION objects:

```
void InitializeCriticalSection( LPCRITICAL_SECTION lpCS );
void InitializeCriticalSectionAndSpinCount(
                             LPCRITICAL_SECTION lpCS,
                             DWORD dwSpinCount );
void EnterCriticalSection( LPCRITICAL_SECTION lpCS );
BOOL TryEnterCriticalSection( LPCRITICAL_SECTION lpCS );
void LeaveCriticalSection( LPCRITICAL_SECTION lpCS );
DWORD SetCriticalSectionSpinCount( LPCRITICAL_SECTION lpCS,
                             DWORD dwSpinCount );
void DeleteCriticalSection( LPCRITICAL_SECTION lpCS );
```

EnterCriticalSection() blocks on a critical section object when it is not available. The non-blocking form of this operation is TryEnterCriticalSection().

Atomic Operations

Acquiring mutexes and other locking primitives can be very expensive. Many modern computer architectures support special instructions that allow programmers to quickly perform common atomic operations without the overhead of acquiring a lock. Microsoft supports the operations through the use of the Interlocked API.

The Interlocked functions perform atomic operations 32-bit and 64-bit variables. These functions enable the following operations:

■ *InterlockedIncrement()* atomically increments a 32-bit variable. The 64-bit version is InterlockedIncrement64().

■ *InterlockedDecrement()* atomically decrements a 32-bit variable. The 64-bit version is InterlockedDecrement64().

■ *InterlockedExchange()* atomically assigns one 32-bit value to another target variable. The 64-bit version is InterlockedExchange64(). To exchange pointers, use the InterlockedExchangePointer() function.

■ *InterlockedExchangeAdd()* provides an atomic version of the C += operator. The function atomically adds a value to a target 32-bit variable and then assigns the resulting sum to the target variable. The 64-bit version is InterlockedExchangeAdd64().

■ *InterlockedCompareExchange()* atomically compares the destination value with a comparison value and updates the destination if the comparison is true. The function takes three parameters: a pointer to the *Destination* variable, an *Exchange* value, which is a 32-bit value to assign to *Destination* if the comparison is true, and *Comperand,* which is the value that *Destination* will be compared with. If *Destination* is equal to *Comperand,* then *Destination* is assigned to the value of *Exchange*. If the comparison fails, then the function doesn't do anything. The 64-bit version of this function is InterlockedCompareExchange64(). To exchange pointers, use InterlockedCompareExchangePointer().

In addition to providing atomic access to variables, the Interlocked functions enable atomic access to singly linked lists. Four operations are defined as part of this class of operations:

■ *InitializeSListHead()* initializes the linked list.

■ *InterlockedPushEntrySList()* atomically adds a node to the front of the list.

■ *InterlockedPopEntrySList()* atomically removes a node from the front of the list.

■ *InterlockedFlushSList()* atomically removes all nodes in the list.

Thread Pools

In certain applications, the developer may need to dynamically allocate a number of threads to perform some task. The number of threads may vary greatly, depending on variables that are completely out of the developer's control. For example, in a Web server application, there may be times where the server is sitting idle, with no work to be done. During other times, the server may be handling thousands of requests at any given time. One approach to handling this scenario in software would be dynamic thread creation. As the system starts receiving more and more work, the programmer would create new threads to handle incoming requests. When the system slows down, the programmer may decide to destroy a number of the threads created during peak load as there isn't any work to be done and the threads are occupying valuable system resources.

A couple of problems are associated with dynamic thread creation. First, thread creation can be an expensive operation. During peak traffic, a Web server will spend more time creating threads than it will spend actually responding to user requests. To overcome that limitation, the developer may decide to create a group of threads when the application starts. These threads would be ready to handle requests as they come in. This certainly helps solve the overhead problem, but other problems still remain. What is the optimal number of threads that should be created? How can these threads be scheduled optimally based on current system load? At the application level, most developers don't have visibility into these parameters, and as a result, it makes sense for the operating system to provide some support for the notion of a thread pool.

Beginning with Windows 2000, Microsoft started providing a thread pool API that greatly reduces the amount of code that the developer needs to write to implement a thread pool. The principal function for using the thread pool is `QueueUserWorkItem()`:

```
BOOL QueueUserWorkItem ( LPTHREAD_START_ROUTINE Function,
                         PVOID Context,
                         ULONG Flags );
```

The first two parameters are of the kind you've seen before in creating Windows threads. The routine `Function()` is a pointer to a function that represents the work the thread in the pool must perform. This function must have the form:

```
DWORD WINAPI Function( LPVOID parameter );
```

The return value is the thread's exit code, which can be obtained by calling `GetExitCodeThread()`. The `parameter` argument contains a pointer to void. This construct is a generic way of allowing a program to pass a single parameter or a structure containing multiple parameters. Simply cast this parameter within the `Function` routine to point to the desired data type. The `Flags` parameter will be examined shortly.

When `QueueUserWorkItem()` is called for the first time, Windows creates a thread pool. One of these threads will be assigned to `Function`. When it completes, the thread is returned to the pool, where it awaits a new assignment. Because Windows relies on this process, `Function()` must not make any calls that terminate the thread. If no threads are available when `QueueUserWorkItem()` is called, Windows has the option of expanding the number of threads in the pool by creating additional threads. The size of the thread pool is dynamic and under the control of Windows, whose internal algorithms determine the best way to handle the current thread workload.

If you know the work you're assigning will take a long time to complete, you can pass `WT_EXECUTELONGFUNCTION` as the third parameter in the call to `QueueUserWorkItem()`. This option helps the thread pool management functions determine how to allocate threads. If all threads are busy when a call is made with this flag set, a new thread is automatically created.

Threads in Windows thread pools come in two types: those that handle asynchronous I/O and those that don't. The former rely on I/O completion ports, a Windows kernel entity that enables threads to be associated with I/O on specific system resources. How to handle I/O with completion ports is a complex process that is primarily the province of server applications. A thorough discussion of I/O completion ports may be found in *Programming Applications for Microsoft Windows* (Richter 1999).

When calling `QueueUserWorkItem()`, you should identify which threads are performing I/O and which ones are not by setting the `WT_EXECUTIONDEFAULT` field into the `QueueUserWorkItem() Flags` parameter. This tells the thread pool that the thread does not perform asynchronous I/O and it should be managed accordingly. Threads that do perform asynchronous I/O should use the `WT_EXECUTEINIOTHREAD` flag.

When using many threads and functional decomposition, consider using the thread pool API to save some programming effort and to allow Windows the best possible opportunities to achieve maximum performance

Thread Priority

All operating systems that support threads use a priority scheme to determine how threads should be allocated time to run on a particular core processor. This enables important work to proceed while lesser tasks wait for processing resources to become available. Every operating system has a different way of handling priorities. Much of the time, priorities are of no great concern; however, every once in a while priorities can be important to know how a particular thread will run in the context of competing threads.

Windows uses a scheme in which threads have priorities that range from 0 (lowest priority) to 31 (highest priority). The Windows scheduler *always* schedules the highest priority threads first. This means that higher-priority threads could hog the system causing lower-priority threads to starve—if it wasn't for priority boosts. Windows can dynamically boost a thread's priority to avoid thread starvation. Windows automatically does this when a thread is brought to the foreground, a window receives a message such as a mouse input, or a blocking condition (event) is released. Priority boosts can somewhat be controlled by the user via the following four functions:

```
SetProcessPriorityBoost( HANDLE hProc, BOOL disable )
SetThreadPriorityBoost( HANDLE hThread, BOOL disable )
GetProcessPriorityBoost( HANDLE hProc, PBOOL disable )
GetThreadPriorityBoost( HANDLE hThread, PBOOL disable )
```

All threads are created, by default, with their priority set to normal. After creation, a thread's priority is changed using this function:

```
BOOL SetThreadPriority( HANDLE threadHandle,
                        int newPriority );
```

The possible values for `newPriority` are specified in Table 5.1, which lists the priorities in descending order. The values are self-explanatory.

Table 5.1 Symbolic Constants for Representing the Priorities Supported by Windows

Symbolic Constant for Thread Priority
THREAD_PRIORITY_TIME_CRITICAL
THREAD_PRIORITY_HIGHEST
THREAD_PRIORITY_ABOVE_NORMAL
THREAD_PRIORITY_NORMAL

| THREAD_PRIORITY_BELOW_NORMAL |
| THREAD_PRIORITY_LOWEST |
| THREAD_PRIORITY_IDLE |

The function that returns a thread's priority level is:

```
int GetThreadPriority( HANDLE threadHandle );
```

This function returns a value that translates into one of the symbolic constants in Table 5.1. Note that Windows does not identify a thread's priority level on the 0 to 31 scale nor does it allow a thread's priority to be set with such specificity. This design enables Microsoft to define new priority levels at a future date.

You will rarely need to boost a thread's priority significantly. However, one unique situation does warrant special consideration. In cases where precise timing is critical, the thread performing the timing might need to boost its priority to the highest level. This measure is used to prevent the thread from being swapped out while it is reading from the system timer. Immediately upon getting the timing information, the thread's priority should be reset back to normal or to its original priority. It's important to realize that while a thread is running at highest priority, other threads are waiting, so it's generally advisable not to abuse this priority level by using it excessively.

Priority levels affect the way a thread is scheduled. On processors with Hyper-Threading Technology (HT Technology), the two logical processors do not interact on the basis of thread priority. Both threads have an equal chance of using a free resource, and their instructions are interleaved in the most efficient way possible, without any consideration paid to thread priority. On multi-core processors, it's important to understand that one cannot rely on priority to provide mutually-exclusive access to a critical section. On a single-core processor, a careless developer might make the assumption that since one thread is always a higher priority than another that it will always execute to completion before the lower-priority thread gets a chance to execute. This is not the case on a multi-core processor; both the high and low priority threads may run simultaneously.

Processor Affinity

When threads are scheduled for execution, Windows chooses which processor should run it. The policy it uses in selecting the processor is called *soft affinity*. This policy suggests to the Windows scheduler that threads should, as much as possible, run on the processor on which they ran previously. The idea is that this policy makes best use of data that might remain in processor cache.

Affinity, or the preference for a thread to run on a given processor, can be set by the developer. This is a desirable thing to do in some situations. For example, say a program uses four threads of which two perform considerable I/O and two perform intensive number crunching. If these threads are running on a dual-core system with HT Technology, four logical processors are available to the program. If both I/O threads run on the same physical processor core and the number-crunching threads run on the other processor core, then the processing load will be poorly balanced. The I/O processor core will spend considerable time waiting as both threads are reading or writing data. Meanwhile, the processor core running the number-crunching threads will be working continuously trying to perform the calculations.

By use of thread affinity, a developer can place one I/O thread and one calculation thread on the same physical processor core, and likewise on the second processor core. Now, when the I/O thread is waiting for data to be read or written, its resources can be temporarily made available to the calculation thread. By this means, the processor makes best use of the delays, and the two threads help each other while keeping both processors completely busy.

To achieve this kind of load balancing between threads and processor cores, you need to tell Windows on which processor to run the thread. Windows must follow this instruction. As a result, unless you know for sure that your preference will improve performance, as in the example, it is best not to specify affinity because doing so will interfere with the scheduler's own optimized scheduling algorithms. Thorough testing is the best way to know with certainty the benefits of this optimization. If you find a compelling reason to set a thread's processor affinity, you do it with the following function:

```
DWORD_PTR SetThreadAffinityMask (
          HANDLE threadHandle,
          DWORD_PTR threadAffinityMask );
```

The `threadAffinityMask` parameter is actually an unsigned integer. It has one bit turned on for every logical processor on which the thread can be scheduled. The first processor core, core 0, is indicated by an affinity mask of 0x01. The second processor core, core 1, is indicated by an affinity mask of 0x02. A thread that can run on either one of these processors will have an affinity mask of 0x03, and so forth.

The affinity mask must be a subset of the program's own affinity mask. Each program, or process, can specify its processor affinity. If the thread attempts to set its affinity to a processor core not within the process's affinity, an error ensues.

To obtain a process's affinity mask, you call:

```
BOOL GetProcessAffinityMask (
    HANDLE processHandle,
    PDWORD_PTR processAffinityMask,
    PDWORD_PTR systemAffinityMask );
```

To call this function, you provide the process handle, and Windows will fill in the process affinity mask and the system's affinity mask. The latter indicates which of the system's processors are capable of handling threads.

If need be, the process's affinity mask can be set from inside the program by calling:

```
BOOL SetProcessorAffinityMask (
    HANDLE processHandle,
    PDWORD_PTR processAffinityMask );
```

The parameters to this function are used and constructed in the same manner as those in `SetThreadAffinityMask()`, discussed previously.

As discussed earlier, using affinity masks to force Windows to place a thread on a given processor core is not always a good move. In some cases, the interference that this practice causes with the scheduler's method of running threads can create delays. As a result, affinity should be implemented judiciously. When testing shows that it realizes substantial benefits, it should be used. However, situations frequently arise where tests indicate a slight-to-moderate lift in using processor affinity. In these cases, you want to use affinity as long as it does not disrupt the Windows scheduler. The function to communicate affinity as a preference rather than a command is:

```
DWORD SetThreadIdealProcessor (
    HANDLE threadHandle,
    DWORD idealProcessor );
```

The second parameter is not an affinity mask, but an integer that indicates the processor core. The manifest constant MAXIMUM_PROCESSORS can be passed for this parameter. This value tells Windows that no particular processor core is preferred. This practice can be useful to disable affinity for a thread that previously had set affinity to a particular processor core. The function returns the previous ideal processor or MAXIMUM_PROCESSORS, if there was no previous ideal processor core.

Important questions arise here: how do you know how many processors a system has and which ones are configured and available? Again, the Windows API provides a solution to this problem. Listing 5.5 shows the code that extracts processor information for the runtime system from the operating system.

```
// program to obtain and display basic
// information about the runtime processor
// hardware on Windows systems

#include <windows.h>
#include <stdio.h>

void main()
{
    SYSTEM_INFO sysInfo;

    // Function loads sysInfo structure with data
    GetSystemInfo ( &sysInfo );
    // Display the data
    printf ( "System hardware information: \n" );
    printf ( "  OEM ID: %u\n", sysInfo.dwOemId );
    printf ( "  Number of processors: %u\n",
              sysInfo.dwNumberOfProcessors );
    printf ( "  Processor type: %u\n",
              sysInfo.dwProcessorType );
    printf ( "  Active processor mask: %u\n",
              sysInfo.dwActiveProcessorMask );
    printf ( "  Page size: %u bytes\n", sysInfo.dwPageSize );
}
```

Listing 5.5   How to Obtain Basic Processor Data from Windows

On a system with HT Technology running Windows XP, the output from this code is:

```
System hardware information:
  OEM ID: 0
  Number of processors: 2
  Processor type: 586
  Active processor mask: 3
    Page size: 4096 bytes
```

Notice that the number of processors is the number of logical processors. In other words, it recognizes the capabilities of HT Technology as distinct processors.

The active processor mask indicates which processors are configured, or available for use by Windows. Each bit is set to 1 for each configured processor, hence the decimal value 3 when the "processors" are configured.

On a dual-core system with HT Technology, the output from running the code in Listing 5.5 is:

```
System hardware information:
  OEM ID: 0
  Number of processors: 4
  Processor type: 586
  Active processor mask: 15
    Page size: 4096 bytes
```

User-level Threading with Fibers

Until this point, only *kernel threads* have been discussed. These are threads that are regularly preempted by other threads the Windows scheduler wants to run. In addition, all these threads have been kernel objects. This means the data regarding their status is created and maintained in the kernel by kernel processes, such as the scheduler.

Windows offers a user-level threading package called fibers. Fibers are completely contained in user space, and use cooperative, rather than preemptive scheduling. Fibers run until you decide to manually swap one out.

Here is how fibers work. A single thread can be broken down into tasks that are swapped in and out by the application. The Windows kernel knows nothing about the fibers; the kernel simply runs threads. The work that the threads are doing is unknown to the kernel. When using fibers, the thread is running the work of whichever fiber the developer has specified in the logic of the code. In other words, the scheduling algorithm is implemented in the application. Therefore, it is up to the developer to manage the scheduling of fibers and when they should run in the context of the thread's time slice. However, a limitation of fibers is that at no time can any single thread ever run more than one fiber at a time. As such, fibers are not a mechanism that enables greater parallelism, which means that they do not gain, at least directly, a performance benefit from HT Technology or multi-core platforms. The primary purpose of fibers is to provide the developer with a convenient method of scheduling multiple tasks that are known to *not* need parallel execution.

The first step in using Windows fibers is to convert the current thread into a fiber. Once this is done, additional fibers can be added. So, the following function is the first one to call:

```
PVOID ConvertThreadToFiber( PVOID parameters );
```

This function returns the address of the fiber's internal data area, which contains housekeeping items. This address should be saved. Later on, when you switch fibers, the address of this data area will be needed. The sole parameter to this function is a pointer to arguments for this fiber. It seems a bit strange for a thread to pass arguments to itself. However, this parameter can be retrieved from the fiber's internal data area using the function:

```
PVOID GetFiberData();
```

There is no point in converting a thread into a fiber unless you plan to run multiple fibers on the thread. So, once you've converted the thread into a fiber, you should next create the other fibers you plan to run. The function to do this is:

```
PVOID CreateFiber ( DWORD fiberStackSize,
                    PFIBER_START_ROUTINE fiberProc,
                    PVOID fiberProcParameters );
```

The first parameter specifies how large the stack for the fiber should be. Normally, a value of 0 is passed here. Passing a 0 will cause Windows to allocate two pages of storage and to limit the stack size to the default 1 MB. The next two parameters should look familiar from thread-creation functions you have previously seen. The first is a pointer to a fiber function; the second is a pointer to the parameters of that function. Note that unlike a thread function this fiber function does not return a value. This function has the form:

```
VOID WINAPI fiberProc( PVOID fiberProcParameters );
```

An important characteristic of the fiber function is that it must not exit. Remember that when using threads and the thread function exits, the thread is terminated. However, with fibers, the effect is more dramatic: the thread and *all* the fibers associated with it are terminated.

Again, it's important to save the address returned by `CreateFiber()` because it is used in the following function to switch among the fibers:

```
VOID SwitchToFiber( PVOID addressOfFiberEnvironment );
```

The sole parameter to this function is the address returned by `CreateFiber()` and `ConvertThreadToFiber()`. Switching to a fiber is the only way to activate a fiber. You can switch anytime you desire to. You basically receive total control over scheduling in exchange for the fact that only one fiber at a time can run on a thread. Only a fiber can switch to another fiber. This explains why you must convert the original thread into a fiber at the start of this process.

The function to delete a fiber is:

```
VOID DeleteFiber( PVOID addressOfFiberEnvironment );
```

A fiber can kill itself this way. However, when it does so, it kills the current thread and all fibers associated with it.

A final function that is useful is

```
PVOID GetCurrentFiber();
```

which returns the address of the fiber environment of the currently executing fiber.

Listing 5.6 shows the code for a program that creates some fibers and has them print their identification.

```
// demonstration of the use of Windows fibers
#define _WIN32_WINNT  0x400

#include <stdio.h>
#include <windows.h>

#define FIBER_COUNT 10
void *fiber_context[FIBER_COUNT];

VOID WINAPI fiberProc ( void * );

void main()
{
    int    i;
    int    fibers[FIBER_COUNT];

    for ( i = 0; i < FIBER_COUNT; i++ )
        fibers[i] = i;

    fiber_context[0] = ConvertThreadToFiber ( NULL );

    for ( i = 1; i < FIBER_COUNT; i++ )
    {
        fiber_context[i] = CreateFiber (
                            0,              // stack size
                            fiberProc,      // function
                            &fibers[i] );   // parameter
```

```
        if ( fiber_context[i] != NULL )
            printf ( "fiber %d created\n", i );
    }

    for ( i = 1; i < FIBER_COUNT; i++ )
    {
        if ( fiber_context[i] != NULL )
            SwitchToFiber ( fiber_context[i] );
    }
}

VOID WINAPI fiberProc ( void *fiber_nbr )
{
    int nbr;

    nbr = *( (int*) fiber_nbr );
    printf ( "Hello from fiber %d\n", nbr );

    // now switch back to the fiber of the main line
    SwitchToFiber ( fiber_context[0] );
}
```

Listing 5.6   Program to Create Fibers that Print an Identifying Message to the Console

Notice the #defined manifest constant at the very start of the listing. Fibers were introduced in Windows NT 4.0. The value of 0x400 in:

```
#define  _WIN32_WINNT  0x400
```

tells the compiler to include features in windows.h that appeared in Microsoft Windows NT 4.0 and later; hence, it includes support for function calls used by the fiber APIs. Failing to include the constant will result in compilation errors. The output from this program is:

```
fiber 1 created
fiber 2 created
fiber 3 created
fiber 4 created
fiber 5 created
fiber 6 created
fiber 7 created
fiber 8 created
fiber 9 created
Hello from fiber 1
Hello from fiber 2
Hello from fiber 3
Hello from fiber 4
Hello from fiber 5
Hello from fiber 6
```

```
Hello from fiber 7
Hello from fiber 8
Hello from fiber 9
```

Notice how the fibers print out their messages in a nice sequential order. This is, of course, attributable to the fact that only one fiber can run at a time and that the main fiber schedules which one runs when.

It might seem that fibers are not valuable in the context of parallel programming because they only run one at a time. However, they have considerable value in certain specific applications. Suppose for example that your application receives numerous requests that you want to handle individually. You could create a thread for each request, but this approach has drawbacks. Threads are expensive to start up and you don't have control over their execution. The former problem can be handled with thread pools, but because pools are generally used for all thread tasks a program must perform, the execution schedule is even more uncertain. In addition, if you have to expand your thread pool, the creation of threads is a kernel call and, hence, expensive.

Fibers, however, are cheap to create because they do not involve user-space to kernel transitions. In fact, several of the fiber functions are implemented as inline functions. Fibers are an efficient mechanism any time you have multiple tasks to perform and are content doing one at a time. Notice that you can emulate parallel processing by swapping fibers as needed. This way, if a fiber is about to wait on a slow process, you can swap in another fiber and give it as much time as you deem necessary. In some situations where the behavior and parallelism of the application is well known, fibers may even provide a performance benefit due to the reduction of synchronization and task-switching overhead.

Compiling and Linking Multi-threaded Applications in Windows

In order to simplify the building of multi-threaded applications for Windows platforms, Microsoft has built in support for multithreading into the Microsoft compiler. The first step in compiling a multi-threaded application is to make sure that the compiler is using the correct runtime libraries. Microsoft provides several different implementations of the standard C runtime library. These versions vary based on three different criteria: linkage (static or dynamic), whether or not the library is re-entrant,[7] and whether or not the library includes debugging symbols. The

---

[7] One library is designed for single-threaded applications; it is not re-entrant. The other library is designed for multi-threaded applications; it is re-entrant.

compiler switches that are used in multi-threaded applications are shown in Table 5.2. These compiler switches can be specified on the command line or by selecting the appropriate option in the "code generation" tab of the project's properties within Visual Studio, as shown in Figure 5.1.

Table 5.2   Command-line Switches for Compiling Multi-threaded Code in Windows.

Switch	Meaning
/MT	Multithreaded with static linkage
/MTd	Multithreaded with debugging enabled
/MD	Multi-threaded dynamic link library (DLL)
/MDd	Multi-threaded DLL with debugging enabled

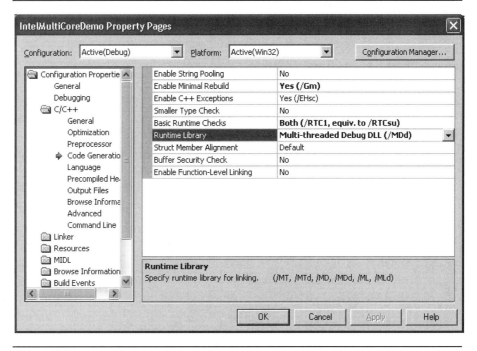

Figure 5.1   Enabling Multi-threading in Microsoft Visual Studio

In addition, the _MT preprocessor value should be defined. This is the agreed convention in Windows for testing code for multithreading. It is set by the /D "_MT" command-line switch.

The appropriate libraries are generally brought in by setting the correct flag from Table 5.2. However, it is important to know more about which libraries are used. This knowledge will help in the case that you need to troubleshoot compiler issues or you want to write custom makefiles. Table 5.3 provides the list of multi-threaded libraries that are used when linking in the Microsoft C runtime library.

Table 5.3 Microsoft's Multi-threaded Libraries for C Programs

Program Type	C Runtime Library
Multithreaded	LIBCMT.lib
Multithreaded with debugging	LIBCMTD.lib
Multi-threaded DLL	MSVCRT.lib (import library for MSVCRT.dll)
Multi-threaded DLL with debugging	MSVCRTD.lib (import library for MSVCRTD.dll)

The libraries for the C++ runtime are different, as shown in Table 5.4

Table 5.4 Microsoft's Multi-threaded Libraries for C++ Programs

Program Type	C++ Runtime library
Multithreaded	LIBCPMT.lib
Multithreaded with debugging	LIBCPMTD.lib
Multithreaded DLL	MSVCPRT.lib (also uses MSVCRT.dll)
Multithreaded DLL with debugging	MSVCPRTD.lib (also uses MSVCRTD.dll)

A word of caution is in order here. Developers should not intermix the use of static and dynamic libraries in a single process space. Multiple copies of the C runtime library within a single process space will result in unstable behavior.[8] The Microsoft linker will prevent this error in the case where the developer tries to link both the static and dynamic versions of the runtime library into a single .exe. However, in the case of a .dll that is used by an .exe, it is the programmer's responsibility to guarantee that the .exe and .dll are built with the same version of the C runtime.

---

[8] Note that this is the second time that using the standard C library routines has introduced an additional level of complexity to using threads in Windows; the first was when using the CreateThread() call. In general, Microsoft encourages the use of the Win32 API over the standard C library, for instance, CreateFile() instead of fopen(). Using the Win32 API exclusively will simplify writing Windows-based multi-threaded applications.

Threading APIs for Microsoft .NET Framework

In 2002, Microsoft introduced a new execution environment, called the Common Language Runtime (CLR), which executes programs in the form of intermediate code, rather than native binaries. This code is conceptually similar to Java bytecodes in that the CLR executes them within a carefully defined virtual machine. And like Java, it frequently uses just-in-time compilation to convert the intermediate code into binary routines on the fly.

The goal of this design was to provide a common execution environment for all the major languages Microsoft supported at the time, notably C++ and Visual Basic, and for a new language, named C#, that Microsoft unveiled with the launch of the CLR and associated technologies. Those technologies included an extensive set of APIs commonly referred to as the .NET Framework. Together, the framework, the CLR, and the tools needed for execution, are referred to as .NET.

The .NET Framework has extensive support for threads. The API provides a substantial subset of the functionality of the Windows API. It does not include some features, such as fibers, but most thread management functions and concepts are present. These are implemented in the .NET Framework class entitled Thread. This section discusses how to use Thread in .NET. The examples are implemented in C#. If you want to use another .NET language, such as C++, Visual Basic .NET, or JScript, consult Microsoft's .NET Framework Class Library Reference, which provides examples of the APIs in all four languages.

Creating Threads

On the whole, .NET APIs tend to be somewhat leaner than their Win32 counterparts. This is especially visible in the call for creating a new thread:

```
using System.Threading;
. . .
Thread t = new Thread( new ThreadStart( ThreadFunc ));
```

The call to `ThreadStart()` constructs a new thread. The parameter is a delegate called `ThreadFunc`. In C#, a *delegate* is the equivalent of an address of a function in C. It's a manner of identifying a function or method without actually invoking it. As with Win32, when `ThreadFunc()` ends, the thread terminates.

Listing 5.7 illustrates a simple creation of a thread and the call to the ThreadFunc.

```
1    using System;
2    using System.Threading;
3
4    public class ThreadDemo1
5    {
6        public static void ThreadFunc()
7        {
8            for ( int i = 0; i < 3; i++ )
9                Console.WriteLine(
10                   "Hello #{0} from ThreadFunc", i );
11               Thread.Sleep( 10000 );
12       }
13
14       // The main entry point for the application.
15       public static void Main()
16       {
17           Thread t =
18               new Thread( new ThreadStart( ThreadFunc ) );
19           t.Start();
20           Thread.Sleep( 40 );
21
22           for ( int j = 0; j < 4; j++ )
23           {
24               Console.WriteLine( "Hello from Main Thread" );
25               Thread.Sleep( 0 );
26           }
27       }
28   }
```

Listing 5.7   Simple Program Showing Thread Creation

A new thread is created using `ThreadStart()` on lines 17–18. The ThreadFunc is defined in lines 6–12. An important difference between the Win32 and .NET APIs appears here. In Win32, the creation of a thread results in a request to the scheduler to execute it. No additional step is necessary. In .NET, this is not so. The thread must be explicitly started by the `start()` method, as shown on line 19. This method changes the status of the thread to `Runnable` inside .NET, which makes it eligible for processing by the scheduler. On a single processor system, however, .NET will not start the thread until the main thread has completed or is suspended. This can cause obvious problems, so it is common to suspend the current, principal thread to enable created threads to begin execution. This is done on line 20 by the call to the Sleep() method. The sole argument to this method is a 32-bit integer that indicates the number of milliseconds to sleep before being awakened, that is, reactivated. As with nearly all things related to threads, nothing is guaranteed. So, the number of milliseconds is simply a request to the operating system. The actual number of milliseconds in the sleeping state might vary considerably from the requested amount.

Because Microsoft is aware that Sleep() must be called to start up waiting threads, it provides a special value of 0 to indicate that the principal thread should be suspended only long enough to start execution of the any waiting threads. On the other end of the scale, the special value Infinite tells the scheduler to suspend the thread indefinitely.

As Listing 5.7 illustrates, the method for creating a function in C# is much more concise than the corresponding function call in C on Win32. This concision comes at a cost, however. The delegate called when a thread is started accepts no parameters, so it is difficult to pass thread-specific information to the delegate. To pass data without making it accessible globally is an advanced topic, which is beyond the scope of this book. (Abrams 2004), however, explains how to do this.

Thread Priority and Other Properties

As discussed in the previous sections on the Win32 API, thread priority determines when the scheduler will schedule execution. Threads with higher priority can grab the processor for themselves and even starve lower priority threads, so managing priority in special circumstances can be beneficial. For the most part, you should accept the default priority that .NET assigns to your threads. However, if you need to change it, you simply specify it as an assignment to the thread.Priority property. For example,

```
Thread nThread = new Thread ( ThreadFunc );
nthread.Priority = AboveNormal;
nThread.Start ();
```

The .NET framework supports five levels of thread priority:
- Highest
- AboveNormal
- Normal (the default level)
- BelowNormal
- Lowest

Each of these levels represents a group of fine-grained levels, which are accessible through Win32. When the thread is started, the scheduler determines where in the group of levels to place the thread. For example, if you specify `BelowNormal`, the scheduler chooses the sub-level within `BelowNormal` to place your thread. You have no control over this decision.

Another useful property .NET provides enables you to name a thread. This option has several benefits, the most important of which is in debugging, where the name makes it much easier for developers to identify which thread is being followed. To name a thread, simply initialize its `.name` property. For example:

```
Thread nThread = new Thread ( ThreadFunc );
nthread.Name = "new_thread1";
nThread.Start ();
```

Having examined thread creation, let's examine how threads are terminated and how their activities can be suspended and restarted.

Managing Threads

The simplest and safest way to terminate a thread is to exit it. Doing so, permits the CLR to perform the necessary clean up without any difficulty. At times, however, it's necessary to terminate some other thread. As part of the .NET threading API, an `Abort()` method is supplied for this purpose. A call to `Abort()` generates a `ThreadAbortException`, where any code should go to handle an abort signal in the middle of an unfinished operation. In addition, the call will execute any code in the aborted thread's `finally` statement. Listing 5.8 shows the calls.

```
1    using System;
2    using System.Threading;
3
4    public class ThreadAbortExample
5    {
6        public static void Thread2()
7        {
8            try
9            {
10                Console.WriteLine( "starting t2" );
11                Thread.Sleep( 500 );
12                Console.WriteLine( "finishing t2" );
13            }
14            catch( ThreadAbortException e )
```

```
15              {
16                  Console.WriteLine( "in t2\'s catch block");
17              }
18              finally
19              {
20                  Console.WriteLine( "in t2\'s finally" );
21              }
22          }
23
24      public static void Main()
25      {
26          Thread t = new Thread( new ThreadStart(Thread2) );
27          Console.WriteLine( "starting main thread" );
28          t.Start();
29          Thread.Sleep( 500 );
30          t.Abort();
31          t.Join();
32          Console.WriteLine( "main thread finished.\n" +
33                             "Press <Enter> to exit" );
34          Console.ReadLine();
35      }
36  }
```

Listing 5.8   How to Abort a Thread in .NET

Lines 26–28 start a second thread, t, as illustrated previously. After a brief pause (line 29), t is aborted. The effect of this is to call the catch code in Thread2's exception handler, followed by the code in the finally clause. The output of this program is:

```
starting main thread
starting t2
finishing t2
in t2's catch block
in t2's finally
main thread finished.
Press <Enter> to exit
```

Calling Abort() results in a more complicated set of actions. The first is that the thread being aborted can thwart the action by calling the System.Threading.Thread.ResertAbort method inside the exception handler.

Another factor should be borne in mind: processing in the finally block might take a substantial amount of time. Because the thread will stay alive throughout the processing of the finally code, the thread might not abort for a substantial period of time, sometimes not until the program itself is finished. Because of these two possibilities of a thread persisting past the initial `Abort()`, it might be necessary to verify that a specific thread has indeed been aborted. The way to do this is to use the `join` method, which is discussed next.

Waiting on a Thread

Threads often need to wait on each other. This concept is presented in the Win32 APIs as "waiting on an event." The .NET Framework borrows the model used by Pthreads—the API employed in Linux and several versions of UNIX. There the concept is known as *joining* a thread, and it simply means waiting for that thread to finish. Line 31 of Listing 5.8 shows how this method is called. In that program, the main thread creates and aborts `Thread2` then joins it. This is the preferred way of knowing with certainty that a given thread has aborted.

It is important to note that the thread calling `Join()` blocks until the joined thread exits. In some circumstances, this might not be desirable because in such cases, `Join()` can be called with a 32-bit integer parameter, which indicates the maximum number of milliseconds to wait for the joined thread to complete. When called, this way, `Join()` returns the Boolean value `true` if the thread terminated, and `false` if the thread did not terminate and the return occurred because the maximum wait expired.

Suspending and Resuming Threads

Earlier in this section, we described the use of the `Sleep()` method to suspend a thread for a time-delimited duration. Examples of its use appear in lines 11 and 20 of Listing 5.8.

There are times, however, when it's desirable to suspend a thread for an indefinite period of time and then resume it at a later point. The pair of methods to do this are `Suspend()` and `Resume()`. Neither of these methods takes an argument or returns a value.

Thread Pools

The creation of a new thread is an expensive operation. A lot of system-level activity is generated to create the new thread of execution, create thread-local storage, and set up the system structures to manage the thread. As a result of this overhead, conservation of created threads is a recommended practice. The effect on performance, especially on slower machines, can be compelling.

However, managing the task of managing multiple threads, some of which might be dormant, and assigning new chunks of work to the threads as the work becomes available, leads to a significant amount of code complexity. In response, the .NET Framework provides a resource called *thread pools*.

A pool of threads is initially created as well as a work queue of sorts. As new chunks of work become available they are queued up for the thread pool, which executes them as threads are available. The process of managing the work queue, waking threads, and assigning them the work is all handled by the .NET Framework. This is a valuable resource. If your program uses more than a few threads, thread pools should be considered as an option.

.NET's ThreadPool class does most of the work of thread pools. The pool is created the first time work is queued for it—a remarkably high-level operation. The exact number of threads created in the pool is dynamic and determined by .NET when the pool is created. However, .NET enforces a maximum of 25 threads per hardware processor. The ThreadPool methods GetMinThreads() and SetMinThreads() can be used to inquire and enforce a minimum number of threads. A corresponding GetMaxThreads() method informs you of the maximum, but there is no method that enables you to increase this value.

Listing 5.9 shows a simple example of a thread pool in use.

```
1    using System;
2    using System.Threading;
3    public class ThreadPoolExample
4    {
5        public static void Main()
6        {
7            // Queue a piece of work
8            ThreadPool.QueueUserWorkItem(
9                    new WaitCallback( WorkToDo ) );
10
11           Console.WriteLine( "Greetings from Main()" );
12           Thread.Sleep( 1000 );
13
14           Console.WriteLine( "Main thread exiting...\n" +
15                               "Press <enter> to close" );
16           Console.ReadLine();
17       }
18
19       // This thread procedure performs the task.
20       static void WorkToDo( Object dataItems )
```

```
21              {
22                  Console.WriteLine("Greetings from thread pool");
23              }
24      }
```

Listing 5.9   Simple Example of Using a Thread Pool in .NET

The thread pool is created by the first call to the work queue, which occurs in line 8. As in thread creation, it is passed a delegate; which, in this case points to the method defined in lines 20–23. As can be seen from the signature on line 20, there is an overloaded version, which permits an object to be passed to the work procedure. Frequently, this data object contains state information about the status of the application when the call work was queued, but it can, in fact, contain any data object.

Notice the call to `Sleep()` on line 12. It is necessary for successful completion of this program. Without this statement, the program could exit without the work queue ever having completed its work. Because the work can be assigned to any available thread, the main thread has no way to join any of the pool's threads, so it has no mechanism for waiting until they complete. Of course, the threads in the pool can modify a data item to indicate activity, but that is a not a .NET-specific solution.

The output from this program is:

```
Greetings from Main()
Greetings from thread pool.
Main thread exiting...
Press <enter> to close
```

In addition to being work engines that consume queued work items, thread pools are effective means of assigning threads to wait on specific events, such as waiting on network traffic and other asynchronous events. The .NET Framework provides several methods for waiting. They require registering a call-back function that is invoked when the waited-for event occurs. One of the basic methods for registering a call-back and waiting is `RegisterWaitForSingleObject()`, which enables you to also specify a maximum wait period. The call-back function is called if the event occurs or the wait period expires. Listing 5.10, which is adapted from a Microsoft example, shows the necessary code.

```
1   using System;
2   using System.Threading;
3   // TaskInfo contains data that is passed to the callback
4   // method.
5   public class TaskInfo
```

```
 6      {
 7          public RegisteredWaitHandle Handle = null;
 8          public string OtherInfo = "default";
 9      }
10
11      public class Example
12      {
13          public static void Main( string[] args )
14          {
15
16              AutoResetEvent ev = new AutoResetEvent( false );
17
18              TaskInfo ti = new TaskInfo();
19              ti.OtherInfo = "First task";
20              ti.Handle =
21                  ThreadPool.RegisterWaitForSingleObject(
22                      ev,
23                      new WaitOrTimerCallback( WaitProc ),
24                      ti,
25                      1000,
26                      false );
27
28              // The main thread waits three seconds,
29              // to demonstrate the time-outs on the queued
30              // thread, and then signals.
31
32              Thread.Sleep( 3100 );
33              Console.WriteLine( "Main thread signals." );
34              ev.Set();
35
36              Thread.Sleep( 1000 );
37              Console.WriteLine( "Press <enter> to close." );
38              Console.ReadLine();
39          }
40
41      // The callback method executes when the registered
42      // wait times-out, or when the WaitHandle (in this
43      // case, AutoResetEvent) is signaled.
44
45          public static void WaitProc( object passedData,
46                                        bool timedOut )
47          {
48              TaskInfo ti = (TaskInfo) passedData;
49
50              string cause = "TIMED OUT";
51              if ( !timedOut )
52              {
53                  cause = "SIGNALED";
54                  if ( ti.Handle != null )
```

```
55                          ti.Handle.Unregister( null );
56                   }
57
58              Console.WriteLine(
59                   "WaitProc({0}) on thread {1}; cause={2}",
60                   ti.OtherInfo,
61                   Thread.CurrentThread.GetHashCode().ToString(),
62                   cause
63              );
64         }
65     }
```

Listing 5.10   Using Callbacks in Thread Pools to Wait on Events

There is a lot going on in this listing. The method that is registered for the callback is `WaitProc`, defined in lines 45-64. As can be seen, it takes two parameters: the first is an object containing data to be passed to the method, the second is a Boolean to indicate whether the call was generated by a time out (`true`) signal from the waited for event (`false`). The passed data object is cast to an object of type `TaskInfo`, which is defined in lines 3-9. The handle property of `TaskInfo` is returned from the call to `RegisterWaitForSingleObject()` on lines 21-26. The parameters to this method are complex. `ev` is a handle for the event being waited for—we'll come back to this shortly. The second parameter is the delegate for the callback function; as can be seen, that delegate must be of type `WaitOrTimerCallback`.

The third parameter is the data object to pass to the callback function. The fourth parameter is the number of milliseconds to wait. And the fifth is a Boolean that indicates whether the event should stop waiting after the delegate has been called (`true`) or keep wait anew (`false`).

As soon as the handle is created, the wait begins. The `Sleep` statement on line 32 allows this wait to expire several times. Because of the parameter on line 26, the wait renews and expires several times, each time calling the method pointed to by the delegate. Line 34 actually triggers the event via a direct call. The callback function is able to distinguish which event triggered the call by the `timedOut` parameter discussed previously. As a result, running this code generates the following output:

```
WaitProc(First task) executes on thread 4; cause=TIMED OUT.
WaitProc(First task) executes on thread 4; cause=TIMED OUT.
WaitProc(First task) executes on thread 6; cause=TIMED OUT.
Main thread signals.
WaitProc(First task) executes on thread 6; cause=SIGNALED.
Press <enter> to close.
```

The number of the thread on which the task is executed will vary from system to system. As can be seen, while the main thread is waiting, the 1-second duration expires three times, as expected. Then, the callback function is called one more time when the signal is sent.

The .NET Framework enables threads to start up based on more than a single event. The `WaitHandle.WaitAll()` and `WaitHandle.Wait-Any()` methods fire when all events in an array have been signaled, or if any one event in an array is signaled, respectively. Events themselves do not need to be automatic as in Listing 5.10; they can also be manual by using `ManualResetEvent()`. The difference is that an automatic reset will issue the signal and then reset itself so that it is not in the signaled state, whereas a manual reset event persists in the signaled state until it is manually reset. The choice between them depends entirely on the application's needs.

As this section has illustrated, thread pools are a very useful mechanism that enables sophisticated threading to be implemented conveniently in many applications. The range of options regarding events and the characteristics of signals give thread pools considerable flexibility.

Thread Synchronization

The mechanisms for synchronizing thread actions in .NET are similar to those found in all other threading APIs, such as Win32 and Pthreads. They include capabilities for mutual exclusion and for atomic actions on specific variables. By and large, .NET maintains the simplicity of expression seen in the previous examples. No synchronization is simpler, in fact, than use of the `lock` keyword in C#.

The usual way to use `lock` is to place it in front of a block of code delimited by braces. Then, that block can be executed by only one thread at a time. For example:

```
lock(this)
{
    shared_var = other_shared_var + 1;
    other_shared_var = 0;
}
```

The C# `lock` statement makes several calls to the .NET Framework. The previous example is syntactically equivalent to the following snippet:

```
Monitor.Enter( this )
try
{
        shared_var = other_shared_var + 1;
```

```
        other_shared_var = 0;
}
finally
{
        Monitor.Exit( this )
}
```

`Monitor` is a class that enforces mutual exclusion and locking in .NET. When used as in the previous example, `Monitor.Enter()` locks a code block. In this respect, it is similar to critical sections in the Win32 API.

Monitor can also be used to lock a data structure by passing that data structure as a parameter to the `Monitor.Enter()` call. `Monitor.Exit()` releases the lock. If `Monitor.Enter()` was called with an object, `Monitor.Exit()` should be called with the same object to release the lock. When `Monitor.Enter()` is called, the .NET Framework sets up two queues: one containing references to threads waiting to obtain the lock once it's released, and another queue containing references to threads that want to be signaled that the lock is available. When `Monitor.Exit()` is called, the next thread in the first queue gets the lock.

Monitors have unusual aspects. For example, the `Monitor.Wait()` method enables a thread to temporarily give up a lock to another thread and then reclaim it. A system of signals called *pulses* are used to notify the original thread that the lock has been released.

As you have learned, mutexes are a similar mechanism for providing mutual exclusion to resources. Mutexes differ from monitors in that they can be used with wait handles, as shown in the following example. They also can be locked multiple times. In such a case, they must be unlocked the same number of times before the lock is actually released.

To use a mutex, one must be created. Then a call to `WaitOne` is issued to grab the lock as soon as it becomes available, if it's not already available. Once the lock is no longer needed, it is made available with the `ReleaseMutex` method.

```
private static Mutex mutx = new Mutex();
. . .

private static void UseResource()
{
    // Wait to enter the locked code.
    mutx.WaitOne();

    Console.WriteLine( " in the locked code " );

    Thread.Sleep( 100 );
```

```
       Console.WriteLine( " leaving locked code ",

       // Release the Mutex.
       mutx.ReleaseMutex();
}
```

This is a simple, effective locking mechanism that is comparable to counterparts in Win32 and Pthreads.

Atomic Actions

Actions are atomic if they can only be performed as a single indivisible act. The term is commonly used in database operations to refer to a series of steps that must all be completed. If any of them can't be completed, all steps so far completed are rolled back, so that at no time does the database record a partial series. It's all or nothing. Threads present similar problems. Consider what happens if a thread is suspended while it is updating the values of an important variable. Suddenly, the application or the system can be left in a degenerate or corrupted state.[9] One solution is the `Interlocked` class. Although not discussed in the Win32 portion of this chapter, the Win32 API does have corresponding APIs.

The three most common methods of the `Interlocked` class are: `Decrement`, `Increment`, and `Exchange`. These are all simple methods to use and should be used anytime a variable shared between threads is being modified.

```
int intCounter = 0;
. . .

// set the value of intCounter to 6
Interlocked.Exchange( ref usingResource, 6 );

// Drop value to 5
Interlocked.Decrement( ref intCounter );

//Raise it back to 6
Interlocked.Increment( ref intCounter );
```

Several aspects are worthy of note. Firstly, the `Interlocked` class uses references to the variables to be modified, not the variables themselves; so make sure to include the `ref` keyword, as in the

---

[9] It might come as a surprise to some readers that incrementing or decrementing a variable is not inherently an indivisible action. It takes three instructions: the variable is copied into a register in the processor core by a process called *loading*, incremented, and then copied from the register back to the variable's location in memory.

previous examples. These references are the equivalent of addresses or pointers from C and C++. Secondly, the Exchange method is not really used for exchanging values but initializing one value to another. In the example, the value of 0 to which intCounter was initialized is exchanged with 6, leaving 6 as the new value of intCounter.

As can be seen from this overview, the .NET Framework's set of threading APIs is more succinct than its counterparts in Win32. It also includes higher-level capabilities, such as advanced thread pool manage-ment functions. The upshot is that programming threads in C# on .NET tends to be easier and overall more productive than at the lower levels of Win32.

POSIX Threads

POSIX threads, or Pthreads, is a portable threading library designed with the intent of providing a consistent programming interface across multiple operating system platforms. Pthreads is now the standard threading interface for Linux and is also widely used on most UNIX platforms. An open-source version for Windows, called pthreads-win32, is available as well. For more information on pthreads-win32, refer to References. If you want to work in C and need a *portable* threading API that provides more direct control than OpenMP, pthreads is a good choice.

Most core Pthreads functions focus on thread creation and destruction, synchronization, plus a few miscellaneous functions. Capabilities like thread priorities are not a part of the core pthreads library, but instead are a part of the optional capabilities that are vendor specific.

Creating Threads

The POSIX threads call to create a thread is pthread_create():

```
pthread_create (
    &a_thread,        // thread ID goes here
    NULL,             // thread attributes (NULL = none)
    PrintThreads,     // function name
    (void *) msg );   // parameter
```

As in Windows, the third parameter represents a pointer to the function called by the launched thread, while the fourth parameter is a pointer to a void, which is used to pass arguments to the called function.

Listing 5.11 illustrates the usage of pthread_create() to create a thread.

```
1    #include <stdio.h>
2    #include <stdlib.h>
3    #include <pthread.h>
4
5    void *PrintThreads ( void * );
6
7    #define NUM_THREADS 9
8
9    int main()
10   {
11       int i, ret;
12       pthread_t a_thread;
13
14       int thdNum [NUM_THREADS];   //thread numbers go here
15
16       for ( i = 0; i < NUM_THREADS; i++ )
17           thdNum[i] = i;
18
19       for ( i = 0; i < NUM_THREADS; i++ )
20       {
21           ret = pthread_create (
22                   &a_thread,
23                   NULL,
24                   PrintThreads,
25                   (void *) &thdNum[i] );
26
27           if ( ret == 0 )
28               printf ( "Thread launched successfully\n" );
29       }
30
31       printf ( "Press any key to exit..." );
32       i = getchar();
33       return ( 0 );
34   }
35
36   // Make the threads print out their thread number.
37
38   void *PrintThreads ( void *num )
39   {
40       int i;
41
42       for ( i = 0; i < 3; i++ )
43           printf ( "Thread number is %d\n",
44               *((int*)num));
45
46       return ( NULL );
47   }
```

Listing 5.11   Creating and Using Threads with Pthreads

The main loop does print a notice when a thread is launched successfully, and then has the thread print its thread number three times. Note that the output from this program does not show an orderly sequence of print statements from each individual thread. Instead, the print statements are printed out in a mixed order.

Managing Threads

When a thread is created under Pthreads, developers have the option of indicating the nature of that thread's interaction with other threads. For example,

```
pthread_detach( pthread_t thread_to_detach );
```

can be used to detach the thread from the other threads when it has no need to interact with them. This option asserts that no other thread will interact with this thread, and that the operating system is free to use this information in managing the thread. The operating system uses this information particularly at thread exit, when it knows that no return value needs to be passed back to some other thread.

The complementary function,

```
pthread_join( pthread_t thread, void **ret_val );
```

tells the operating system to block the calling thread until the specified thread exits. Attaching to a thread in this way is called *joining*, just as we saw in the section on .NET threads. The function takes two parameters: the `pthread_t` identifier of the thread being joined, and a pointer to a pointer to `void` where the thread's return value should be placed. If the thread does not return a value, `NULL` can be passed as the second parameter.

To wait on multiple threads, simply join all those threads. Listing 5.12 shows how this is done.

```
int main()
{
    int i, ret;

    pthread_t thdHandle [NUM_THREADS]; //thread identifiers
    int thdNum [NUM_THREADS];          //thread numbers go here

    for ( i = 0; i < NUM_THREADS; i++ )
        thdNum[i] = i;

    for ( i = 0; i < NUM_THREADS; i++ )
```

```
{
    ret = pthread_create (
            &thdHandle[i],
            NULL,
            PrintThreads,
            (void *) &thdNum[i] );

    if ( ret == 0 )
        printf ( "Thread launched successfully\n" );
}

// join all the threads and wait...
for ( i = 0; i < NUM_THREADS; i++ )
    pthread_join ( thdHandle[i], NULL );

printf ( "Press any key to exit..." );
i = getchar();
return ( 0 );
}
```

Listing 5.12   Coordinating Thread Execution with `pthread_join`

One caveat should be noted: two threads cannot join the same thread. Once a thread has been joined, no other threads can join it. To have two or more threads wait on a thread's execution, other devices such as those presented in the section on signaling can be used.

Thread Synchronization

The Pthreads library has mutexes that function similarly to those in Win32 and .NET. Terminology and coding syntax, predictably, are different; as are some details of implementation.

Whereas Windows refers to mutexes as being signaled, that is, available or unlocked, Pthreads refers to mutexes by the more intuitive terms *locked* and *unlocked*. Obviously, when a mutex is locked, the code it's protecting is not accessible. The syntax of the Pthreads API calls follows this nomenclature:

```
pthread_mutex_lock( &aMutex );
    ... code to be protected goes here ...
pthread_mutex_unlock( &aMutex );
```

The sole parameter to both functions is the address of a previously declared mutex object:

```
pthread_mutex_t aMutex = PTHREAD_MUTEX_INITIALIZER;
```

`PTHREAD_MUTEX_INITIALIZER` is a macro that initializes the opaque data type `pthread_mutex_t`. Certain uncommon forms of mutex creation can use other macros; however, the vast majority of the time you create a mutex, this is the initialization code you'll want.

Using a mutex, the code for the `PrintThreads()` routine of Listing 5.11 (lines 38–47) would now looks like this:

```
void *PrintThreads( void *num )
{
    int i;

    pthread_mutex_lock( &testMutex );

    for ( i = 0; i < 3; i++ )
        printf ( "Thread number is %d\n",
            *((int*)num));

    pthread_mutex_unlock( &testMutex );

    return ( NULL );
}
```

Earlier in the program, at the global level, the following definition appeared:

```
pthread_mutex_t testMutex = PTHREAD_MUTEX_INITIALIZER;
```

In the discussion of Win32 mutexes, we saw that calling `WaitForSingleObject(hMutex, 0)` would test `hMutex` right away and return. By examining the return value and comparing it to `WAIT_TIMEOUT`, we can tell whether the mutex was locked. The Pthreads library has a similar function, `pthread_mutex_trylock(&mutex)`, which tests the mutex to see whether it's locked and then returns. If it returns `EBUSY`, the mutex is already locked. It's important to note in both the Windows and Pthreads version of this function, if the mutex is unlocked, this call *will* lock it. It behooves you therefore to check the return value, so as to avoid inadvertently locking a mutex simply because you were trying to see whether it was available. It is expected that you will use this test-and-lock behavior in situations where you would like to lock a mutex, but if the mutex is already locked, you might want to perform other activities before testing the mutex again.

Signaling

Many multi-threading programmers find the event model of communication error prone. As a result, certain APIs exclude them. The Pthreads model has no direct counterpart to the Windows concept of events. Rather, two separate constructs can be used to achieve the same ends. They are condition variables and the semaphore.

Condition Variables

A *condition variable* is a mechanism that is tightly bound to a mutex and a data item. It is used when one or more threads are waiting for the value of the data item to change. Rather than spinning, the threads block on the condition variable and wait for it to be signaled by some other thread. This signal notifies the waiting threads that the data item has changed and enables the threads to begin or resume processing.

This works in a very mechanical way. The data item is declared, for instance, with a flag that tells a consumer thread that the producer thread has data ready for it, and that the data is protected by a mutex. The data item and the mutex together are associated with a condition variable. When the producer thread changes the flag, after unlocking and relocking the mutex, it signals the condition variable, which announces that the flag has changed value. This announcement can be sent optionally to a single thread or broadcast to all threads blocking on the condition variable. In addition to the announcement, the signal unblocks the waiting thread or threads.

Listing 5.13 illustrates how this works by showing two threads waiting on a condition variable. The listing is somewhat longer than the others presented in this book, but it shows how to address a very typical problem in programming with threads.

```
1       #include <stdio.h>
2       #include <stdlib.h>
3
4       #include <pthread.h>
5
6       #define BLOCK_SIZE     100
7       #define BUF_SIZE    1000000
8
9       size_t bytesRead;
10
11      typedef struct {
12         pthread_mutex_t  mutex; // mutex
13         pthread_cond_t   cv;    // condition variable
14         int              data;  // data item used as a flag
15      } flag;
16
17      flag ourFlag = {                // default initialization
18            PTHREAD_MUTEX_INITIALIZER,
```

```
19                 PTHREAD_COND_INITIALIZER,
20                 0 };                    // data item set to 0
21
22     pthread_t hThread1, hThread2;     // the waiting threads
23     void* PrintCountRead( void* );    // the thread function
24
25     int main( int argc, char *argv[] )
26     {
27         FILE *infile;
28         char *inbuf;
29         int  status;
30
31         if ( argc != 2 )
32         {
33             printf( "Usage GetSetEvents filename\n" );
34             return( -1 );
35         }
36
37         infile = fopen( argv[1], "r+b" );
38         if ( infile == NULL )
39         {
40             printf( "Error opening %s\n", argv[1] );
41             return( -1 );
42         }
43
44         inbuf = (char*) malloc ( BUF_SIZE );
45         if ( inbuf == NULL )
46         {
47             printf( "Could not allocate read buffer\n" );
48             return( -1 );
49         }
50
51         // now start up two threads
52         pthread_create( &hThread1, NULL,
53                         PrintCountRead, (void *) NULL );
54         pthread_create( &hThread2, NULL,
55                         PrintCountRead, (void *) NULL );
56
57         bytesRead = fread( inbuf, 1, BLOCK_SIZE, infile );
58         if ( bytesRead < BLOCK_SIZE )
59         {
60             printf( "Need a file longer than %d bytes\n",
61                     BLOCK_SIZE );
62             return( -1 );
63         }
64         else  // now we tell the waiting thread(s)
65         {
66             // first, lock the mutex
67             status = pthread_mutex_lock( &ourFlag.mutex );
68             if ( status != 0 )
```

```
69          {
70              printf( "error locking mutex in main func.\n" );
71              exit( -1 );
72          }
73
74          ourFlag.data = 1; // change the data item
75                            // then broadcast the change
76          status = pthread_cond_broadcast( &ourFlag.cv ) ;
77          if ( status != 0 )
78          {
79              printf( "error broadcasting condition var\n" );
80              exit( -1 );
81          }
82
83          // unlock the mutex
84          status = pthread_mutex_unlock( &ourFlag.mutex );
85          if ( status != 0 )
86          {
87              printf( "error unlocking mutex in waiting \
88                      function\n" );
89              exit( -1 );
90          }
91      }
92
93      while ( !feof( infile ) &&
94              bytesRead < BUF_SIZE - BLOCK_SIZE )
95          bytesRead += fread(inbuf, 1, BLOCK_SIZE, infile );
96
97      printf("Read a total of %d bytes\n", (int)bytesRead);
98      return( 0 );
99  }
100
101 // the thread function, which waits on the
102 // condition variable
103 void *PrintCountRead( void* pv )
104 {
105     int status;
106
107     // lock the mutex
108     status = pthread_mutex_lock( &ourFlag.mutex );
109     if ( status != 0 )
110     {
111         printf( "error locking mutex in waiting func.\n" );
112         exit( -1 );
113     }
114
115     // now wait on the condition variable
116     // (loop should spin once only)
117     while ( ourFlag.data == 0 )
118     {
```

```
119            status = pthread_cond_wait( &ourFlag.cv,
120                                     &ourFlag.mutex );
121            if ( status != 0 )
122            {
123                printf("error waiting on condition variable\n");
124                exit( -1 );
125            }
126        }
127
128        if ( ourFlag.data != 0 )
129        {
130            printf( "Condition was signaled. "
131                    "Main thread has read %06d bytes\n",
132                    (int) bytesRead );
133        }
134
135        // unlock the mutex
136        status = pthread_mutex_unlock( &ourFlag.mutex );
137        if ( status != 0 )
138        {
139            printf("error unlocking mutex in waiting func.\n");
140            exit( -1 );
141        }
142
143        return( pv );
144    }
```

Listing 5.13   Waking Two Threads through a Broadcast to Condition Variables in
Pthreads

Several subtleties come into play. Before examining them, let's go
over what this code does. At a global level (lines 11–21), the code creates
a structure that includes a mutex, a condition variable, and a data item
that serves as a flag. This code also initializes both the mutex and the
condition variable to the Pthreads defaults, and 0 for the flag.

The code opens and reads a file that is specified on the command
line. Then, two threads are created (lines 51-55); they both use the same
thread function, `PrintCountRead()`. This function locks the mutex
(lines 108-113) and then starts a loop that waits on the value of the flag.
The function then calls `pthread_cond_wait()` (lines 119–120), which
is the code that registers with the system that it wants to be awakened
when the condition variable is signaled. At this point, the thread blocks
while waiting for a signal. When the signal arrives, the thread wakes up
and proceeds. The condition variable is signaled from the `main` function
after the flag's value is changed to 1 (lines 74-76). The loop condition

now proves false, and execution flows to the next statement. Here, the flag's value is checked again (line 128-130) and the dependent action—printing the number of bytes read by the principal thread—is performed. The mutex is then unlocked (lines 135-141) and the worker thread exits.

After starting up the two worker threads, which are both blocked waiting for their condition variables to be signaled, the main thread reads one buffer of data (line 57). When this read is successful, it signals the worker threads that they can proceed. It does this by locking the mutex and broadcasting the signal to all waiting threads via `pthread_cond_broadcast()` (line 76). It then unlocks the mutex and finishes reading the file. This routine could have instead used `pthread_cond_signal()` to emit the signal. However, that call would have signaled only one waiting thread, rather than all of them. Such an option would be useful if several waiting threads are all waiting to do the same thing, but the desired activity cannot be parallelized.

The program in Listing 5.14 generates the following output when run on a file consisting of 435,676 bytes.

```
Condition was signaled. Main thread has read 002700 bytes
Condition was signaled. Main thread has read 011200 bytes
Read a total of 435676 bytes
```

You might be tempted to use condition variables without the required mutex. This will lead to problems. Pthreads is designed to use a mutex with condition variables, as can be seen in the parameters in `pthread_cond_wait()`, which takes a pointer to the condition variable and one to the mutex. In fact, without the mutex, the code will not compile properly. The mutex is needed by the Pthreads architecture to correctly record the occurrence of the signal used by the condition variable.

The code in Listing 5.14 is typical of producer/consumer situations. In those, typically, the program starts up a bunch of threads. The producer threads—in this case, the one reading the file—must generate data or actions for the consumer or worker threads to process. Typically, the consumer threads are all suspended pending a signal sent when there is data to consume. In this situation, .NET implements handles via a thread pool; however, Pthreads has no built-in thread pool mechanism.

Semaphores

The *semaphore* is comparable to those in the Win32 APIs, described earlier. A semaphore is a counter that can have any nonnegative value. Threads wait on a semaphore. When the semaphore's value is 0, all threads are forced to wait. When the value is nonzero, a waiting thread is released to work. The thread that gets released is determined first by thread priority, then by whoever attached to the semaphore first. When a thread releases, that is, becomes unblocked, it decrements the value of the semaphore. In typical constructs, the semaphore is set to 0 (blocking), which forces dependent threads to wait. Another thread increments the semaphore; this process is known as *posting*. One waiting thread is thereby released and in releasing, it decrements the semaphore back to 0. This blocks all other threads still waiting on the semaphore. This design makes the semaphore a convenient way to tell a single waiting thread that it has work to be performed.

Technically speaking, Pthreads does not implement semaphores; they are a part of a different POSIX specification. However, semaphores are used in conjunction with Pthreads' thread-management functionality, as you shall see presently. Listing 5.14 illustrates the use of Pthreads with semaphores. The program reads a file and signals another thread to print the count of bytes read. Nonessential parts of the listing have been removed.

```
1    #include <stdio.h>
2    #include <stdlib.h>
3
4    #include <pthread.h>
5    #include <semaphore.h>
6
7    #define BLOCK_SIZE     100
8    #define BUF_SIZE    1000000
9
10   size_t bytesRead;
11
12   sem_t sReadOccurred;        // the semaphore we'll use
13   pthread_t hThread;          // the waiting thread
14   void*
15      PrintCountRead( void* ); // the thread function
16
17   int main( int argc, char *argv[] )
18   {
19      . . . open the input file here. . .
20
21      // first initialize the semaphore
22      sem_init( &sReadOccurred, // address of the semaphore
23          0,   // 0 = share only with threads in this program
24          0 ); // initial value. 0 = make threads wait
25
26      // now start up the thread
```

```
27          pthread_create(
28                  &hThread,
29                  NULL,
30                  PrintCountRead,
31                  (void *) NULL );
32
33          bytesRead = fread( inbuf, 1, BLOCK_SIZE, infile );
34          if ( bytesRead < BLOCK_SIZE )
35          {
36              printf( "Need a file longer than %d bytes\n",
37                      BLOCK_SIZE );
38              return( -1 );
39          }
40          else
41              sem_post( &sReadOccurred ); // release the
42                                          // waiting threads
43
44      . . . finish reading file and print total bytes read. . .
45
46          return( 0 );
47      }
48
49      // the thread function, which waits for the event before
50      // proceeding
51      void *PrintCountRead( void* pv )
52      {
53          int i;
54
55          sem_wait( &sReadOccurred ); // wait on the semaphore
56          printf( "Have now read %06d bytes\n",
57                  (int) bytesRead );
58          return( pv );
59      }
```

Listing 5.14   Using a Pthreads Semaphore to Indicate Program Status

The code opens an input file, creates a semaphore (lines 21–25) and starts up a thread (lines 26–32) before it reads any data. Notice that the semaphore refers to the semaphore data item on line 12. In line 55, we see that the created thread, which will report the number of bytes read, is waiting for the semaphore to signal. After the first read occurs, the semaphore is signaled (line 41) and releases the waiting thread to begin reporting the number of input bytes read. Even though the reporting thread was started up prior to any reads, it is incapable of reporting 0 bytes read because it has blocked on the semaphore until after the first read completed.

This use of a semaphore is valuable in the producer-consumer model. The consumer thread function is set up to contain an infinite loop, such as with `while(1)`. When the producer has placed data in a data structure, generally a queue, it signals the semaphore, thereby releasing the consumer thread's main loop. This release resets the semaphore; once the consumer routine is complete and loops anew, it will block on the semaphore until the producer thread releases it again. If the producer thread should post to the semaphore while the consumer thread is working, the thread will discover upon looping that the semaphore is already unlocked and so it will continue processing without stopping. By this means, the producer thread can directly control when and how often the consumer thread performs its work.

The difficulty with semaphores is that they are limited when dealing with multiple consumer threads. To solve this problem, developers using the Pthreads library rely on condition variables.

Compilation and Linking

Pthreads code should include the pthread.h header file. On the compilation command line, the Pthreads library should be specified to the linker on UNIX and Linux environments using the `-lpthread` command-line switch. For the pthreads-win32 version mentioned earlier, include the bundled header file and link to the DLL, and the Pthreads programs will compile and run correctly on Windows.

Key Points

This chapter provided an overview of two threading APIs: the Microsoft Windows model, and the POSIX threads (Pthreads) model. When developing applications based on these APIs, you should keep the following points in mind:

- Multi-threaded applications targeting Microsoft Windows can be written in either native or managed code.

- Since the `CreateThread()` function does not perform per-thread initialization of C runtime datablocks and variables, you cannot reliably use `CreateThread()` in any application that uses the C runtime library. Use `_beginthreadex()` function instead.

- Thread termination should be handled very carefully. Avoid using functions such as `TerminateThread()`.

- Threads can communicate with one another using Events.

- Thread synchronization may be accomplished through the use of Mutexes, Semaphores, CriticalSections, and Interlocked functions.

- Thread pool support is built into the API.

- Windows supports multiple thread-priority levels.

- Processor affinity is a mechanism that allows the programmer to specify which processor a thread should try to run on.

- POSIX threads (Pthreads) is a portable threading API that is supported on a number of platforms.

- Different platforms support different Pthreads capabilities. Features may not be available in all Pthreads environments.

Chapter 6

OpenMP†:
A Portable Solution
for Threading

The major CPU vendors are shifting gears, choosing to add parallelism support on-chip with multi-core processors in order to avoid many of the technological hurdles in boosting speeds, while still offering a better performing processor. However, if your software does not take advantage of these multiple cores, it may not run any faster. That is where OpenMP† plays a key role by providing an easy method for threading applications without burdening the programmer with the complications of creating, synchronizing, load balancing, and destroying threads.

The OpenMP standard was formulated in 1997 as an API for writing portable, multithreaded applications. It started as a Fortran-based standard, but later grew to include C and C++. The current version is OpenMP Version 2.5, which supports Fortran, C, and C++. Intel C++ and Fortran compilers support the OpenMP Version 2.5 standard (www.openmp.org). The OpenMP programming model provides a platform-independent set of compiler pragmas, directives, function calls, and environment variables that explicitly instruct the compiler how and where to use parallelism in the application. Many loops can be threaded by inserting only one pragma right before the loop, as demonstrated by examples in this chapter. By leaving the nitty-gritty details to the compiler and OpenMP runtime library, you can spend more time determining which loops should be threaded and how to best restructure the algorithms for performance on multi-core processors. The full potential of OpenMP is realized when it is used to thread the most time-consuming loops, that is, the hot spots.

135

Tackling the topic of OpenMP in a single chapter is an intimidating task. Therefore, this chapter serves as a bridge for you, allowing you to reach a point where you have a fundamental understanding of threading with OpenMP from which you can build your broader practical knowledge. The power and simplicity of OpenMP can be demonstrated by looking at an example. The following loop converts each 32-bit RGB (red, green, blue) pixel in an array into an 8-bit grayscale pixel. The one pragma, which has been inserted immediately before the loop, is all that is needed for parallel execution under OpenMP.

```
#pragma omp parallel for
    for ( i = 0; i < numPixels; i++)
    {
        pGrayScaleBitmap[i] = (unsigned BYTE)
            ( pRGBBitmap[i].red    * 0.299 +
              pRGBBitmap[i].green  * 0.587 +
              pRGBBitmap[i].blue   * 0.114 );
    }
```

Let's take a closer look at the loop. First, the example uses *work-sharing*, which is the general term that OpenMP uses to describe distributing work across threads. When work-sharing is used with the `for` construct, as shown in this example, the iterations of the loop are distributed among multiple threads. The OpenMP implementation determines how many threads to create and how best to manage them. All the programmer needs to do is to tell OpenMP which loop should be threaded. No need for programmers to add a lot of codes for creating, initializing, managing, and killing threads in order to exploit parallelism. OpenMP compiler and runtime library take care of these and many other details behind the scenes.

In the current OpenMP specification Version 2.5, OpenMP places the following five restrictions on which loops can be threaded:

■ The loop variable must be of type signed integer. Unsigned integers will not work. Note: this restriction is to be removed in the future OpenMP specification Version 3.0.

■ The comparison operation must be in the form `loop_variable` `<`, `<=`, `>`, or `>=` `loop_invariant_integer`.

■ The third expression or increment portion of the `for` loop must be either integer addition or integer subtraction and by a loop-invariant value.

- If the comparison operation is < or <=, the loop variable must increment on every iteration; conversely, if the comparison operation is > or >=, the loop variable must decrement on every iteration.

- The loop must be a single entry and single exit loop, meaning no jumps from the inside of the loop to the outside or outside to the inside are permitted with the exception of the exit statement, which terminates the whole application. If the statements `goto` or `break` are used, they must jump within the loop, not outside it. The same goes for exception handling; exceptions must be caught within the loop.

Although these restrictions may sound somewhat limiting, most loops can easily be rewritten to conform to them. The restrictions listed above must be observed so that the compiler can parallelize loops via OpenMP. However, even when the compiler parallelizes the loop, you must still ensure the loop is functionally correct by watching out for the issues in the next section.

Challenges in Threading a Loop

Threading a loop is to convert independent loop iterations to threads and run these threads in parallel. In some sense, this is a re-ordering transformation in which the original order of loop iterations can be converted to into an undetermined order. In addition, because the loop body is not an atomic operation, statements in the two different iterations may run simultaneously. In theory, it is valid to convert a sequential loop to a threaded loop if the loop carries no dependence. Therefore, the first challenge for you is to identify or restructure the hot loop to make sure that it has no loop-carried dependence before adding OpenMP pragmas.

Loop-carried Dependence

Even if the loop meets all five loop criteria and the compiler threaded the loop, it may still not work correctly, given the existence of data dependencies that the compiler ignores due to the presence of OpenMP pragmas. The theory of data dependence imposes two requirements that must be met for a statement S_2 and to be data dependent on statement S_1.

- There must exist a possible execution path such that statement S_1 and S_2 both reference the same memory location L.

- The execution of S_1 that references L occurs before the execution of S_2 that references L.

In order for S_2 to depend upon S_1, it is necessary for some execution of S_1 to *write* to a memory location L that is later *read* by an execution of S_2. This is also called *flow dependence*. Other dependencies exist when two statements *write* the same memory location L, called an *output dependence*, or a *read* occurs before a *write*, called an *anti-dependence*. This pattern can occur in one of two ways:

- S_1 can reference the memory location L on one iteration of a loop; on a subsequent iteration S_2 can reference the same memory location L.

- S_1 and S_2 can reference the same memory location L on the same loop iteration, but with S_1 preceding S_2 during execution of the loop iteration.

The first case is an example of *loop-carried* dependence, since the dependence exists when the loop is iterated. The second case is an example of *loop-independent* dependence; the dependence exists because of the position of the code within the loops. Table 6.1 shows three cases of loop-carried dependences with dependence distance d, where $1 \leq d \leq n$, and n is the loop upper bound.

Table 6.1   The Different Cases of Loop-carried Dependences

	iteration k	iteration $k + d$
	Loop-carried flow dependence	
statement S_1	write L	
statement S_2		read L
	Loop-carried anti-dependence	
statement S_1	read L	
statement S_2		write L
	Loop-carried output dependence	
statement S_1	write L	
statement S_2		write L

Let's take a look at the following example where $d = 1$ and $n = 99$. The *write* operation is to location x[k] at iteration k in S$_1$, and a *read* from it at iteration $k+1$ in S$_2$, thus a loop-carried flow dependence occurs. Furthermore, with the *read* from location y[$k-1$] at iteration k in S$_1$, a *write* to it is performed at iteration $k+1$ in S$_2$, hence, the loop-carried anti-dependence exists. In this case, if a `parallel for` pragma is inserted for threading this loop, you will get a wrong result.

```
// Do NOT do this. It will fail due to loop-carried
// dependencies.

x[0] = 0;
y[0] = 1;

#pragma omp parallel for private(k)

    for ( k = 1; k < 100; k++ ) {
        x[k] = y[k-1] + 1;   // S1
        y[k] = x[k-1] + 2;   // S2
    }
```

Because OpenMP directives are commands to the compiler, the compiler will thread this loop. However, the threaded code will fail because of loop-carried dependence. The only way to fix this kind of problem is to rewrite the loop or to pick a different algorithm that does not contain the loop-carried dependence. With this example, you can first predetermine the initial value of x[49] and y[49]; then, you can apply the loop strip-mining technique to create a loop-carried dependence-free loop m. Finally, you can insert the `parallel for` to parallelize the loop m. By applying this transformation, the original loop can be executed by two threads on a dual-core processor system.

```
// Effective threading of the loop using strip-mining
// transformation.

x[0] = 0;
y[0] = 1;
x[49] = 74; //derived from the equation x(k)=x(k-2)+3
y[49] = 74; //derived from the equation y(k)=y(k-2)+3

#pragma omp parallel for private(m, k)

    for (m=0, m<2; m++) {
        for ( k = m*49+1; k < m*50+50; k++ ) {
            x[k] = y[k-1] + 1;    // S1
            y[k] = x[k-1] + 2;    // S2
        }
    }
```

Besides using the `parallel for` pragma, for the same example, you can also use the `parallel sections` pragma to parallelize the original loop that has loop-carried dependence for a dual-core processor system.

```
// Effective threading of a loop using parallel sections

#pragma omp parallel sections private(k)
    { {   x[0] = 0; y[0] = 1;
        for ( k = 1; k < 49; k++ ) {
            x[k] = y[k-1] + 1;      // S1
            y[k] = x[k-1] + 2;      // S2
        }
    }

#pragma omp section
    {   x[49] = 74; y[49] = 74;
        for ( k = 50; k < 100; k++ ) {
            x[k] = y[k-1] + 1;      // S3
            y[k] = x[k-1] + 2;      // S4
        }
    }
}
```

With this simple example, you can learn several effective methods from the process of parallelizing a loop with loop-carried dependences. Sometimes, a simple code restructure or transformation is necessary to get your code threaded for taking advantage of dual-core and multi-core processors besides simply adding OpenMP pragmas.

Data-race Conditions

Data-race conditions that are mentioned in the previous chapters could be due to output dependences, in which multiple threads attempt to update the same memory location, or variable, after threading. In general, the OpenMP C++ and Fortran compilers do honor OpenMP pragmas or directives while encountering them during compilation phase, however, the compiler does not perform or ignores the detection of data-race conditions. Thus, a loop similar to the following example, in which multiple threads are updating the variable x will lead to undesirable results. In such a situation, the code needs to be modified via privatization or synchronized using mechanisms like mutexes. For example, you can simply add the `private(x)` clause to the `parallel for` pragma to eliminate the data-race condition on variable x for this loop.

```
// A data race condition exists for variable x;
// you can eliminate it by adding private(x) clause.

#pragma omp parallel for
for ( k = 0; k < 80; k++ )
{
    x = sin(k*2.0)*100 + 1;
    if ( x > 60 ) x = x % 60 + 1;
    printf ( "x %d = %d\n", k, x );
}
```

As discussed previously, data-race conditions can sometimes be difficult to spot; that is, more difficult than shown in this example. When using the full thread synchronization tools in the Windows API or in Pthreads, developers are more likely to avoid these issues because data is designed from the start to be managed with threading contention and race conditions in mind. However, when using OpenMP, it is easier to overlook data-race conditions. One tool that helps identify such situations is Intel® Thread Checker, which is an add-on to Intel VTune™ Performance Analyzer. Intel Thread Checker is discussed in more detail in Chapter 11.

Managing Shared and Private Data

In writing multithreaded programs, understanding which data is shared and which is private becomes extremely important, not only to performance, but also for program correctness. OpenMP makes this distinction apparent to the programmer through a set of clauses such as shared, private, and default, and it is something that you can set manually. With OpenMP, it is the developer's responsibility to indicate to the compiler which pieces of memory should be shared among the threads and which pieces should be kept private. When memory is identified as shared, all threads access the exact same memory location. When memory is identified as private, however, a separate copy of the variable is made for each thread to access in private. When the loop exits, these private copies become undefined.

By default, all the variables in a parallel region are shared, with three exceptions. First, in parallel for loops, the loop index is private. In the next example, the k variable is private. Second, variables that are local to the block of the parallel region are private. And third, any variables listed in the private, firstprivate, lastprivate, or reduction clauses are private. The privatization is done by making a distinct copy of each of these variables for each thread.

Each of the four clauses takes a list of variables, but their semantics are all different. The private clause says that each variable in the list should have a private copy made for each thread. This private copy is initialized with its default value, using its default constructor where appropriate. For example, the default value for variables of type `int` is 0. In OpenMP, memory can be declared as private in the following three ways.

- Use the `private`, `firstprivate`, `lastprivate`, or `reduction` clause to specify variables that need to be private for each thread.

- Use the `threadprivate` pragma to specify the global variables that need to be private for each thread.

- Declare the variable inside the loop—really inside the OpenMP parallel region—without the `static` keyword. Because static variables are statically allocated in a designated memory area by the compiler and linker, they are not truly private like other variables declared within a function, which are allocated within the stack frame for the function.

The following loop fails to function correctly because the variable x is shared. It needs to be private. Given example below, it fails due to the loop-carried output dependence on the variable x. The x is shared among all threads based on OpenMP default shared rule, so there is a data-race condition on the x while one thread is reading x, another thread might be writing to it

```
#pragma omp parallel for
     for ( k = 0; k < 100; k++ ) {
         x = array[k];
         array[k] = do_work(x);
     }
```

This problem can be fixed in either of the following two ways, which both declare the variable x as private memory.

```
// This works. The variable x is specified as private.

#pragma omp parallel for private(x)
for ( k = 0; k < 100; k++ )
{
    x = array[i];
    array[k] = do_work(x);
}
```

```
// This also works. The variable x is now private.

#pragma omp parallel for
for ( k = 0; k < 100; k++ )
{
    int x; // variables declared within a parallel
           // construct are, by definition, private
    x = array[k];
    array[k] = do_work(x);
}
```

Every time you use OpenMP to parallelize a loop, you should carefully examine all memory references, including the references made by called functions.

Loop Scheduling and Partitioning

To have good load balancing and thereby achieve optimal performance in a multithreaded application, you must have effective loop scheduling and partitioning. The ultimate goal is to ensure that the execution cores are busy most, if not all, of the time, with minimum overhead of scheduling, context switching and synchronization. With a poorly balanced workload, some threads may finish significantly before others, leaving processor resources idle and wasting performance opportunities. In order to provide an easy way for you to adjust the workload among cores, OpenMP offers four scheduling schemes that are appropriate for many situations: *static*, *dynamic*, *runtime*, and *guided*. The Intel C++ and Fortran compilers support all four of these scheduling schemes.

A poorly balanced workload is often caused by variations in compute time among loop iterations. It is usually not too hard to determine the variability of loop iteration compute time by examining the source code. In most cases, you will see that loop iterations consume a uniform amount of time. When that's not true, it may be possible to find a set of iterations that do consume similar amounts of time. For example, sometimes the set of all even iterations consumes about as much time as the set of all odd iterations, or the set of the first half of the loop consumes about as much time as the second half. On the other hand, it may be impossible to find sets of loop iterations that have a uniform execution time. In any case, you can provide loop scheduling information via the `schedule(kind [, chunksize])` clause, so that the compiler and runtime library can better partition and distribute the iterations of the loop across the threads, and therefore the cores, for optimal load balancing.

By default, an OpenMP `parallel for` or worksharing `for` loop uses static-even scheduling. This means the iterations of a loop are distributed among the threads in a roughly equal number of iterations. If m iterations and N threads are in the thread team, each thread gets m/N iterations, and the compiler and runtime library correctly handles the case when m is not evenly divisible by N.

With the static-even scheduling scheme, you could minimize the chances of memory conflicts that can arise when more than one processor is trying to access the same piece of memory. This approach is workable because loops generally touch memory sequentially, so splitting up the loop into large chunks results in little chance of overlapping memory and a reasonable chance of good processor cache efficiency. Consider the following simple loop when executed using static-even scheduling and two threads.

```
#pragma omp parallel for
for ( k = 0; k < 1000; k++ ) do_work(k);
```

OpenMP will execute loop iterations 0 to 499 on one thread and 500 to 999 on the other thread. While this partition of work might be a good choice for memory issues, it could be bad for load balancing. Unfortunately, the converse is also true: what might be good for load balancing could be bad for memory performance. Therefore, performance engineers must strike a balance between optimal memory usage and optimal load balancing by measuring performance to see what method produces the best results.

Loop-scheduling and partitioning information is conveyed to the compiler and runtime library on the OpenMP `for` construct with the schedule clause.

```
#pragma omp for schedule(kind [, chunk-size])
```

The four schedule schemes specified in the OpenMP standard are summarized in Table 6.2. The optional parameter `chunk-size`, when specified, must be a loop-invariant positive integer constant or integer expression.

Be careful when you adjust the chunk size, because performance can be adversely affected. As the chunk size shrinks, the number of times a thread needs to retrieve work from the work queue increases. As a result, the overhead of going to the work queue increases, thereby reducing performance and possibly offsetting the benefits of load balancing.

Table 6.2   The Four Schedule Schemes in OpenMP

Schedule Type	Description
static (default with no chunk size)	Partitions the loop iterations into equal-sized chunks or as nearly equal as possible in the case where the number of loop iterations is not evenly divisible by the number of threads multiplied by the chunk size. When chunk size is not specified, the iterations are divided as evenly as possible, with one chunk per thread. Set chunk to 1 to interleave the iterations.
dynamic	Uses an internal work queue to give a chunk-sized block of loop iterations to each thread as it becomes available. When a thread is finished with its current block, it retrieves the next block of loop iterations from the top of the work queue. By default, chunk size is 1. Be careful when using this scheduling type because of the extra overhead required.
guided	Similar to dynamic scheduling, but the chunk size starts off large and shrinks in an effort to reduce the amount of time threads have to go to the work queue to get more work. The optional chunk parameter specifies the minimum size chunk to use, which, by default, is 1.
runtime	Uses the OMP_SCHEDULE environment variable at runtime to specify which one of the three loop-scheduling types should be used. OMP_SCHEDULE is a string formatted exactly the same as it would appear on the parallel construct.

For dynamic scheduling, the chunks are handled with the first-come, first-serve scheme, and the default chunk size is 1. Each time, the number of iterations grabbed is equal to the chunk size specified in the schedule clause for each thread, except the last chunk. After a thread has finished executing the iterations given to it, it requests another set of chunk-size iterations. This continues until all of the iterations are completed. The last set of iterations may be less than the chunk size. For example, if the chunk size is specified as 16 with the `schedule(dynamic,16)` clause and the total number of iterations is 100, the partition would be `16,16,16,16,16,16,4` with a total of seven chunks.

For guided scheduling, the partitioning of a loop is done based on the following formula with a start value of β_0 = number of loop iterations.

$$\pi_k = \left\lceil \frac{\beta_k}{2N} \right\rceil$$

where N is the number of threads, π_k denotes the size of the k'th chunk, starting from the 0'th chunk, and β_k denotes the number of remaining unscheduled loop iterations while computing the size of k'th chunk.

When π_k gets too small, the value gets clipped to the chunk size S that is specified in the `schedule (guided, chunk-size)` clause. The default chunk size setting is 1, if it is not specified in the `schedule` clause. Hence, for the guided scheduling, the way a loop is partitioned depends on the number of threads (N), the number of iterations (β_0) and the chunk size (S).

For example, given a loop with $\beta_0 = 800$, $N = 2$, and $S = 80$, the loop partition is {200, 150, 113, 85, 80, 80, 80, 12}. When π_4 is smaller than 80, it gets clipped to 80. When the number of remaining unscheduled iterations is smaller than S, the upper bound of the last chunk is trimmed whenever it is necessary. The guided scheduling supported in the Intel C++ and Fortran compilers are a compliant implementation specified in the OpenMP Version 2.5 standard.

With dynamic and guided scheduling mechanisms, you can tune your application to deal with those situations where each iteration has variable amounts of work or where some cores (or processors) are faster than others. Typically, guided scheduling performs better than dynamic scheduling due to less overhead associated with scheduling.

The runtime scheduling scheme is actually not a scheduling scheme per se. When `runtime` is specified in the schedule clause, the OpenMP runtime uses the scheduling scheme specified in the `OMP_SCHEDULE` environment variable for this particular `for` loop. The format for the `OMP_SCHEDULE` environment variable is `schedule-type[,chunk-size]`. For example:

```
export OMP_SCHEDULE=dynamic,16
```

Using runtime scheduling gives the end-user some flexibility in selecting the type of scheduling dynamically among three previously mentioned scheduling mechanisms through the `OMP_SCHEDULE` environment variable, which is set to `static` by default.

Furthermore, understanding the loop scheduling and partitioning schemes will significantly help you to choose the right scheduling scheme, help you to avoid false-sharing for your applications at runtime, and lead to good load balancing. Considering the following example:

```
float x[1000], y[1000];
#pragma omp parallel for schedule(dynamic, 8)
        for (k=0; k<1000; k++) {
            x[k] = cos(k) * x[k] + sin(k) * y[k]
        }
```

Assume you have a dual-core processor system and the cache line size is 64 bytes. For the sample code shown above, two chunks (or array sections) can be in the same cache line because the chunk size is set to 8 in the `schedule` clause. So each chunk of array x takes 32 bytes per cache line, which leads to two chunks placed in the same cache line. Because two chunks can be read and written by two threads at the same time, this will result in many cache line invalidations, although two threads do not read/write the same chunk. This is called false-sharing, as it is not necessary to actually share the same cache line between two threads. A simple tuning method is to use `schedule(dynamic,16)`, so one chunk takes the entire cache line to eliminate the false-sharing. Eliminating false-sharing through the use of a chunk size setting that is aware of cache line size will significantly improve your application performance.

Effective Use of Reductions

In large applications, you can often see the reduction operation inside hot loops. Loops that reduce a collection of values to a single value are fairly common. Consider the following simple loop that calculates the sum of the return value of the integer-type function call `func(k)` with the loop index value as input data.

```
sum = 0;
for ( k = 0; k < 100; k++ ){
  sum = sum + func(k); // "func" has no side-effects
}
```

It looks as though the loop-carried dependence on `sum` would prevent threading. However, if you have a dual-core processor system, you can perform the privatization—that is, create a stack variable "`temp`" from which memory is allocated from automatic storage for each thread—and perform loop partitioning to sum up the value of two sets of calls in parallel, as shown in the following example.

Thread 0:	Thread 1:
| ```
temp = 0;
for (k=0; k<50; k++) {
  temp = temp + func(k);
}

lock (&sum)
sum = sum + temp
unlock (&sum)
``` | ```
temp = 0;
for (k=50; k<100; k++) {
    temp = temp + func(k)
}

lock(&sum)
sum = sum + temp
unlock(&sum)
``` |

At the synchronization point, you can combine the partial sum results from each thread to generate the final sum result. In order to perform this form of recurrence calculation in parallel, the operation must be mathematically associative and commutative. You may notice that the variable sum in the original sequential loop must be shared to guarantee the correctness of the multithreaded execution of the loop, but it also must be private to permit access by multiple threads using a lock or a critical section for the atomic update on the variable sum to avoid data-race condition. To solve the problem of both sharing and protecting sum without using a lock inside the threaded loop, OpenMP provides the reduction clause that is used to efficiently combine certain associative arithmetical reductions of one or more variables in a loop. The following loop uses the reduction clause to generate the correct results.

```
sum = 0;
#pragma omp parallel for reduction(+:sum)
    for (k = 0; k < 100; k++) {
        sum = sum + func(k);
    }
```

Given the reduction clause, the compiler creates private copies of the variable sum for each thread, and when the loop completes, it adds the values together and places the result in the original variable sum.

Other reduction operators besides "+" exist. Table 6.3 lists those C++ reduction operators specified in the OpenMP standard, along with the initial values—which are also the mathematical identity value—for the temporary private variables. You can also find a list of Fortran reduction operators along with their initial values in OpenMP specification Version 2.5.

Table 6.3   Reduction Operators and Reduction Variable's Initial Value in OpenMP

Operator	Initialization Value
+ (addition)	0
- (subtraction)	0
* (multiplication)	1
& (bitwise and)	~0
| (bitwise or)	0
^ (bitwise exclusive or)	0
&& (conditional and)	1
|| (conditional or)	0

For each variable specified in a `reduction` clause, a private copy is created, one for each thread, as if the `private` clause is used. The private copy is then initialized to the initialization value for the operator, as specified in Table 6.3. At the end of the region or the loop for which the `reduction` clause was specified, the original reduction variable is updated by combining its original value with the final value of each of the private copies, using the operator specified. While identifying the opportunities to explore the use of the `reduction` clause for threading, you should keep the following three points in mind.

- The value of the original reduction variable becomes undefined when the first thread reaches the region or loop that specifies the `reduction` clause and remains so until the reduction computation is completed.

- If the `reduction` clause is used on a loop to which the `nowait` is also applied, the value of original reduction variable remains undefined until a barrier synchronization is performed to ensure that all threads have completed the reduction.

- The order in which the values are combined is unspecified. Therefore, comparing sequential and parallel runs, even between two parallel runs, does not guarantee that bit-identical results will be obtained or that side effects, such as floating-point exceptions, will be identical.

Minimizing Threading Overhead

Using OpenMP, you can parallelize loops, regions, and sections or straight-line code blocks, whenever dependences do not forbids them being executed in parallel. In addition, because OpenMP employs the simple fork-join execution model, it allows the compiler and run-time library to compile and run OpenMP programs efficiently with lower threading overhead. However, you can improve your application performance by further reducing threading overhead.

Table 6.4 provides measured costs of a set of OpenMP constructs and clauses on a 4-way Intel Xeon® processor-based system running at 3.0 gigahertz with the Intel compiler and runtime library. You can see that the cost for each construct or clause is small. Most of them are less than 7 microseconds except the `schedule(dynamic)` clause. The `schedule (dynamic)` clause takes 50 microseconds, because its default chunk size is 1, which is too small. If you use `schedule(dynamic,16)`, its cost is reduced to 5.0 microseconds. Note that all measured costs are subject to change if you measure these costs on a different processor or under a different system configuration. The key point is that no matter how well the compiler and runtime are developed and tuned to minimize the overhead of OpenMP constructs and clauses, you can always find ways to reduce the overhead by exploring the use of OpenMP in a more effective way.

Table 6.4   Measured Cost of OpenMP Constructs and Clauses

Constructs	Cost (in microseconds)	Scalability
parallel	1.5	Linear
Barrier	1.0	Linear or $O(\log(n))$
schedule(static)	1.0	Linear
schedule(guided)	6.0	Depends on contention
schedule(dynamic)	50	Depends on contention
ordered	0.5	Depends on contention
Single	1.0	Depends on contention
Reduction	2.5	Linear or $O(\log(n))$
Atomic	0.5	Depends on data-type and hardware
Critical	0.5	Depends on contention
Lock/Unlock	0.5	Depends on contention

Earlier, you saw how the `parallel for` pragma could be used to split the iterations of a loop across multiple threads. When the compiler generated thread is executed, the iterations of the loop are distributed among threads. At the end of the parallel region, the threads are suspended and they wait for the next parallel region, loop, or sections. A suspend or resume operation, while significantly lighter weight than create or terminate operations, still creates overhead and may be unnecessary when two parallel regions, loops, or sections are adjacent as shown in the following example.

```
#pragma omp parallel for for
( k = 0; k < m; k++ ) {
    fn1(k); fn2(k);
}

#pragma omp parallel for // adds unnecessary overhead
for ( k = 0; k < m; k++ ) {
    fn3(k); fn4(k);
}
```

The overhead can be removed by entering a parallel region once, then dividing the work within the parallel region. The following code is functionally identical to the preceding code but runs faster, because the overhead of entering a parallel region is performed only once.

```
#pragma omp parallel
{
    #pragma omp for
    for ( k = 0; k < m; k++ ) {
        fn1(k); fn2(k);
    }

    #pragma omp for
    for ( k = 0; k < m; k++ ) {
        fn3(k); fn4(k);
    }
}
```

Ideally, all performance-critical portions of the application would be executed within a parallel region. Since very few programs are comprised only of loops, additional constructs are used to handle non-loop code. A work-sharing section is one such construct.

Work-sharing Sections

The work-sharing `sections` construct directs the OpenMP compiler and runtime to distribute the identified sections of your application among threads in the team created for the parallel region. The following example uses work-sharing `for` loops and work-sharing `sections` together within a single parallel region. In this case, the overhead of forking or resuming threads for `parallel` `sections` is eliminated.

```
#pragma omp parallel
{
    #pragma omp for
    for ( k = 0; k < m; k++ ) {
        x = fn1(k) + fn2(k);
    }

    #pragma omp sections private(y, z)
    {
        #pragma omp section
            { y = sectionA(x); fn7(y); }
        #pragma omp section
            { z = sectionB(x); fn8(z); }
    }
}
```

Here, OpenMP first creates several threads. Then, the iterations of the loop are divided among the threads. Once the loop is finished, the sections are divided among the threads so that each section is executed exactly once, but in parallel with the other sections. If the program contains more sections than threads, the remaining sections get scheduled as threads finish their previous sections. Unlike loop scheduling, the schedule clause is not defined for sections. Therefore, OpenMP is in complete control of how, when, and in what order threads are scheduled to execute the sections. You can still control which variables are shared or private, using the `private` and `reduction` clauses in the same fashion as the loop construct.

Performance-oriented Programming

OpenMP provides a set of important pragmas and runtime functions that enable thread synchronization and related actions to facilitate correct parallel programming. Using these pragmas and runtime functions effectively with minimum overhead and thread waiting time is extremely important for achieving optimal performance from your applications.

Using Barrier and Nowait

Barriers are a form of synchronization method that OpenMP employs to synchronize threads. Threads will wait at a barrier until all the threads in the parallel region have reached the same point. You have been using implied barriers without realizing it in the work-sharing `for` and work-sharing `sections` constructs. At the end of the `parallel`, `for`, `sections`, and `single` constructs, an implicit barrier is generated by the compiler or invoked in the runtime library. The barrier causes execution to wait for all threads to finish the work of the loop, sections, or region before any go on to execute additional work. This barrier can be removed with the `nowait` clause, as shown in the following code sample.

```
#pragma omp parallel
{
    #pragma omp for nowait
    for ( k = 0; k < m; k++ ) {
        fn10(k); fn20(k);
    }

    #pragma omp sections private(y, z)
    {
        #pragma omp section
            { y = sectionD(); fn70(y); }
```

```
            #pragma omp section
                { z = sectionC(); fn80(z); }
    }
}
```

In this example, since data is not dependent between the first work-sharing `for` loop and the second work-sharing `sections` code block, the threads that process the first work-sharing `for` loop continue immediately to the second work-sharing `sections` without waiting for all threads to finish the first loop. Depending upon your situation, this behavior may be beneficial, because it can make full use of available resources and reduce the amount of time that threads are idle. The `nowait` clause can also be used with the work-sharing `sections` construct and `single` construct to remove its implicit barrier at the end of the code block.

Adding an explicit barrier is also supported by OpenMP as shown in the following example through the `barrier` pragma.

```
#pragma omp parallel shared(x, y, z) num_threads(2)
{
    int tid = omp_get_thread_num();
    if (tid == 0) {
        y = fn70(tid);
    }
    else {
        z = fn80(tid);
    }

#pragma omp barrier

#pragma omp for
    for ( k = 0; k < 100; k++ ) {
        x[k] = y + z + fn10(k) + fn20(k);
    }
}
```

In this example, the OpenMP code is to be executed by two threads; one thread writes the result to the variable y, and another thread writes the result to the variable z. Both y and z are read in the work-sharing `for` loop, hence, two flow dependences exist. In order to obey the data dependence constraints in the code for correct threading, you need to add an explicit `barrier` pragma right before the work-sharing `for` loop to guarantee that the value of both y and z are ready for read. In real applications, the `barrier` pragma is especially useful when all threads need to finish a task before any more work can be completed, as would be the case, for example, when updating a graphics frame buffer before displaying its contents.

Interleaving Single-thread and Multi-thread Execution

In large real-world applications, a program may consist of both serial and parallel code segments due to various reasons such as data dependence constraints and I/O operations. A need to execute something only once by only one thread will certainly be required within a parallel region, especially because you are making parallel regions as large as possible to reduce overhead. To handle the need for single-thread execution, OpenMP provides a way to specify that a sequence of code contained within a parallel section should only be executed one time by only one thread. The OpenMP runtime library decides which single thread will do the execution. If need be, you can specify that you want only the master thread, the thread that actually started the program execution, to execute the code, as in the following example.

```
#pragma omp parallel
{   // every thread calls this function
    int tid = omp_get_thread_num();

    // this loop is divided among the threads
    #pragma omp for nowait
    for ( k = 0; k < 100; k++ ) x[k] = fn1(tid);
    // no implicit barrier at the end of the above loop causes
    // all threads to synchronize here

    #pragma omp master
    y = fn_input_only();// only the master thread calls this

    // adding an explicit barrier to synchronize all threads
    // to make sure x[0-99] and y is ready for use
    #pragma omp barrier

    // again, this loop is divided among the threads
    #pragma omp for nowait
    for ( k = 0; k < 100; k++ ) x[k] = y + fn2(x[k]);
    // The above loop does not have an implicit barrier, so
    // threads will not wait for each other.

    // One thread - presumbly the first one done with above --
    // will continue and execute the following code.
    #pragma omp single
    fn_single_print(y); // only one of threads calls this

    // The above single construct has an implicit barrier,
    // so all threads synchronize here before printing x[].

    #pragma omp master
    fn_print_array(x); // only one of threads prints x[]
}
```

As can be seen from the comments in this code, a remarkable amount of synchronization and management of thread execution is available in a comparatively compact lexicon of pragmas. Note that all low-level details are taken care of by the OpenMP compiler and runtime. What you need to focus on is to specify parallel computation and synchronization behaviors you expected for correctness and performance. In other words, using `single` and `master` pragmas along with the `barrier` pragma and `nowait` clause in a clever way, you should be able to maximize the scope of a parallel region and the overlap of computations to reduce threading overhead effectively, while obeying all data dependences and I/O constraints in your programs.

Data Copy-in and Copy-out

When you parallelize a program, you would normally have to deal with how to copy in the initial value of a private variable to initialize its private copy for each thread in the team. You would also copy out the value of the private variable computed in the last iteration/section to its original variable for the master thread at the end of parallel region. OpenMP standard provides four clauses—`firstprivate`, `lastprivate`, `copyin`, and `copyprivate`—for you to accomplish the data copy-in and copy-out operations whenever necessary based on your program and parallelization scheme. The following descriptions summarize the semantics of these four clauses:

- `firstprivate` provides a way to initialize the value of a private variable for each thread with the value of variable from the master thread. Normally, temporary private variables have an undefined initial value saving the performance overhead of the copy.

- `lastprivate` provides a way to copy out the value of the private variable computed in the last iteration/section to the copy of the variable in the master thread. Variables can be declared both `firstprivate` and `lastprivate` at the same time.

- `copyin` provides a way to copy the master thread's `threadprivate` variable to the `threadprivate` variable of each other member of the team executing the parallel region.

- `copyprivate` provides a way to use a private variable to broadcast a value from one member of threads to other members of the team executing the parallel region. The `copyprivate` clause is allowed to associate with the `single` construct; the broadcast action is completed before any of threads in the team left the barrier at the end of construct.

Considering the code example, let's see how it works. The following code converts a color image to black and white.

```
for ( row = 0; row < height; row++ ) {
    for ( col = 0; col < width; col++ ) {
        pGray[col] = (BYTE)
            ( pRGB[row].red    * 0.299 +
              pRGB[row].green  * 0.587 +
              pRGB[row].blue   * 0.114 );
    }
    pGray += GrayStride;
    pRGB += RGBStride;
}
```

The issue is how to move the pointers pGray and pRGB to the correct place within the bitmap while threading the outer "row" loop. The address computation for each pixel can be done with the following code:

```
pDestLoc = pGray + col + row * GrayStride;
pSrcLoc  = pRGB + col + row * RGBStride;
```

The above code, however, executes extra math on each pixel for the address computation. Instead, the firstprivate clause can be used to perform necessary initialization to get the initial address of pointer pGray and pRGB for each thread. You may notice that the initial addresses of the pointer pGray and pRGB have to be computed only once based on the "row" number and their initial addresses in the master thread for each thread; the pointer pGray and pRGB are induction pointers and updated in the outer loop for each "row" iteration. This is the reason the bool-type variable doInit is introduced with an initial value TRUE to make sure the initialization is done only once for each to compute the initial address of pointer pGray and pRGB. The parallelized code follows:

```
#pragma omp parallel for private (row, col) \
                    firstprivate(doInit, pGray, pRGB)
for ( row = 0; row < height; row++ ) {
    // Need this init test to be able to start at an
    // arbitrary point within the image after threading.
    if (doInit == TRUE) {
        doInit = FALSE;
        pRGB  += ( row * RGBStride );
        pGray += ( row * GrayStride );
    }
    for ( col = 0; col < width; col++ ) {
        pGray[col] = (BYTE) ( pRGB[row].red    * 0.299 +
                              pRGB[row].green * 0.587 +
                              pRGB[row].blue  * 0.114 );
```

```
    }
    pGray += GrayStride;
    pRGB += RGBStride;
}
```

If you take a close look at this code, you may find that the four variables `GrayStride`, `RGBStride`, `height`, and `width` are read-only variables. In other words, no write operation is performed to these variables in the parallel loop. Thus, you can also specify them on the `parallel for` loop by adding the code below:

```
firstprivate (GrayStride, RGBStride, height, width)
```

You may get better performance in some cases, as the privatization helps the compiler to perform more aggressive registerization and code motion as their loop invariants reduce memory traffic.

Protecting Updates of Shared Variables

The `critical` and `atomic` pragmas are supported by the OpenMP standard for you to protect the updating of shared variables for avoiding data-race conditions. The code block enclosed by a critical section and an atomic pragma are areas of code that may be entered only when no other thread is executing in them. The following example uses an unnamed critical section.

```
#pragma omp critical
{
    if ( max < new_value ) max = new_value
}
```

Global, or unnamed, critical sections will likely and unnecessarily affect performance because every thread is competing to enter the same global critical section, as the execution of every thread is serialized. This is rarely what you want. For this reason, OpenMP offers *named* critical sections. Named critical sections enable fine-grained synchronization, so only the threads that need to block on a particular section will do so. The following example shows the code that improves the previous example. In practice, named critical sections are used when more than one thread is competing for more than one critical resource.

```
#pragma omp critical(maxvalue)
{
    if ( max < new_value ) max = new_value
}
```

With named critical sections, applications can have multiple critical sections, and threads can be in more than one critical section at a time. It is important to remember that entering nested critical sections runs the risk of deadlock. The following code example code shows a deadlock situation:

```
void dequeue(NODE *node)
{
  #pragma omp critical (x)
  {
    node = node->next;
  }
}

void do_work(NODE *node)
{
  #pragma omp critical (x)
  {
    node->next->data = fn1(node->data);
    node = dequeue(node)
  }
}
```

In the previous code, the dynamically nested critical sections are used. When the function do_work is called inside a parallel loop, multiple threads compete to enter the outer critical section. The thread that succeeds in entering the outer critical section will call the dequeue function; however, the dequeue function cannot make any further progress, as the inner critical section attempts to enter the same critical section in the do_work function. Thus, the do_work function could never complete. This is a deadlock situation. The simple way to fix the problem in the previous code is to do the inlining of the dequeue function in the do_work function as follows:

```
void do_work(NODE *node)
{
  #pragma omp critical (x)
  {
    node->next->data = fn1(node->data);
    node = node->next;
  }
}
```

When using multiple critical sections, be very careful to examine critical sections that might be lurking in subroutines. In addition to using critical sections, you can also use the atomic pragma for updating shared variables. When executing code in parallel, it is impossible to know when an operation will be interrupted by the thread scheduler.

However, sometimes you may require that a statement in a high-level language complete in its entirety before a thread is suspended. For example, a statement *x++* is translated into a sequence of machine instructions such as:

```
load   reg, [x];
add    reg 1;
store  [x], reg;
```

It is possible that the thread is swapped out between two of these machine instructions. The atomic pragma directs the compiler to generate code to ensure that the specific memory storage is updated atomically. The following code example shows a usage of the atomic pragma.

```
int main()
{ float y[1000];
  int    k, idx[1000];

  #pragma omp parallel for shared(y, idx)
  for ( k = 0; k < 8000; k++) {
    idx[k] = k % 1000;
    y[idx[k]] = 8.0;
  }

  #pragma omp parallel for shared(y, idx)
  for ( k = 0; k < 8000; k++) {
    #pragma omp atomic
    y[idx[k]] += 8.0 * (k % 1000);
  }
  return 0;
}
```

An expression statement that is allowed to use the atomic pragma must be with one of the following forms:

- *x binop = expr*

- *x++*

- *++x*

- *x –*

- *– x*

In the preceding expressions, *x* is an lvalue expression with scalar type; *expr* is an expression with scalar type and does not reference the object designed by *x*; *binop* is not an overloaded operator and is one of +, *, -, /, &, ^, |, <<, or >> for the C/C++ language.

It is worthwhile to point out that in the preceding code example, the advantage of using the atomic pragma is that it allows update of two different elements of array *y* to occur in parallel. If a critical section were used instead, then all updates to elements of array *y* would be executed serially, but not in a guaranteed order. Furthermore, in general, the OpenMP compiler and runtime library select the most efficient method to implement the `atomic` pragma given operating system features and hardware capabilities. Thus, whenever it is possible you should use the `atomic` pragma before using the critical section in order to avoid data-race conditions on statements that update a shared memory location.

Intel Taskqueuing Extension to OpenMP

The Intel Taskqueuing extension to OpenMP allows a programmer to parallelize control structures such as recursive function, dynamic-tree search, and pointer-chasing while loops that are beyond the scope of those supported by the current OpenMP model, while still fitting into the framework defined by the OpenMP specification. In particular, the taskqueuing model is a flexible programming model for specifying units of work that are not pre-computed at the start of the work-sharing construct. Take a look the following example.

```
void tq_func(LIST *p)
{
  #pragma intel omp parallel taskq shared(p)
  {  while (p!= NULL)  {
      #pragma intel omp task captureprivate(p)
       {   tq_work1(p, 70);   }
      #pragma intel omp task captureprivate(p)
       {   tq_work2(p, 80);   }
      p= p->next;
    }
  }
}
```

The `parallel taskq` pragma directs the compiler to generate code to create a team of threads and an environment for the `while` loop to enqueue the units of work specified by the enclosed `task` pragma. The loop's control structure and the enqueuing are executed by one thread, while the other threads in the team participate in dequeuing the work from the `taskq` queue and executing it. The `captureprivate` clause ensures that a private copy of the link pointer *p* is captured at the time each task is being enqueued, hence preserving the sequential semantics. The taskqueuing execution model is shown in Figure 6.1.

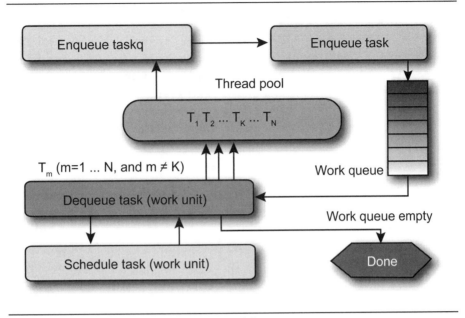

Figure 6.1   Taskqueuing Execution Model

Essentially, for any given program with `parallel taskq` constructs, a team of threads is created by the runtime library when the main thread encounters a parallel region. The runtime thread scheduler chooses one thread T_K to execute initially from all the threads that encounter a `taskq` pragma. All the other threads wait for work to be put on the task queue. Conceptually, the `taskq` pragma triggers this sequence of actions:

1. Causes an empty queue to be created by the chosen thread T_K

2. Enqueues each task that it encounters

3. Executes the code inside the `taskq` block as a single thread

The task pragma specifies a unit of work, potentially to be executed by a different thread. When a task pragma is encountered lexically within a `taskq` block, the code inside the task block is placed on the queue associated with the `taskq` pragma. The conceptual queue is disbanded when all work enqueued on it finishes and the end of the `taskq` block is reached. The Intel C++ compiler has been extended throughout its various components to support the taskqueuing model for generating multithreaded codes corresponding to taskqueuing constructs.

OpenMP Library Functions

As you may remember, in addition to pragmas, OpenMP provides a set of functions calls and environment variables. So far, only the pragmas have been described. The pragmas are the key to OpenMP because they provide the highest degree of simplicity and portability, and the pragmas can be easily switched off to generate a non-threaded version of the code.

In contrast, the OpenMP function calls require you to add the conditional compilation in your programs as shown below, in case you want to generate a serial version.

```
#include <omp.h>

#ifdef _OPENMP
    omp_set_num_threads(4);
#endif
```

When in doubt, always try to use the pragmas and keep the function calls for the times when they are absolutely necessary. To use the function calls, include the `<omp.h>` header file. The compiler automatically links to the correct libraries.

The four most heavily used OpenMP library functions are shown in Table 6.5. They retrieve the total number of threads, set the number of threads, return the current thread number, and return the number of available cores, logical processors or physical processors, respectively. To view the complete list of OpenMP library functions, please see the OpenMP Specification Version 2.5, which is available from OpenMP web site at www.openmp.org.

Table 6.5　The Most Heavily Used OpenMP Library Functions

Function Name	Description
int omp_get_num_threads (void);	Returns the number of threads currently in use. If called outside a parallel region, this function will return 1.
int omp_set_num_threads (int NumThreads);	This function sets the number of threads that will be used when entering a parallel section. It overrides the OMP_NUM_THREADS environment variable.
int omp_get_thread_num (void);	Returns the current thread number between 0 (master thread) and total number of threads - 1.
int omp_get_num_procs (void);	Returns the number of available cores (or processors). A core or processor with Hyper-Threading Technology enabled will count as two cores (or two processors).

Figure 6.2 uses these functions to perform data processing for each element in array *x*. This example illustrates a few important concepts when using the function calls instead of pragmas. First, your code must be rewritten, and with any rewrite comes extra documentation, debugging, testing, and maintenance work. Second, it becomes difficult or impossible to compile without OpenMP support. Finally, because thread values have been hard coded, you lose the ability to have loop-scheduling adjusted for you, and this threaded code is not scalable beyond four cores or processors, even if you have more than four cores or processors in the system.

```
float x[8000];
omp_set_num_threads(4);
#pragma omp parallel private(k)
{ // This code has a shortcoming. Can you find it?
  int num_thds = omp_get_num_threads();
  int ElementsPerThread = 8000 / num_thds;
  int Tid = omp_get_thread_num();
  int LowBound   = Tid*ElementsPerThread;
  int UpperBound = LowBound + ElementsPerThread;

  for ( k = LowBound; k < UpperBound; k++ )
      DataProcess(x[k]);
}
```

Figure 6.2   Loop that Uses OpenMP Functions and Illustrates the Drawbacks

OpenMP Environment Variables

The OpenMP specification defines a few environment variables. Occasionally the two shown in Table 6.6 may be useful during development.

Table 6.6   Most Commonly Used Environment Variables for OpenMP

Environment Variable	Description	Example
OMP_SCHEDULE	Controls the scheduling of the for-loop work-sharing construct.	set OMP_SCHEDULE = "guided, 2"
OMP_NUM_THREADS	Sets the default number of threads. The omp_set_num_threads() function call can override this value.	set OMP_NUM_THREADS = 4

Additional compiler-specific environment variables are usually available. Be sure to review your compiler's documentation to become familiar with additional variables.

Compilation

Using the OpenMP pragmas requires an OpenMP-compatible compiler and thread-safe runtime libraries. The Intel C++ Compiler version 7.0 or later and the Intel Fortran compiler both support OpenMP on Linux and Windows. This book's discussion of compilation and debugging will focus on these compilers. Several other choices are available as well, for instance, Microsoft supports OpenMP in Visual C++ 2005 for Windows and the Xbox™ 360 platform, and has also made OpenMP work with managed C++ code. In addition, OpenMP compilers for C/C++ and Fortran on Linux and Windows are available from the Portland Group.

The /Qopenmp command-line option given to the Intel C++ Compiler instructs it to pay attention to the OpenMP pragmas and to create multithreaded code. If you omit this switch from the command line, the compiler will ignore the OpenMP pragmas. This action provides a very simple way to generate a single-threaded version without changing any source code. Table 6.7 provides a summary of invocation options for using OpenMP.

Table 6.7 Compiler Switches for OpenMP (C/C++ and Fortran)

Windows	Linux	Semantics
-Qopenmp	-openmp	Generate multithreaded code for Intel® Pentium® III, Pentium 4 with Hyper-Threading Technology, Pentium M, and multi-core processors.
-Qopenmp-profile	-openmp-profile	Link with instrumented OpenMP runtime library to generate OpenMP profiling information for use with the OpenMP component of VTune™ Performance Analyzer.
-Qopenmp-stubs	-openmp-stubs	Enable the user to compile OpenMP programs in sequential mode. The openmp directives are ignored and a stub OpenMP library is linked for sequential execution.

Windows	Linux	Semantics
-Qopenmp-report	-openmp-report	Control level of reports:
0 1 2	0 1 2	0 - Disable parallelization diagnostics 1 - report successfully threaded code [default] 2 – 1 + report successfully code generation for master, single, critical, and atomic.

For conditional compilation, the compiler defines _OPENMP. If needed, this definition can be tested in this manner:

```
#ifdef _OPENMP
    printf ( "Hello World, I'm using OpenMP!\n" );
#endif
```

The thread-safe runtime libraries are selected and linked automatically when the OpenMP related compilation switch is used.

The Intel compilers support the OpenMP Specification Version 2.5 except the `workshare` construct. Be sure to browse the release notes and compatibility information supplied with the compiler for the latest information. The complete OpenMP specification is available from the OpenMP Web site, listed in References. To review details about OpenMP for the Intel Compiler, see Chapter 11.

Debugging

Debugging multithreaded applications has always been a challenge due to the nondeterministic execution of multiple instruction streams caused by runtime thread-scheduling and context switching. Also, debuggers may change the runtime performance and thread scheduling behaviors, which can mask race conditions and other forms of thread interaction. Even print statements can mask issues because they use synchronization and operating system functions to guarantee thread-safety.

Debugging an OpenMP program adds some difficulty, as OpenMP compilers must communicate all the necessary information of private variables, shared variables, threadprivate variables, and all kinds of constructs to debuggers after threaded code generation; additional code that is impossible to examine and step through without a specialized OpenMP-aware debugger. Therefore, the key is narrowing down the problem to a small code section that causes the same problem. It would be even better if you could come up with a very small test case that can reproduce the problem. The following list provides guidelines for debugging OpenMP programs.

1. Use the binary search method to identify the parallel construct causing the failure by enabling and disabling the OpenMP pragmas in the program.

2. Compile the routine causing problem with no /Qopenmp switch and with /Qopenmp_stubs switch; then you can check if the code fails with a serial run, if so, it is a serial code debugging. If not, go to Step 3.

3. Compile the routine causing problem with /Qopenmp switch and set the environment variable OMP_NUM_THREADS=1; then you can check if the threaded code fails with a serial run. If so, it is a single-thread code debugging of threaded code. If not, go to Step 4.

4. Identify the failing scenario at the lowest compiler optimization level by compiling it with /Qopenmp and one of the switches such as /Od, /O1, /O2, /O3, and/or /Qipo.

5. Examine the code section causing the failure and look for problems such as violation of data dependence after parallelization, race conditions, deadlock, missing barriers, and uninitialized variables. If you can not spot any problem, go to Step 6.

6. Compile the code using /Qtcheck to perform the OpenMP code instrumentation and run the instrumented code inside the Intel Thread Checker.

Problems are often due to race conditions. Most race conditions are caused by shared variables that really should have been declared private, reduction, or threadprivate. Sometimes, race conditions are also caused by missing necessary synchronization such as critica and atomic protection of updating shared variables. Start by looking at the variables inside the parallel regions and make sure that the variables are declared private when necessary. Also, check functions called within parallel constructs. By default, variables declared on the stack are private but the C/C++ keyword `static` changes the variable to be placed on the global heap and therefore the variables are shared for OpenMP loops. The `default(none)` clause, shown in the following code sample, can be used to help find those hard-to-spot variables. If you specify `default(none)`, then every variable must be declared with a data-sharing attribute clause.

```
#pragma omp parallel for default(none) private(x,y) shared(a,b)
```

Another common mistake is uninitialized variables. Remember that private variables do not have initial values upon entering or exiting a parallel construct. Use the `firstprivate` or `lastprivate` clauses discussed previously to initialize or copy them. But do so only when necessary because this copying adds overhead.

If you still can't find the bug, perhaps you are working with just too much parallel code. It may be useful to make some sections execute serially, by disabling the parallel code. This will at least identify the location of the bug. An easy way to make a parallel region execute in serial is to use the `if` clause, which can be added to any parallel construct as shown in the following two examples.

```
#pragma omp parallel if(0)
printf("Executed by thread %d\n", omp_get_thread_num());

#pragma omp parallel for if(0)
for ( x = 0; x < 15; x++ ) fn1(x);
```

In the general form, the `if` clause can be any scalar expression, like the one shown in the following example that causes serial execution when the number of iterations is less than 16.

```
#pragma omp parallel for if(n>=16)
for ( k = 0; k < n; k++ ) fn2(k);
```

Another method is to pick the region of the code that contains the bug and place it within a critical section, a single construct, or a master construct. Try to find the section of code that suddenly works when it is within a critical section and fails without the critical section, or executed with a single thread.

The goal is to use the abilities of OpenMP to quickly shift code back and forth between parallel and serial states so that you can identify the locale of the bug. This approach only works if the program does in fact function correctly when run completely in serial mode. Notice that only OpenMP gives you the possibility of testing code this way without rewriting it substantially. Standard programming techniques used in the Windows API or Pthreads irretrievably commit the code to a threaded model and so make this debugging approach more difficult.

Performance

OpenMP paves a simple and portable way for you to parallelize your applications or to develop threaded applications. The threaded application performance with OpenMP is largely dependent upon the following factors:

■ The underlying performance of the single-threaded code.

■ The percentage of the program that is run in parallel and its scalability.

■ CPU utilization, effective data sharing, data locality and load balancing.

■ The amount of synchronization and communication among the threads.

■ The overhead introduced to create, resume, manage, suspend, destroy, and synchronize the threads, and made worse by the number of serial-to-parallel or parallel-to-serial transitions.

■ Memory conflicts caused by shared memory or falsely shared memory.

■ Performance limitations of shared resources such as memory, write combining buffers, bus bandwidth, and CPU execution units.

Essentially, threaded code performance boils down to two issues: how well does the single-threaded version run, and how well can the work be divided up among multiple processors with the least amount of overhead?

Performance always begins with a well-designed parallel algorithm or well-tuned application. The wrong algorithm, even one written in hand-optimized assembly language, is just not a good place to start. Creating a program that runs well on two cores or processors is not as desirable as creating one that runs well on any number of cores or processors. Remember, by default, with OpenMP the number of threads is chosen by the compiler and runtime library—not you—so programs that work well regardless of the number of threads are far more desirable.

Once the algorithm is in place, it is time to make sure that the code runs efficiently on the Intel Architecture and a single-threaded version can be a big help. By turning off the OpenMP compiler option you can generate a single-threaded version and run it through the usual set of optimizations. A good reference for optimizations is *The Software Optimization Cookbook* (Gerber 2006). Once you have gotten the single-threaded performance that you desire, then it is time to generate the multithreaded version and start doing some analysis.

First look at the amount of time spent in the operating system's idle loop. The Intel VTune Performance Analyzer is great tool to help with the investigation. Idle time can indicate unbalanced loads, lots of blocked synchronization, and serial regions. Fix those issues, then go back to the VTune Performance Analyzer to look for excessive cache misses and memory issues like false-sharing. Solve these basic problems, and you will have a well-optimized parallel program that will run well on multi-core systems as well as multiprocessor SMP systems.

Optimizations are really a combination of patience, trial and error, and practice. Make little test programs that mimic the way your application uses the computer's resources to get a feel for what things are faster than others. Be sure to try the different scheduling clauses for the parallel sections. Chapter 7 provides additional advice on how to tune parallel code for performance and Chapter 11 covers the tools you'll need.

Key Points

Keep the following key points in mind while programming with OpenMP:

- The OpenMP programming model provides an easy and portable way to parallelize serial code with an OpenMP-compliant compiler.

- OpenMP consists of a rich set of pragmas, environment variables, and a runtime API for threading.

- The environment variables and APIs should be used sparingly because they can affect performance detrimentally. The pragmas represent the real added value of OpenMP.

- With the rich set of OpenMP pragmas, you can incrementally parallelize loops and straight-line code blocks such as sections without re-architecting the applications. The Intel Task queuing extension makes OpenMP even more powerful in covering more application domain for threading.

- If your application's performance is saturating a core or processor, threading it with OpenMP will almost certainly increase the application's performance on a multi-core or multiprocessor system.

- You can easily use pragmas and clauses to create critical sections, identify private and public variables, copy variable values, and control the number of threads operating in one section.

■ OpenMP automatically uses an appropriate number of threads for the target system so, where possible, developers should consider using OpenMP to ease their transition to parallel code and to make their programs more portable and simpler to maintain. Native and quasi-native options, such as the Windows threading API and Pthreads, should be considered only when this is not possible.

Chapter 7

Solutions to Common Parallel Programming Problems

Parallel programming has been around for decades, though before the advent of multi-core processors, it was an esoteric discipline. Numerous programmers have tripped over the common stumbling blocks by now. By recognizing these problems you can avoid stumbling. Furthermore, it is important to understand the common problems *before* designing a parallel program, because many of the problems arise from the overall decomposition of the program, and cannot be easily patched later. This chapter surveys some of these common problems, their symptoms, and ways to circumvent them.

Too Many Threads

It may seem that if a little threading is good, then a lot must be better. In fact, having too many threads can seriously degrade program performance. The impact comes in two ways. First, partitioning a fixed amount of work among too many threads gives each thread too little work, so that the overhead of starting and terminating threads swamps the useful work. Second, having too many concurrent software threads incurs overhead from having to share fixed hardware resources.

When there are more software threads than hardware threads, the operating system typically resorts to round robin scheduling. The scheduler gives each software thread a short turn, called a *time slice*, to run on one of the hardware threads. When a software thread's time slice runs out, the scheduler preemptively suspends the thread in order to run another software thread on the same hardware thread. The software thread freezes in time until it gets another time slice.

Time slicing ensures that all software threads make some progress. Otherwise, some software threads might hog all the hardware threads and starve other software threads. However, this equitable distribution of hardware threads incurs overhead. When there are too many software threads, the overhead can severely degrade performance. There are several kinds of overhead, and it helps to know the culprits so you can spot them when they appear.

The most obvious overhead is the process of saving and restoring a thread's register state. Suspending a software thread requires saving the register values of the hardware thread, so the values can be restored later, when the software thread resumes on its next time slice. Typically, thread schedulers allocate big enough time slices so that the save/restore overheads for registers are insignificant, so this obvious overhead is in fact not much of a concern.

A more subtle overhead of time slicing is saving and restoring a thread's cache state. Modern processors rely heavily on cache memory, which can be about 10 to 100 times faster than main memory. Accesses that hit in cache are not only much faster; they also consume no bandwidth of the memory bus. Caches are fast, but finite. When the cache is full, a processor must evict data from the cache to make room for new data. Typically, the choice for eviction is the least recently used data, which more often than not is data from an earlier time slice. Thus threads tend to evict each other's data. The net effect is that too many threads hurt performance by fighting each other for cache.

A similar overhead, at a different level, is thrashing virtual memory. Most systems use virtual memory, where the processors have an address space bigger than the actual available memory. Virtual memory resides on disk, and the frequently used portions are kept in real memory. Similar to caches, the least recently used data is evicted from memory when necessary to make room. Each software thread requires virtual memory for its stack and private data structures. As with caches, time slicing causes threads to fight each other for real memory and thus hurts performance. In extreme cases, there can be so many threads that the program runs out of even virtual memory.

The cache and virtual memory issues described arise from sharing limited resources among too many software threads. A very different, and often more severe, problem arises called *convoying,* in which software threads pile up waiting to acquire a lock. Consider what happens when a thread's time slice expires while the thread is holding a lock. All threads waiting for the lock must now wait for the holding thread to wake up and release the lock. The problem is even worse if the lock implementation is *fair,* in which the lock is acquired in first-come first-served order. If a waiting thread is suspended, then *all* threads waiting behind it are blocked from acquiring the lock.

The solution that usually works best is to limit the number of "runnable" threads to the number of hardware threads, and possibly limit it to the number of outer-level caches. For example, a dual-core Intel® Pentium® Processor Extreme Edition has two physical cores, each with Hyper-Threading Technology, and each with its own cache. This configuration supports four hardware threads and two outer-level caches. Using all four runnable threads will work best unless the threads need so much cache that it causes fighting over cache, in which case maybe only two threads is best. The only way to be sure is to experiment. Never "hard code" the number of threads; leave it as a tuning parameter.

Runnable threads, not blocked threads, cause time-slicing overhead. When a thread is blocked waiting for an external event, such as a mouse click or disk I/O request, the operating system takes it off the round-robin schedule. Hence a blocked thread does not cause time-slicing overhead. A program may have many more software threads than hardware threads, and still run efficiently if most of the OS threads are blocked.

A helpful organizing principle is to separate compute threads from I/O threads. Compute threads should be the threads that are runnable most of the time. Ideally, the compute threads never block on external events, and instead feed from task queues that provide work. The number of compute threads should match the processor resources. The I/O threads are threads that wait on external events most of the time, and thus do not contribute to having too many threads.

Because building efficient task queues takes some expertise, it is usually best to use existing software to do this. Common useful practices are as follows:

■ Let OpenMP do the work. OpenMP lets the programmer specify loop iterations instead of threads. OpenMP deals with managing the threads. As long as the programmer does not request a particular number of threads, the OpenMP implementation will strive to use the optimal number of software threads.

■ Use a thread pool, which is a construct used to maintain a set of long lived software threads and eliminates the overhead of initialization process of threads for short lived tasks. A thread pool is a collection of tasks which are serviced by the software threads in the pool. Each software thread finishes a task before taking on another. For example, Windows has a routine QueueUserWorkItem. Clients add tasks by calling QueueUserWorkItem with a callback and pointer that define the task. Hardware threads feed from this queue. For managed code, Windows .NET has a class ThreadPool. Java has a class Executor for similar purposes. Unfortunately, there is no standard thread pool support in POSIX threads.

■ Experts may wish to write their own task scheduler. The method of choice is called *work stealing*, where each thread has its own private collection of tasks. When a thread runs out of tasks, it steals from another thread's collection. Work stealing yields good cache usage and load balancing. While a thread is working on its own tasks, it tends to be reusing data that is hot in its cache. When it runs out of tasks and has to steal work, it balances the load. The trick to effective task stealing is to bias the stealing towards large tasks, so that the thief can stay busy for a while. The early Cilk scheduler (Blumofe 1995) is a good example of how to write an effective task-stealing scheduler.

Data Races, Deadlocks, and Live Locks

Unsynchronized access to shared memory can introduce race conditions, where the program results depend nondeterministically on the relative timings of two or more threads. Figure 7.1 shows two threads trying to add to a shared variable x, which has an initial value of 0. Depending upon the relative speeds of the threads, the final value of x can be 1, 2, or 3.

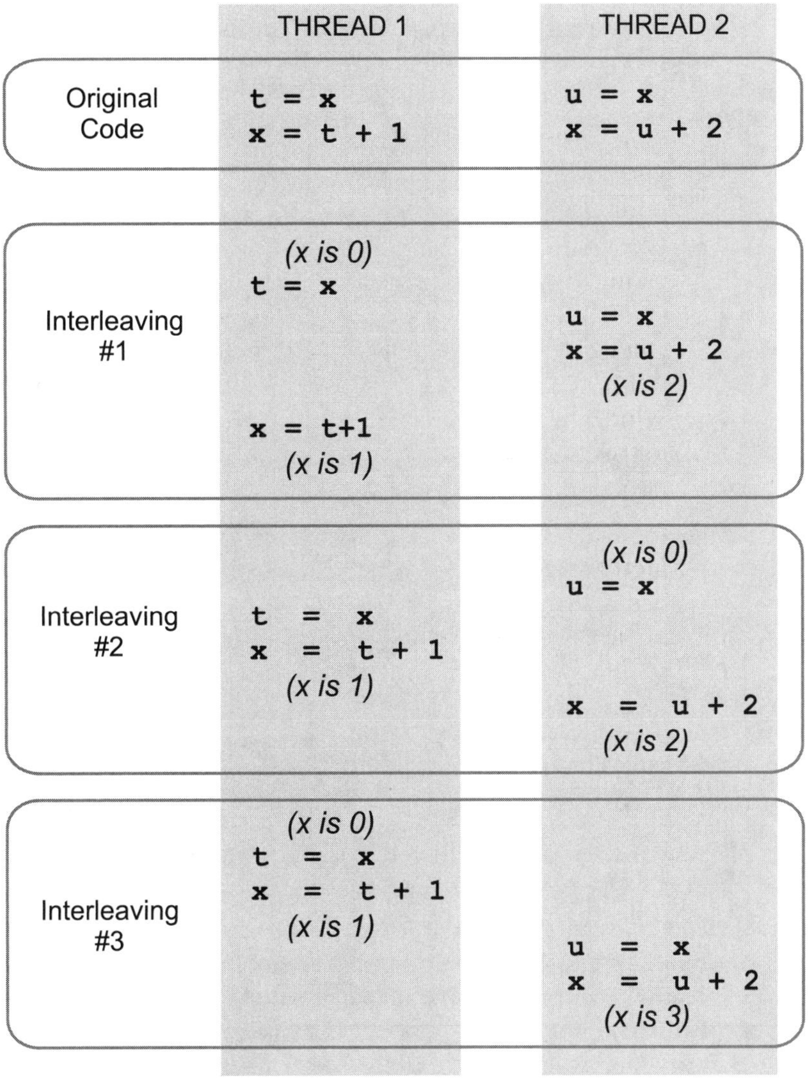

	THREAD 1	THREAD 2
Original Code	`t = x` `x = t + 1`	`u = x` `x = u + 2`

Interleaving #1	*(x is 0)*
	`t = x`
	
	`x = t+1`
	(x is 1)
		`u = x`
		`x = u + 2`
		(x is 2)

Interleaving #2	`t = x`
	`x = t + 1`
	(x is 1)
		(x is 0)
		`u = x`
		
		`x = u + 2`
		(x is 2)

Interleaving #3	*(x is 0)*
	`t = x`
	`x = t + 1`
	(x is 1)
		`u = x`
		`x = u + 2`
		(x is 3)

Figure 7.1   Unsynchronized Threads Racing against each Other Lead to Nondeterministic Outcome

Parallel programming would be a lot easier if races were as obvious as in Figure 7.1. But the same race can be hidden by language syntax in a variety of ways, as shown by the examples in Figure 7.2. Update operations such as += are normally just shorthand for "temp = x; x = temp+1", and hence can result in interleaving. Sometimes the shared location is accessed by different expressions. Sometimes the shared location is hidden by function calls. Even if each thread uses a single instruction to fetch and update the location, there could be interleaving, because the hardware might break the instruction into interleaved reads and writes.

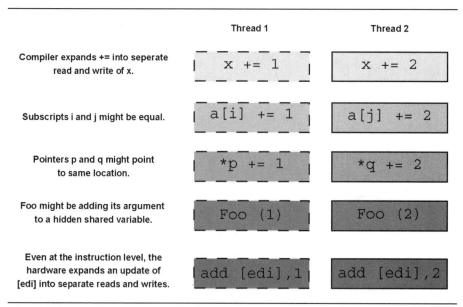

Figure 7.2   Race Conditions Hiding behind Language Syntax

Intel Thread Checker is a powerful tool for detecting potential race conditions. It can see past all the varieties of camouflage shown in Figure 7.2 because it deals in terms of actual memory locations, not their names or addressing expressions. Chapter 11 says more about Thread Checker.

Sometimes deliberate race conditions are intended and useful. For example, threads may be reading a location that is updated asynchronously with a "latest current value." In such a situation, care must be taken that the writes and reads are atomic. Otherwise, garbled data may be written or read. For example, reads and writes of structure types are often done a word at a time or a field at a time. Types longer than the natural word size, such as 80-bit floating-point, might not be read or written atomically, depending on the architecture. Likewise, misaligned loads and stores, when supported, are usually not atomic. If such an access straddles a cache line, the processor performs the access as two separate accesses to the two constituent cache lines.

Data races can arise not only from unsynchronized access to shared memory, but also from synchronized access that was synchronized at too low a level. Figure 7.3 shows such an example. The intent is to use a list to represent a set of keys. Each key should be in the list at most once. Even if the individual list operations have safeguards against races, the combination suffers a higher level race. If two threads both attempt to insert the same key at the same time, they may simultaneously determine that the key is not in the list, and then both would insert the key. What is needed is a lock that protects not just the list, but that also protects the invariant "no key occurs twice in list."

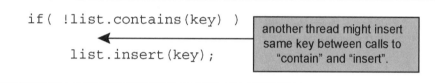

Figure 7.3   A Higher-Level Race Condition Example.

Adding the necessary lock to correct Figure 7.3 exposes the frustrating performance problem of locks. Building locks into low-level components is often a waste of time, because the high-level components that use the components will need higher-level locks anyway. The lower-level locks then become pointless overhead. Fortunately, in such a scenario the high-level locking causes the low-level locks to be uncontended, and most lock implementations optimize the uncontended case. Hence the performance impact is somewhat mitigated, but for best performance the superfluous locks should be removed. Of course there are times when components should provide their own internal locking. This topic is discussed later in the discussion of thread-safe libraries.

Deadlock

Race conditions are typically cured by adding a lock that protects the invariant that might otherwise be violated by interleaved operations. Unfortunately, locks have their own hazards, most notably deadlock. Figure 7.4 shows a deadlock involving two threads. Thread 1 has acquired lock A. Thread 2 has acquired lock B. Each thread is trying to acquire the other lock. Neither thread can proceed.

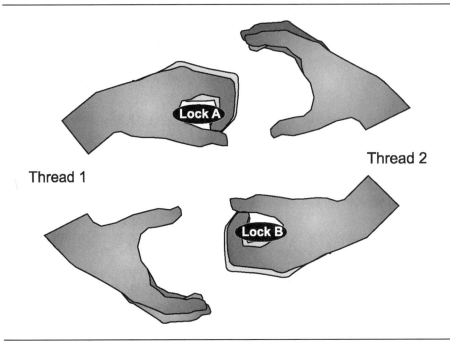

Figure 7.4   Deadlock Caused by Cycle

Though deadlock is often associated with locks, it can happen any time a thread tries to acquire exclusive access to two more shared resources. For example, the locks in Figure 7.4 could be files instead, where the threads are trying to acquire exclusive file access.

Deadlock can occur only if the following four conditions hold true:

1. Access to each resource is exclusive.

2. A thread is allowed to hold one resource while requesting another.

3. No thread is willing to relinquish a resource that it has acquired.

4. There is a cycle of threads trying to acquire resources, where each resource is held by one thread and requested by another.

Deadlock can be avoided by breaking any one of these conditions.

Often the best way to avoid deadlock is to replicate a resource that requires exclusive access, so that each thread can have its own private copy. Each thread can access its own copy without needing a lock. The copies can be merged into a single shared copy of the resource at the end if necessary. By eliminating locking, replication avoids deadlock and has the further benefit of possibly improving scalability, because the lock that was removed might have been a source of contention.

If replication cannot be done, that is, in such cases where there really must be only a single copy of the resource, common wisdom is to always acquire the resources (locks) in the same order. Consistently ordering acquisition prevents deadlock cycles. For instance, the deadlock in Figure 7.4 cannot occur if threads always acquire lock A before they acquire lock B.

The ordering rules that are most convenient depend upon the specific situation. If the locks all have associated names, even something as simple as alphabetical order works. This order may sound silly, but it has been successfully used on at least one large project.

For multiple locks in a data structure, the order is often based on the topology of the structure. In a linked list, for instance, the agreed upon order might be to lock items in the order they appear in the list. In a tree structure, the order might be a pre-order traversal of the tree. Somewhat similarly, components often have a nested structure, where bigger components are built from smaller components. For components nested that way, a common order is to acquire locks in order from the outside to the inside.

If there is no obvious ordering of locks, a solution is to sort the locks by address. This approach requires that a thread know all locks that it needs to acquire before it acquires any of them. For instance, perhaps a thread needs to swap two containers pointed to by pointers x and y, and each container is protected by a lock. The thread could compare "x < y" to determine which container comes first, and acquire the lock on the first container before acquiring a lock on the second container, as Figure 7.5 illustrates.

```
void AcquireTwoLocksViaOrdering( Lock& x, Lock& y ) {
    assert( &x!=&y );
    if( &x<&y ) {
        acquire x
        acquire y
    } else {
        acquire y
        acquire x
    }
}
```

Figure 7.5   Locks Ordered by their Addresses

In large software projects, different programmers construct different components, and by necessity should not have to understand the inner workings of the other components. It follows that to prevent accidental deadlock, software components should try to avoid holding a lock while calling code outside the component, because the call chain may cycle around and create a deadlock cycle.

The third condition for deadlock is that no thread is willing to give up its claim on a resource. Thus another way of preventing deadlock is for a thread to give up its claim on a resource if it cannot acquire the other resources. For this purpose, mutexes often have some kind of "try lock" routine that allows a thread to attempt to acquire a lock, and give up if it cannot be acquired. This approach is useful in scenarios where sorting the locks is impractical. Figure 7.6 sketches the logic for using a "try lock" approach to acquire two locks, A and B. In Figure 7.6, a thread tries to acquire both locks, and if it cannot, it release both locks and tries again.

```
void AcquireTwoLocksViaBackoff( Lock& x, Lock& y ) {
    for( int t=1; ; t*=2 ) {
        acquire x
        try to acquire y
        if( y was acquired ) break;
        release x
        wait for random amount of time between 0 and t
    }
}
```

Figure 7.6   "Try and Back Off" Logic

Figure 7.6 has some timing delays in it to prevent the hazard of *live lock*. Live lock occurs when threads continually conflict with each other and back off. Figure 7.6 applies exponential backoff to avoid live lock. If a thread cannot acquire all the locks that it needs, it releases any that it acquired and waits for a random amount of time. The random time is chosen from an interval that doubles each time the thread backs off. Eventually, the threads involved in the conflict will back off sufficiently that at least one will make progress. The disadvantage of backoff schemes is that they are not fair. There is no guarantee that a particular thread will make progress. If fairness is an issue, then it is probably best to use lock ordering to prevent deadlock.

Heavily Contended Locks

Proper use of lock to avoid race conditions can invite performance problems if the lock becomes highly contended. The lock becomes like a tollgate on a highway. If cars arrive at the tollgate faster than the toll taker can process them, the cars will queue up in a traffic jam behind the tollgate. Similarly, if threads try to acquire a lock faster than the rate at which a thread can execute the corresponding critical section, then program performance will suffer as threads will form a "convoy" waiting to acquire the lock. Indeed, this behavior is sometimes referred to as *convoying*.

As mentioned in the discussion of time-slicing woes, convoying becomes even worse for fair locks, because if a thread falls asleep, all threads behind it have to wait for it to wake up. Imagine that software threads are cars and hardware threads are the drivers in those cars. This might seem like a backwards analogy, but from a car's perspective, people exist solely to move cars between parking places. If the cars form a convoy, and a driver leaves his or her car, everyone else behind is stuck.

Priority Inversion

Some threading implementations allow threads to have priorities. When there are not enough hardware threads to run all software threads, the higher priority software threads get preference. For example, foreground tasks might be running with higher priorities than background tasks. Priorities can be useful, but paradoxically, can lead to situations where a low-priority thread blocks a high-priority thread from running.

Figure 7.7 illustrates priority inversion. Continuing our analogy with software threads as cars and hardware threads as drivers, three cars are shown, but there is only a single driver. A low-priority car has acquired a lock so it can cross a single-lane "critical section" bridge. Behind it waits a high-priority car. But because the high-priority car is blocked, the driver is attending the highest-priority runnable car, which is the medium-priority one. As contrived as this sounds, it actually happened on the NASA Mars Pathfinder mission.

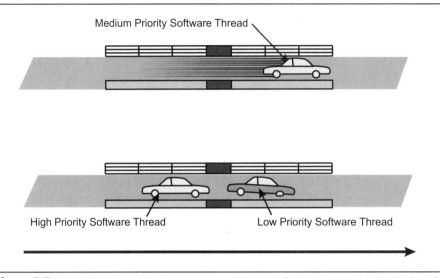

Figure 7.7 Priority Inversion Scenario, Where High Priority Gets Blocked and Medium Priority Gets the Cycles

In real life, the problem in Figure 7.7 would be solved by bumping up the priority of the blocking car until it is out of the way. With locks, this is called *priority inheritance*. When a high-priority thread needs to acquire a lock held by a low-priority thread, the scheduler bumps up the priority of the blocking thread until the lock is released. Indeed, the Mars Pathfinder problem was solved by turning on priority inheritance (Reeves 1998).

An alternative is *priority ceilings* in which a priority, called the ceiling, is assigned to the mutex. The ceiling is the highest priority of any thread that is expected to hold the mutex. When a thread acquires the mutex, its priority is immediately bumped up to the ceiling value for the duration that it holds the mutex. The priority ceilings scheme is eager to bump up a thread's priority. In contrast, the priority inheritance scheme is lazy by not bumping up a thread's priority unless necessary.

Windows mutexes support priority inheritance by default. Pthreads mutexes support neither the priority inheritance nor priority ceiling protocols. Both protocols are optional in the pthreads standard. If they exist in a particular implementation, they can be set for a mutex via the function `pthread_mutexattr_setprotocol` and inspected with the function `pthread_mutexattr_getprotocol`. Read the manual pages on these functions to learn whether they are supported for the target system.

Programmers "rolling their own" locks or busy waits may encounter priority inversion if threads with different priorities are allowed to acquire the same lock. Hand-coded spin locks are a common example. If neither priority inheritance nor priority ceilings can be built into the lock or busy wait, then it is probably best to restrict the lock's contenders to threads with the same priority.

Solutions for Heavily Contended Locks

Upon encountering a heavily contended lock, the first reaction of many programmers is "I need a faster lock." Indeed, some implementations of locks are notoriously slow, and faster locks are possible. However, no matter how fast the lock is, it must inherently serialize threads. A faster lock can thus help performance by a constant factor, but will never improve scalability. To improve scalability, either eliminate the lock or spread out the contention.

The earlier discussion of deadlock mentioned the technique of eliminating a lock by replicating the resource. That is certainly the method of choice to eliminate lock contention if it is workable. For example, consider contention for a counter of events. If each thread can have its own private counter, then no lock is necessary. If the total count is required, the counts can be summed after all threads are done counting.

If the lock on a resource cannot be eliminated, consider partitioning the resource and using a separate lock to protect each partition. The partitioning can spread out contention among the locks. For example, consider a hash table implementation where multiple threads might try to do insertions at the same time. A simple approach to avoid race conditions is to use a single lock to protect the entire table. The lock allows only one thread into the table at a time. The drawback of this approach is that all threads must contend for the same lock, which could become a serial bottleneck. An alternative approach is to create an array of sub-tables, each with its own lock, as shown in Figure 7.8. Keys can be mapped to the sub-tables via a hashing function. For a given key, a thread can figure out which table to inspect by using a hash function that returns a sub-table index. Insertion of a key commences by hashing the key to one of the sub-tables, and then doing the insertion on that sub-table while holding the sub-table's lock. Given enough sub-tables and a good hash function, the threads will mostly not contend for the same sub-table and thus not contend for the same lock.

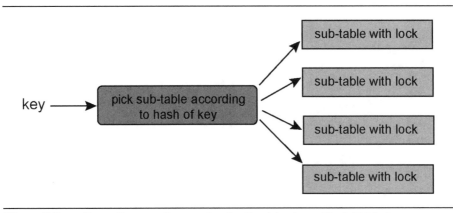

key ⟶ pick sub-table according to hash of key

sub-table with lock

sub-table with lock

sub-table with lock

sub-table with lock

Figure 7.8   Spreading out Contention by Partitioning a Hash Table into Multiple Sub-tables

Pursuit of the idea of spreading contention among multiple locks further leads to *fine-grained locking*. For example, hash tables are commonly implemented as an array of buckets, where each bucket holds keys that hashed to the same array element. In fine-grained locking, there might be a lock on each bucket. This way multiple threads can concurrently access different buckets in parallel. This is straightforward to implement if the number of buckets is fixed. If the number of buckets has to be grown, the problem becomes more complicated, because resizing the array may require excluding all but the thread doing the resizing. A reader-writer lock helps solve this problem, as will be explained shortly. Another pitfall is that if the buckets are very small, the space overhead of the lock may dominate.

If a data structure is frequently read, but infrequently written, then a reader-writer lock may help deal with contention. A reader-write lock distinguishes readers from writers. Multiple readers can acquire the lock at the same time, but only one writer can acquire it at a time. Readers cannot acquire the lock while a writer holds it and vice-versa. Thus readers contend only with writers.

The earlier fine-grained hash table is a good example of where reader-write locks can help if the array of buckets must be dynamically resizable. Figure 7.9 shows a possible implementation. The table consists of an array descriptor that specifies the array's size and location. A reader-writer mutex protects this structure. Each bucket has its own plain mutex protecting it. To access a bucket, a thread acquires two locks: a reader lock on the array descriptor, and a lock on the bucket's mutex. The thread acquires a reader lock, not a writer lock, on the reader-writer mutex even if it is planning to modify a bucket, because the reader-writer mutex protects the array descriptor, not the buckets. If a thread needs to resize the array, it requests a writer lock on the reader-writer mutex. Once granted, the thread can safely modify the array descriptor without introducing a race condition. The overall advantage is that during times when the array is not being resized, multiple threads accessing different buckets can proceed concurrently. The principle disadvantage is that a thread must obtain two locks instead of one. This increase in locking overhead can overwhelm the advantages of increased concurrency if the table is typically not subject to contention.

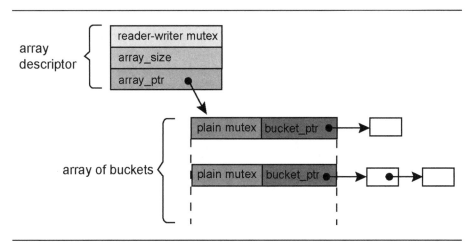

Figure 7.9   Hash Table with Fine-grained Locking

If writers are infrequent, reader-writer locks can greatly reduce contention. However, reader-writer locks have limitations. When the rate of incoming readers is very high, the lock implementation may suffer from memory contention problems. Thus reader-writer locks can be very useful for medium contention of readers, but may not be able to fix problems with high contention. The reliable way to deal with high contention is to rework the parallel decomposition in a way that lowers the contention. For example, the schemes in Figures 7.8 and 7.9 might be combined, so that a hash table is represented by a fixed number of sub-tables, each with fine-grained locking.

Non-blocking Algorithms

One way to solve the problems introduced by locks is to not use locks. Algorithms designed to do this are called *non-blocking*. The defining characteristic of a non-blocking algorithm is that stopping a thread does not prevent the rest of the system from making progress. There are different non-blocking guarantees:

- *Obstruction freedom*. A thread makes progress as long as there is no contention, but live lock is possible. Exponential backoff can be used to work around live lock.

- *Lock freedom*. The system as a whole makes progress.

- *Wait freedom*. Every thread makes progress, even when faced with contention. Very few non-blocking algorithms achieve this.

Non-blocking algorithms are immune from lock contention, priority inversion, and convoying. Non-blocking algorithms have a lot of advantages, but with these come a new set of problems that need to be understood.

Non-blocking algorithms are based on atomic operations, such as the methods of the `Interlocked` class discussed in Chapter 5. A few non-blocking algorithms are simple. Most are complex, because the algorithms must handle all possible interleaving of instruction streams from contending processors.

A trivial non-blocking algorithm is counting via an interlocked increment instead of a lock. The interlocked instruction avoids lock overhead and pathologies. However, simply using atomic operations is not enough to avoid race conditions, because as discussed before, composing thread-safe operations does not necessarily yield a thread-safe procedure. As an example, the C code in Figure 7.10 shows the wrong way and right way to decrement and test a reference count `p->ref_count`. In the wrong code, if the count was originally 2, two threads executing the wrong code might both decrement the count, and then both see it as zero at the same time. The correct code performs the decrement and test as a single atomic operation.

WRONG

```
InterlockedDecrement(&p->ref_count);

if (p->ref_count==0) {
    delete p;
```

another thread might
decrement ref_count
right before the if executes

CORRECT

```
if (InterlockedDecrement(&p->ref_count)==0)
    delete p;
```

Figure 7.10   Atomic Operations and Race Conditions

Most non-blocking algorithms involve a loop that attempts to perform an action using one or more compare-and-swap (CAS) operations, and retries when one of the CAS operations fails. A simple and useful example is implementing a thread-safe fetch-and-op. A fetch-and-op reads a value from a location, computes a new value from it, and stores the new value. Figure 7.11 illustrates both a locked version and a non-blocking version that operate on a location x. The non-blocking version reads location x into a local temporary x_old, and computes a new value x_new = op(x_old). The routine InterlockedCompareExchange stores the new value, unless x is now different than x_old. If the store fails, the code starts over until it succeeds.

```
void LockedFetchAndOp( long& x ) {
    acquire lock
    x = op(x);
    release lock
}

void NonBlockingFetchAndOp( volatile long& x ) {
    long x_old, x_new, x_was;
    do {
        x_old = x;
        x_new = op(x_old);
        x_was = InterlockedCompareExchange(&x, x_new,
                                           x_old);
    } while( x_was!=x_old );
}
```

Figure 7.11   Comparison of Locked and Lockless Code for Fetch-and-op

Fetch-and-op is useful as long as the order in which various threads perform *op* does not matter. For example, op might be "multiply by 2." The location x must have a type for which a compare-and-exchange instruction is available.

ABA Problem

In Figure 7.11, there is a time interval between when a thread executes "x_old = x" and when the thread executes InterlockedCompareExchange. During this interval, other processors might perform other fetch-and-op operations. For example, suppose the initial value read is A. An intervening sequence of fetch-and-op operations by other processors might change x to B and then back to A. When the original thread executes InterlockedCompareExchange, it will be as if the other processor's actions never happened. As long as the order in which op is executed does not matter, there is no problem. The net result is the same as if the fetch-and-op operations were reordered such that the intervening sequence happens before the first read.

But sometimes fetch-and-op has uses where changing x from A to B to A does make a difference. The problem is indeed known as the *ABA problem*. Consider the lockless implementation of a stack shown in Figure 7.12. It is written in the fetch-and-op style, and thus has the advantage of not requiring any locks. But the "op" is no longer a pure function, because it deals with another shared memory location: the field "next." Figure 7.13 shows a sequence where the function BrokenLockLessPop corrupts the linked stack. When thread 1 starts out, it sees B as next on stack. But intervening pushes and pops make C next on stack. But Thread 1's final InterlockedCompareExchange does not catch this switch because it only examines Top.

```
Node* Top;  // Pointer to top item on stack.

void BrokenLocklessPush( Node* node ) {
    Item *t_old, t_was;
    do {
        Item* t_old = Top;
        n->next = t_old;
        t_was = InterlockedCompareExchange(&Top,node,t_old);
    } while( t_was!=t_old );
}
```

```
Item* BrokenLocklessPop() {
    Item *t_old, *t_was, *t_new;
    do {
        t_old = Top;
        t_new = t_old->next;
        // ABA problem may strike below!
        t_was = InterlockedCompareExchange(&Top,t_new,t_old);
    } while( t_was!=t_old );
    return t_old;
}
```

Figure 7.12   Lockless Implementation of a Linked Stack that May Suffer from ABA Problem

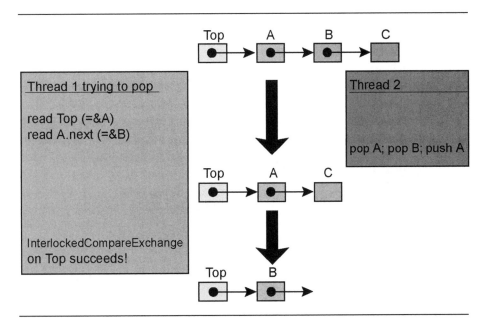

Figure 7.13   Sequence Illustrates ABA Problem for Code in Figure 7.12

The solution to the ABA problem is to never reuse A. In a garbage-collected environment such as Java or .NET, this is simply a matter of not recycling nodes. That is, once a node has been popped, never push it again. Instead allocate a fresh node. The garbage collector will do the hard work of checking that the memory for node A is not recycled until all extant references to it are gone.

In languages with garbage collection, the problem is harder. An old technique dating back to the IBM 370 changes ABA to ABA′. In other words, make A slightly different each time. This is typically done by appending a serial number to the pointer. A special instruction that can do a double-wide compare-exchange is required. On IA-32, the instruction is cmpxchg8b, which does a compare-exchange on eight bytes. On processors with Intel EM64T, it is cmpxchg16b. On Itanium® processors, there is cmp8xchg16, which is not quite the same, because it compares only the first eight bytes, but exchanges all 16. However, as long as the serial number is the first eight bytes, it works for turning ABA into ABA′.

Another solution is to build a miniature garbage collector that handles pointers involved in compare-exchange operations. These pointers are called *hazard pointers*, because they present a hazard to lockless algorithms. Maged Michael's paper on hazard pointers (Michael 2004) explains how to implement hazard pointers. Hazard pointers are a nontrivial exercise and make assumptions about the environment, so tread with caution.

Cache Line Ping-ponging

Non-blocking algorithms can cause a lot of traffic on the memory bus as various hardware threads keep trying and retrying to perform operations on the same cache line. To service these operations, the cache line bounces back and forth ("ping-pongs") between the contending threads. A locked algorithm may outperform the non-blocking equivalent if lock contention is sufficiently distributed and each lock says "hand off my cache line until I'm done." Experimentation is necessary to find out whether the non-blocking or locked algorithm is better. A rough guide is that a fast spin lock protecting a critical section with no atomic operations may outperform an alternative non-blocking design that requires three or more highly contended atomic operations.

Memory Reclamation Problem

Memory reclamation is the dirty laundry of many non-blocking algorithms. For languages such as C/C++ that require the programmer to explicitly free memory, it turns out to be surprisingly difficult to call free on a node used in a non-blocking algorithm. Programmers planning to use non-blocking algorithms need to understand when this limitation arises, and how to work around it.

The problem occurs for algorithms that remove nodes from linked structures, and do so by performing compare-exchange operations on fields in the nodes. For example, non-blocking algorithms for queues do this. The reason is that when a thread removes a node from a data structure, without using a lock to exclude other threads, it never knows if another thread still looking at the node. The algorithms are usually designed so that the other thread will perform a failing compare-exchange on a field in the removed node, and thus know to retry. Unfortunately, if in the meantime the node is handed to `free`, the field might be coincidentally set to the value that the compare-exchange expects to see.

The solution is to use a garbage collector or mini-collector like hazard pointers. Alternatively you may associate a free list of nodes with the data structure and not free any nodes until the data structure itself is freed.

Recommendations

Non-blocking algorithms are currently a hot topic in research. Their big advantage is avoiding lock pathologies. Their primary disadvantage is that they are much more complicated than their locked counterparts. Indeed, the discovery of a lockless algorithm is often worthy of a conference paper. Non-blocking algorithms are difficult to verify. At least one incorrect algorithm has made its way into a conference paper. Non-experts should consider the following advice:

■ Atomic increment, decrement, and fetch-and-add are generally safe to use in an intuitive fashion.

■ The fetch-and-op idiom is generally safe to use with operations that are commutative and associative.

■ The creation of non-blocking algorithms for linked data structures should be left to experts. Use algorithms from the peer-reviewed literature. Be sure to understand any memory reclamation issues.

Otherwise, for now, stick with locks. Avoid having more runnable software threads than hardware threads, and design programs to avoid lock contention. This way, the problems solved by non-blocking algorithms will not come up in the first place.

Thread-safe Functions and Libraries

The Foo example in Figure 7.2 underscores the importance of documenting thread safety. Defining a routine like Foo that updates unprotected hidden shared state is a poor programming practice. In general, routines should be *thread safe*; that is, concurrently callable by clients. However, complete thread safety is usually unrealistic, because it would require that every call do some locking, and performance would be pathetic. Instead, a common convention is to guarantee that instance routines are thread safe when called concurrently on different objects, but not thread safe when called concurrently on the same object.

This convention is implicit when objects do not share state. For objects that do share state, the burden falls on the implementer to protect the shared state. Figure 7.14 shows a reference-counted implementation of strings where the issue arises. From the client's viewpoint, each string object is a separate string object, and thus threads should be able to concurrently operate on each object. In the underlying implementation, however, a string object is simply a pointer to a shared object that has the string data, and a reference count of the number of string objects that point to it. The implementer should ensure that concurrent accesses do not corrupt the shared state. For example, the updates to the reference count should use atomic operations.

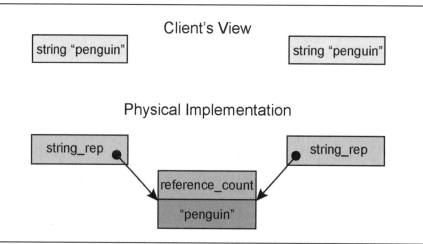

Figure 7.14   Implementer Should Ensure Thread Safety of Hidden Shared State

When defining interfaces, care should be taken to ensure that they can be implemented efficiently in a thread-safe manner. Interfaces should not update hidden global state, because with multiple threads, it may not be clear whose global state is being updated. The C library function strtok is one such offender. Clients use it to tokenize a string. The first call sets the state of a hidden parser, and each successive call advances the parser. The hidden parser state makes the interface thread unsafe. Thread safety can be obtained by having the implementation put the parser in thread-local storage. But this introduces the complexity of a threading package into something that really should not need it in the first place. A thread-safe redesign of strtok would make the parser object an explicit argument. Each thread would create its own local parser object and pass it as an argument. That way, concurrent calls could proceed blissfully without interference.

Some libraries come in thread-safe and thread-unsafe versions. Be sure to use the thread-safe version for multi-threaded code. For example, on Windows, the compiler option /MD is required to dynamically link with the thread-safe version of the run-time library. For debugging, the corresponding option is /MDd, which dynamically links with the "debug" version of the thread-safe run-time. Read your compiler documentation carefully about these kinds of options. Because the compilers date back to the single-core era, the defaults are often for code that is not thread safe.

Memory Issues

When most people perform calculations by hand, they are limited by how fast they can do the calculations, not how fast they can read and write. Early microprocessors were similarly constrained. In recent decades, microprocessors have grown much faster in speed than in memory. A single microprocessor core can execute hundreds of operations in the time it takes to read or write a value in main memory. Programs now are often limited by the memory bottleneck, not processor speed. Multi-core processors can exacerbate the problem unless care is taken to conserve memory bandwidth and avoid memory contention.

Bandwidth

To conserve bandwidth, pack data more tightly, or move it less frequently between cores. Packing the data tighter is usually straightforward, and benefits sequential execution as well. For example, pack Boolean arrays into one Boolean value per bit, not one value per byte. Use the shortest integer type that can hold values in the required range. When declaring structures in C/C++, declare fields in order of descending size. This strategy tends to minimize the extra padding that the compiler must insert to maintain alignment requirements, as exemplified in Figure 7.15.

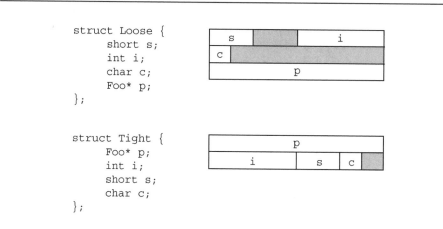

Figure 7.15 Order Fields by Decreasing Size to Reduce Padding

Some compilers also support "#pragma pack" directives that pack structures even more tightly, possibly by removing all padding. Such very tight packing may be counterproductive, however, because it causes misaligned loads and stores that may be significantly slower than aligned loads and stores.

Working in the Cache

Moving data less frequently is a more subtle exercise than packing, because mainstream programming languages do not have explicit commands to move data between a core and memory. Data movement arises from the way the cores read and write memory. There are two categories of interactions to consider: those between cores and memory, and those between cores.

Data movement between a core and memory also occurs in single-core processors, so minimizing data movement benefits sequential programs as well. There exist numerous techniques. For example, a technique called *cache-oblivious blocking* recursively divides a problem into smaller and smaller subproblems. Eventually the subproblems become so small that they each fit in cache. The *Fastest Fourier Transform in the West* (Frigo 1997) uses this approach and indeed lives up to its name. Another technique for reducing the cache footprint is to reorder steps in the code. Sometimes this is as simple as interchanging loops. Other times it requires more significant restructuring.

The Sieve of Eratosthenes is an elementary programming exercise that demonstrates such restructuring and its benefits. Figure 7.16 presents the Sieve of Eratosthenes for enumerating prime numbers up to n. This version has two nested loops: the outer loop finds primes, and the inner loop, inside function Strike, strikes out composite numbers. This version is unfriendly to cache, because the inner loop is over the full length of array composite, which might be much larger than what fits in cache.

```
inline long Strike( bool composite[], long i,
                    long stride, long limit ) {
    for( ; i<=limit; i+=stride )
        composite[i] = true;
    return i;
}
long CacheUnfriendlySieve( long n ) {
    long count = 0;
    long m = (long)sqrt((double)n);
    bool* composite = new bool[n+1];
    memset( composite, 0, n );
    for( long i=2; i<=m; ++i )
        if( !composite[i] ) {
            ++count;
            // Strike walks array of size n here.
            Strike( composite, 2*i, i, n );
        }
    for( long i=m+1; i<=n; ++i )
        if( !composite[i] )
            ++count;
    delete[] composite;
    return count;
}
```

Figure 7.16   Cache-Unfriendly Sieve of Eratosthenes

Figure 7.17 shows how the sieve can be restructured to be cache friendly. Instead of directly representing the conceptual sieve as one big array, it represents it as a small window into the conceptual sieve. The window size is approximately $\sqrt{n}$ bytes. The restructuring requires that the original inner loop be stopped when it reaches the end of a window, and restarted when processing the next window. The array `striker` stores the indices of these suspended loops, and has an element for each prime up to $\sqrt{n}$. The data structures grow much more slowly than n, and so fit in a 10^6 byte cache even when n approaches values as large as 10^{11}. Of course, allocating array `composite` to hold 10^{11} bytes is impractical on most machines. The later discussion of multi-threading the sieve describes how to reduce `composite` to $\sqrt{n}$ bytes instead of n bytes.

```
long CacheFriendlySieve( long n ) {
    long count = 0;
    long m = (long)sqrt((double)n);
    bool* composite = new bool[n+1];
    memset( composite, 0, n );
    long* factor = new long[m];
    long* striker = new long[m];
    long n_factor = 0;
    for( long i=2; i<=m; ++i )
        if( !composite[i] ) {
            ++count;
            striker[n_factor] = Strike( composite, 2*i, i, m );
            factor[n_factor++] = i;
        }
    // Chops sieve into windows of size ≈ sqrt(n)
    for( long window=m+1; window<=n; window+=m ) {
        long limit = min(window+m-1,n);
        for( long k=0; k<n_factor; ++k )
            // Strike walks window of size sqrt(n) here.
            striker[k] = Strike( composite, striker[k], factor[k],
                                 limit );
            for( long i=window; i<=limit; ++i )
                if( !composite[i] )
                    ++count;
    }
    delete[] striker;
    delete[] factor;
    delete[] composite;
    return count;
}
```

Figure 7.17   Cache-Friendly Sieve of Eratosthenes

The restructuring introduces extra complexity and bookkeeping operations. But because processor speed so greatly outstrips memory speed, the extra bookkeeping pays off dramatically. Figure 7.18 shows this performance difference. On this log plot, the cache friendly code has a fairly straight performance plot, while the cache unfriendly version's running time steps up from one straight line to another when n reaches approximately 10^6. The step is characteristic of algorithms that transition from running in cache to running out of cache as the problem size increases. The restructured version is five times faster than the original version when n significantly exceeds the cache size, despite the extra processor operations required by the restructuring.

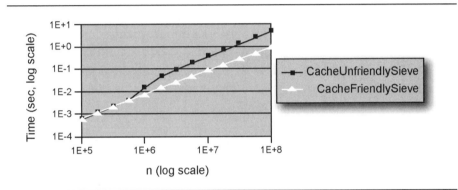

Figure 7.18   Performance Difference between Figure 7.16 and Figure 7.17

Memory Contention

For multi-core programs, working within the cache becomes trickier, because data is not only transferred between a core and memory, but also between cores. As with transfers to and from memory, mainstream programming languages do not make these transfers explicit. The transfers arise implicitly from patterns of reads and writes by different cores. The patterns correspond to two types of data dependencies:

■ *Read-write dependency*. A core writes a cache line, and then a different core reads it.

■ *Write-write dependency*. A core writes a cache line, and then a different core writes it.

An interaction that does *not* cause data movement is two cores repeatedly reading a cache line that is not being written. Thus if multiple cores only read a cache line and do not write it, then no memory bandwidth is consumed. Each core simply keeps its own copy of the cache line.

To minimize memory bus traffic, minimize core interactions by minimizing shared locations. Hence, the same patterns that tend to reduce lock contention also tend to reduce memory traffic, because it is the shared state that requires locks and generates contention. Letting each thread work on its own local copy of the data and merging the data after all threads are done can be a very effective strategy.

Consider writing a multi-threaded version of the function CacheFriendlySieve from Figure 7.17. A good decomposition for this problem is to fill the array `factor` sequentially, and then operate on the windows in parallel. The sequential portion takes time $O(\sqrt{n})$, and hence has minor impact on speedup for large n. Operating on the windows in parallel requires sharing some data. Looking at the nature of the sharing will guide you on how to write the parallel version.

- The array `factor` is read-only once it is filled. Thus each thread can share the array.

- The array `composite` is updated as primes are found. However, the updates are made to separate windows, so they are unlikely to interfere except at window boundaries that fall inside a cache line. Better yet, observe that the values in the window are used only while the window is being processed. The array composite no longer needs to be shared, and instead each thread can have a private portion that holds only the window of interest. This change benefits the sequential version too, because now the space requirements for the sieve have been reduced from O(n) to $O(\sqrt{n})$. The reduction in space makes counting primes up to 10^{11} possible on even a 32-bit machine.

- The variable `count` is updated as primes are found. An atomic increment could be used, but that would introduce memory contention. A better solution, as shown in the example, is to give each thread perform a private partial count, and sum the partial counts at the end.

- The array `striker` is updated as the window is processed. Each thread will need its own private copy. The tricky part is that `striker` induces a loop-carried dependence between windows. For each window, the initial value of `striker` is the last value it had for the previous window. To break this dependence, the initial values in `striker` have to be computed from scratch. This computation is not difficult. The purpose of `striker[k]` is to keep track of the current multiple of `factor[k]`.

■ The variable `base` is new in the parallel version. It keeps track of the start of the window for which `striker` is valid. If the value of base differs from the start of the window being processed, it indicates that the thread must recompute striker from scratch. The recomputation sets the initial value of `striker[k]` to the lowest multiple of `factor[k]` that is inside or after the window.

Figure 7.19 shows the multi-threaded sieve. A further refinement that cuts the work in half would be to look for only odd primes. The refinement was omitted from the examples because it obfuscates understanding of the multi-threading issues.

```
long ParallelSieve( long n ) {
    long count = 0;
    long m = (long)sqrt((double)n);
    long n_factor = 0;
    long* factor = new long[m];

#pragma omp parallel
    {
        bool* composite = new bool[m+1];
        long* striker = new long[m];

#pragma omp single
        {
            memset( composite, 0, m );
            for( long i=2; i<=m; ++i )
                if( !composite[i] ) {
                    ++count;
                    Strike( composite, 2*i, i, m );
                    factor[n_factor++] = i;
                }
        }
        long base = -1;

#pragma omp for reduction (+:count)
        for( long window=m+1; window<=n; window+=m ) {
            memset( composite, 0, m );
            if( base!=window ) {
                // Must compute striker from scratch.
                base = window;
```

```
        for( long k=0; k<n_factor; ++k )
            striker[k] = (base+factor[k]-1)/factor[k] *
                             factor[k] - base;
    }
    long limit = min(window+m-1,n) - base;
    for( long k=0; k<n_factor; ++k )
        striker[k] = Strike( composite, striker[k],
                             factor[k], limit ) - m;
    for( long i=0; i<=limit; ++i )
        if( !composite[i] )
            ++count;
        base += m;
    }
    delete[] striker;
    delete[] composite;
}
delete[] factor;
return count;
}
```

Figure 7.19   Parallel Sieve of Eratosthenes

Cache-related Issues

As remarked earlier in the discussion of time-slicing issues, good performance depends on processors fetching most of their data from cache instead of main memory. For sequential programs, modern caches generally work well without too much thought, though a little tuning helps. In parallel programming, caches open up some much more serious pitfalls.

False Sharing

The smallest unit of memory that two processors interchange is a cache line or cache sector. Two separate caches can share a cache line when they both need to read it, but if the line is written in one cache, and read in another, it must be shipped between caches, even if the locations of interest are disjoint. Like two people writing in different parts of a log book, the writes are independent, but unless the book can be ripped apart, the writers must pass the book back and forth. In the same way, two hardware threads writing to different locations contend for a cache sector to the point where it becomes a ping-pong game.

Figure 7.20 illustrates such a ping-pong game. There are two threads, each running on a different core. Each thread increments a different location belonging to the same cache line. But because the locations belong to the same cache line, the cores must pass the sector back and forth across the memory bus.

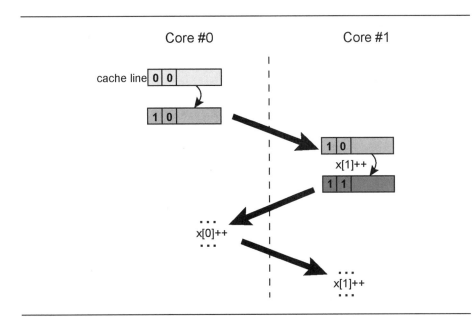

Figure 7.20 Cache Line Ping Ponging Caused by False Sharing

Figure 7.21 shows how bad the impact can be for a generalization of Figure 7.20. Four single-core processors, each enabled with Hyper-Threading Technology (HT Technology), are used to give the flavor of a hypothetical future eight-core system. Each hardware thread increments a separate memory location. The ith thread repeatedly increments x[i*stride]. The performance is worse when the locations are adjacent, and improves as they spread out, because the spreading puts the locations into more distinct cache lines. Performance improves sharply at a stride of 16. This is because the array elements are 4-byte integers. The stride of 16 puts the locations $16 \times 4 = 64$ bytes apart. The data is for a Pentium 4 based processor with a cache sector size of 64 bytes. Hence when the locations were 64 bytes part, each thread is hitting on a separate cache sector, and the locations become private to each thread. The resulting performance is nearly one hundredfold better than when all threads share the same cache line.

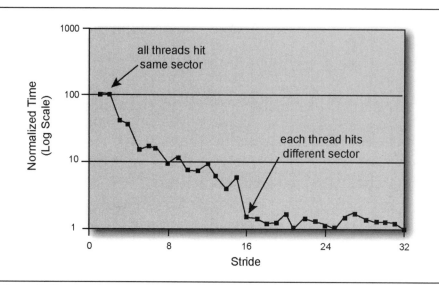

Figure 7.21   Performance Impact of False Sharing

Avoiding false sharing may require aligning variables or objects in memory on cache line boundaries. There are a variety of ways to force alignment. Some compilers support alignment pragmas. The Windows compilers have a directive __declspec(align(n)) that can be used to specify n-byte alignment. Dynamic allocation can be aligned by allocating extra pad memory, and then returning a pointer to the next cache line in the block. Figure 7.22 shows an example allocator that does this. Function CacheAlignedMalloc uses the word just before the aligned block to store a pointer to the true base of the block, so that function CacheAlignedFree can free the true block. Notice that if malloc returns an aligned pointer, CacheAlignedMalloc still rounds up to the next cache line, because it needs the first cache line to store the pointer to the true base.

It may not be obvious that there is always enough room before the aligned block to store the pointer. Sufficient room depends upon two assumptions:

- A cache line is at least as big as a pointer.

- A `malloc` request for at least a cache line's worth of bytes returns a pointer aligned on boundary that is a multiple of `sizeof(char*)`.

These two conditions hold for IA-32 and Itanium-based systems. Indeed, they hold for most architecture because of alignment restrictions specified for `malloc` by the C standard.

```
// Allocate block of memory that starts on cache line
void* CacheAlignedMalloc( size_t bytes, void* hint ) {
    size_t m = (cache line size in bytes);
    assert( (m & m-1)==0 );   // m must be power of 2
    char* base = (char*)malloc(m+bytes);

    // Round pointer up to next line
    char * result = (char*)((UIntPtr)(base+m)&-m);

    // Record where block actually starts.
    ((char**)result)[-1] = base;

    return result;
}

// Free block allocated by CacheAlignedMalloc
void CacheAlignedFree( void* p ) {

    // Recover where block actually starts
    char* base = ((byte**)p)[-1];

    // Failure of following assertion indicates memory
    // was not allocated with CacheAlignedMalloc.
    assert( (void*)((UIntPtr)
            (base+NFS_LineSize)&-NFS_LineSize) == p);
    free( base );
}
```

Figure 7.22   Memory Allocator that Allocates Blocks Aligned on Cache Line Boundaries

The topic of false sharing exposes a fundamental tension between efficient use of a single-core processor and efficient use of a multi-core processor. The general rule for efficient execution on a single core is to pack data tightly, so that it has as small a footprint as possible. But on a multi-core processor, packing shared data can lead to a severe penalty from false sharing. Generally, the solution is to pack data tightly, give each thread its own private copy to work on, and merge results afterwards. This strategy extends naturally to task stealing. When a thread steals a task, it can clone the shared data structures that might cause cache line ping ponging, and merge the results later.

Memory Consistency

At any given instant in time in a sequential program, memory has a well defined state. This is called *sequential consistency.* In parallel programs, it all depends upon the viewpoint. Two writes to memory by a hardware thread may be seen in a different order by another thread. The reason is that when a hardware thread writes to memory, the written data goes through a path of buffers and caches before reaching main memory. Along this path, a later write may reach main memory sooner than an earlier write. Similar effects apply to reads. If one read requires a fetch from main memory and a later read hits in cache, the processor may allow the faster read to "pass" the slower read. Likewise, reads and writes might pass each other. Of course, a processor has to see its own reads and writes in the order it issues them, otherwise programs would break. But the processor does not have to guarantee that other processors see those reads and writes in the original order. Systems that allow this reordering are said to exhibit *relaxed consistency.*

Because relaxed consistency relates to how hardware threads observe each other's actions, it is not an issue for programs running time sliced on a single hardware thread. Inattention to consistency issues can result in concurrent programs that run correctly on single-threaded hardware, or even hardware running with HT Technology, but fail when run on multi-threaded hardware with disjoint caches.

The hardware is not the only cause of relaxed consistency. Compilers are often free to reorder instructions. The reordering is critical to most major compiler optimizations. For instance, compilers typically hoist loop-invariant reads out of a loop, so that the read is done once per loop instead of once per loop iteration. Language rules typically grant the compiler license to presume the code is single-threaded, even if it is not. This is particularly true for older languages such as Fortran, C, and C++ that evolved when parallel processors were esoteric. For recent languages, such as Java and C#, compilers must be more circumspect, but only when the keyword `volatile` is present. Unlike hardware reordering, compiler reordering can affect code even when it is running time sliced on a single hardware thread. Thus the programmer must be on the lookout for reordering by the hardware or the compiler.

Current IA-32 Architecture

IA-32 approximates sequential consistency, because it evolved in the single-core age. The virtue is how IA-32 preserves legacy software. Extreme departures from sequential consistency would have broken old code. However, adhering to sequential consistency would have yielded poor performance, so a balance had to be struck. For the most part, the balance yields few surprises, yet achieves most of the possible performance improvements (Hill 1998). Two rules cover typical programming:

- *Relaxation for performance.* A thread sees other threads' reads and writes in the original order, except that a read may pass a write to a different location. This reordering rule allows a thread to read from its own cache even if the read follows a write to main memory. This rule does not cover "nontemporal" writes, which are discussed later.

- *Strictness for correctness.* An instruction with the LOCK prefix acts as a memory fence. No read or write may cross the fence. This rule stops relaxations from breaking typical synchronization idioms based on the LOCK instructions. Furthermore, the instruction `xchg` has an implicit LOCK prefix in order to preserve old code written before the LOCK prefix was introduced.

This slightly relaxed memory consistency is called *processor order.* For efficiency, the IA-32 architecture also allows loads to pass loads but hides this from the programmer. But if the processor detects that the reordering might have a visible effect, it squashes the affected instructions and reruns them. Thus the only visible relaxation is that reads can pass writes.

The IA-32 rules preserve most idioms, but ironically break the textbook algorithm for mutual exclusion called Dekker's Algorithm[1]. This algorithm enables mutual exclusion for processors without special atomic instructions. Figure 7.23(a) demonstrates the key sequence in Dekker's Algorithm. Two variables X and Y are initially zero. Thread 1

---

[1] The first published software-only, two-process mutual exclusion algorithm.

writes X and reads Y. Thread 2 writes Y and reads X. On a sequentially consistent machine, no matter how the reads and writes are interleaved, no more than one of the threads reads a zero. The thread reading the zero is the one allowed into the exclusion region. On IA-32, and just about every other modern processor, both threads might read 0, because the reads might pass the writes. The code behaves as if written in Figure 7.23(b).

Initial Conditions:
int X=0;   int Y=0;

	Thread 1	Thread 2
(a) Key sequence in Dekker's Alogrithm intends to set at least one of registers r1 or r2 to one.	`x = 1;` `r1 = y;`	`y = 1;` `r2 = x;`
(b) IA-32 allows reads to pass upwards over writes causing sequences (a) to behave as i written as shown, which can cause both r1 and r2 to be set to zero.	`r1 = y` `x = 1;`	`r2 = y;` `x = 1;`

(c) mfence instruction prevents hardware from moving the reads upward over the writes. The_asm syntax here is recognized by compilers for Windows.	`x - 1;`
	`_asm mfence;`
	`r1 = y;`
		`y - 1;`
		`_asm mfence;`
		`r2 = x`

Figure 7.23   Why Relaxed Consistency Breaks Dekker's Algorithm

Figure 7.23(c) shows how make the sequence work by inserting explicit memory fence instructions. The fences keep the reads from passing the writes. Table 7.1 summarizes the three types of IA-32 fence instructions.

Table 7.1   Types of IA-32 Fence Instructions

Mnemonic	Name	Description
mfence	Memory **fence**	neither reads nor writes may cross
lfence	load **fence**	reads may not cross
sfence	Store **fence**	writes may not cross

The fences serve to tighten memory ordering when necessary for correctness. The order of writes can be loosened with nontemporal store instructions, which are not necessarily seen by other processors in the order they were issued by the issuing processor. Some IA-32 string operations, such as MOVS and STOS, can be nontemporal. The looser memory ordering allows the processor to maximize bus efficiency by combining writes. However, the processor consuming such data might not be expecting to see the writes out of order, so the producer should issue a sfence before signaling the consumer that the data is ready.

IA-32 also allows memory consistency rules to be varied for specific memory ranges. For instance, a range with "write combining" permits the processor to temporarily record writes in a buffer, and commit the results to cache or main memory later in a different order. Such a range behaves as if all stores are nontemporal. In practice, in order to preserve legacy code, most environments configure IA-32 systems to use processor order, so the page-by-page rules apply only in special environments. Section 7.2 of Volume 2 of *IA-32 Intel® Architecture Software Developer's Manual* describes the memory ordering rules in more detail.

Itanium® Architecture

The Itanium architecture had no legacy software to preserve, and thus could afford a cutting-edge relaxed memory model. The model theoretically delivers higher performance than sequential consistency by giving the memory system more freedom of choice. As long as locks are properly used to avoid race conditions, there are no surprises. However, programmers writing multiprocessor code with deliberate race conditions must understand the rules. Though far more relaxed than IA-32, the rules for memory consistency on Itanium processors are simpler to remember because they apply uniformly. Furthermore, compilers for Itanium-based systems interpret `volatile` in a way that makes most idioms work.

Figure 7.24(a) shows a simple and practical example where the rules come into play. It shows two threads trying to pass a message via memory. Thread 1 writes a message into variable `Message`, and Thread 2 reads the message. Synchronization is accomplished via the flag `IsReady`. The writer sets `IsReady` after it writes the message. The reader busy waits for `IsReady` to be set, and then reads the message. If the writes or reads are reordered, then Thread 2 may read the message before Thread 1 is done writing it. Figure 7.24(b) shows how the Itanium architecture may reorder the reads and writes. The solution is to declare the flag `IsReady` as `volatile`, as shown in 7.24(c). Volatile writes are compiled as "store with release" and volatile reads are compiled as "load with acquire." Memory operations are never allowed to move downwards over a "release" or upwards over an "acquire," thus enforcing the necessary orderings.

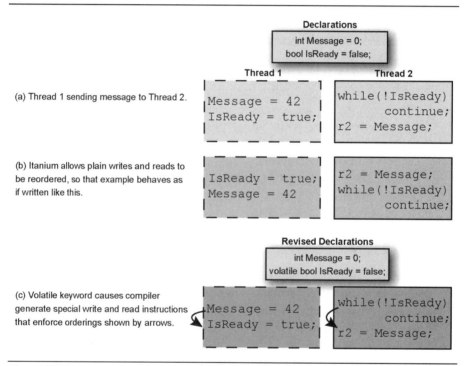

Figure 7.24   Use of Volatile Keyword for Itanium® Architecture

The details of the Itanium architecture's relaxed memory model can be daunting, but the two of the idioms over most practice. Figure 7.25 illustrates these two idioms. The animals represent memory operations whose movement is constrained by animal trainers who represent acquire and release fences. The first idiom is *message passing*, which is a generalization of Figure 7.24. A sender thread writes some data, and then signals a receiver thread that it is ready by modifying a flag location. The modification might be a write, or some other atomic operation. As long as the sender performs a release operation after writing the data, and the receiver performs an acquire operation before reading the data, the desired ordering will be maintained. Typically, these conditions are guaranteed by declaring the flag volatile, or using an atomic operation with the desired acquire/release characteristics.

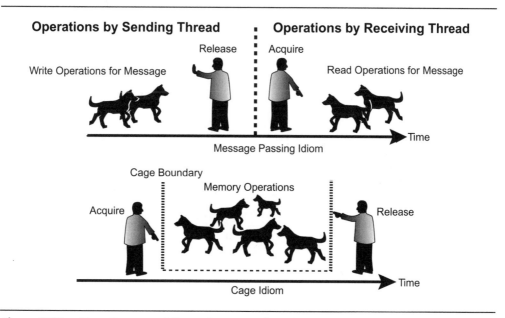

Figure 7.25 Two Common Idioms for Using Shared Memory without a Lock

The second idiom is *memory cage*. A memory cage starts with an acquire fence and ends in a release fence. These fences keep any memory operations inside the cage from escaping. However, be aware that memory cages keep things inside from getting out, and not vice-versa. It is possible for disjoint cages to become overlapped by instruction reordering, because an acquire that begins a cage can float backwards over the release that ends a previous cage. For similar reasons, trying to fix Dekker's Algorithm with acquiring reads and releasing writes does not fix the algorithm—the fix needs to stop reads from floating backwards over writes, but acquiring reads can nonetheless float backwards over releasing writes. The proper fix is to add a full memory fence, for instance, call the __memory_barrier() intrinsic.

A subtle example of fencing is the widely used *double-check* idiom. The idiom is commonly used for lazy initialization in multi-threaded code. Figure 7.26 shows a correct implementation of double check for the Itanium architecture. The critical feature is declaring the flag as volatile so that the compiler will insert the correct acquire and release fences. Double-check is really the message-passing idiom, where the message is the initialized data structure. This implementation is not guaranteed to be correct by the ISO C and C++ standards, but is nonetheless correct for the Itanium architecture because the Itanium processor's interpretation of volatile reads and writes implies fences.

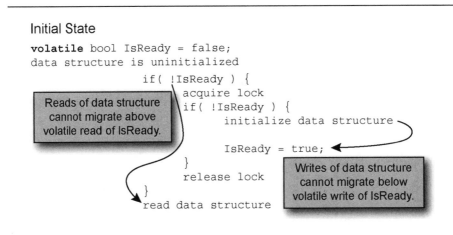

Initial State

```
volatile bool IsReady = false;
data structure is uninitialized
                    if( !IsReady ) {
                        acquire lock
                        if( !IsReady ) {
                            initialize data structure
                            IsReady = true;
                        }
                        release lock
                    }
                    read data structure
```

Reads of data structure cannot migrate above volatile read of IsReady.

Writes of data structure cannot migrate below volatile write of IsReady.

Figure 7.26 Use of Volatile in Double Check Idiom on Itanium® Architecture

A common analysis error is to think that the acquire fence between the outer if and read data structure is redundant, because it would seem that the hardware must perform the if before the read data structure. But an ordinary read could in fact be hoisted above the if were it on the same cache line as another read before the if. Likewise, without the fence, an aggressive compiler might move the read upwards over the if as a speculative read. The acquire fence is thus critical.

High-level Languages

When writing portable code in a high-level language, the easiest way to deal with memory consistency is through the language's existing synchronization primitives, which normally have the right kind of fences built in. Memory consistency issues appear only when programmers "roll their own" synchronization primitives. If you must roll your own synchronization, the rules depend on the language and hardware. Here are some guidelines:

■ *C* and *C++*. There is no portable solution at present. The ISO C++ committee is considering changes that would address the issue. For Windows compilers for IA-32, use inline assembly code to embed fence instructions. For the Itanium processor family, try to stick to the "message passing" and "cage" idioms, and declare the appropriate variables as volatile.

■ *.NET*. Use volatile declarations as for the Itanium architecture and the code should be portable to any architecture.

■ *Java*. The recent JSR-133 revision of the Java memory makes it similar to Itanium architecture with .NET, so likewise, use volatile declarations.

Avoiding Pipeline Stalls on IA-32

When writing a parallel program for performance, first get the decomposition right. Then tune for cache usage, including avoidance of false sharing. Then, as a last measure, if trying to squeeze the last cycles out, concern yourself with the processor's pipeline. The Pentium 4 and Pentium D processors have deep pipelines that permit high execution rates of instructions typical of single-threaded code. The execution units furthermore reorder instructions so that instructions waiting on memory accesses do not block other instructions. Deep pipelines and out of order execution are usually a good thing, but make some operations relatively expensive.

Particularly expensive are *serializing* instructions. These are instructions that force all prior instructions to complete before any subsequent instructions. Common serializing instructions include those with the LOCK prefix, memory fences, and the CPUID instruction. The XCHG instruction on memory is likewise serializing, even without the LOCK prefix. These instructions are essential when serving their purpose, but it can pay to avoid them, or at least minimize them, when such alternatives exist.

On processors with HT Technology, spin waits can be a problem because the spinning thread might consume all the hardware resources. In the worst case, it might starve the thread on which the spinner is waiting! On the Pentium 4 processor and later processors, the solution is to insert a PAUSE instruction. On Itanium processors, the similar instruction is HINT 0. These instructions notify the hardware that the thread is waiting; that is, that hardware resources should be devoted to other threads. Furthermore, on IA-32, spinning on a read can consume bus bandwidth, so it is typically best to incorporate exponential backoff too. Figure 7.27 shows a spin-wait with a PAUSE instruction incorporated. In more complicated waits based on exponential backoff, the PAUSE instruction should go in the delay loop.

```
while( !IsReady )
    _asm pause;

R2 = Message;
```

Figure 7.27   Busy-wait Loop with IA-32 Pause Instruction

Data Organization for High Performance

The interactions of memory, cache, and pipeline can be daunting. It may help to think of a program's locations as divided into four kinds of locality:

■ *Thread private.* These locations are private to a given thread and never shared with other threads. A hardware thread tends to keep this memory in cache, as long as it fits. Hence accesses to thread private locations tend to be very fast and not consume bus bandwidth.

■ *Thread shared read only.* These locations are shared by multiple threads, but never written by those threads. Lookup tables are a common example. Because there are no writes, a hardware thread tends to keep its own copy in cache, as long as it fits.

■ *Exclusive access.* These locations are read and written, but protected by a lock. Once a thread acquires the lock and starts operating on the data, the locations will migrate into cache. Once a thread releases the lock, the locations will migrate back to memory or to the next hardware thread that acquires the lock.

■ *Wild West.* These locations are read and written by unsynchronized threads. Depending upon the lock implementation, these locations may include the lock objects themselves, because by their nature, locks are accessed by unsynchronized threads that the lock will synchronize. Whether a lock object counts as part of the Wild West depends upon whether the lock object holds the real "guts" of the lock, or is just a pointer off to the real guts.

A location's locality may change as the program runs. For instance, a thread may create a lookup table privately, and then publish its location to other threads so that it becomes a read-only table.

A good decomposition favors thread-private storage and thread-shared read-only storage, because these have low impact on the bus and do not need synchronization. Furthermore, locations of a given locality should not be mixed on the same cache line, because false sharing issues arise. For example, putting thread-private data and Wild West data on the same line hinders access to the thread-private data as the Wild West accesses ping pong the line around. Furthermore, Wild West locations are often candidates for putting on a separate cache line, unless the locations tend to be accessed by the same thread at nearly the same time, in which case packing them onto the same cache line may help reduce memory traffic.

Key Points

The key to successful parallel programming is choosing a good program decomposition. Keep the following points in mind when choosing a decomposition:

■ Match the number of runnable software threads to the available hardware threads. Never hard-code the number of threads into your program; leave it as a tuning parameter.

■ Parallel programming for performance is about finding the zone between too little and too much synchronization. Too little synchronization leads to incorrect answers. Too much synchronization leads to slow answers.

■ Use tools like Intel Thread Checker to detect race conditions.

■ Keep locks private. Do not hold a lock while calling another package's code.

■ Avoid deadlock by acquiring locks in a consistent order.

- Consider memory bandwidth and contention issues when picking a decomposition for parallel execution. Pack data tightly to minimize bandwidth and cache footprint. Put data meant for different processors on different cache lines. Separate shared read-only data from writable data.

- Spread out lock contention by using multiple distributed locks where possible.

- Lockless algorithms have both advantages and disadvantages. They are particularly tricky in languages without garbage collection. Tread with caution.

- Cache lines are the quanta of information interchange between hardware threads.

- If writing your own synchronization code, understand the memory consistency model for the target platform.

- Serializing instructions, such as atomic operation and memory fences, are useful when needed, but relatively expensive compared to other instructions.

Chapter 8

Multi-threaded Debugging Techniques

Debugging multi-threaded applications can be a challenging task. The increased complexity of multi-threaded programs results in a large number of possible states that the program may be in at any given time. Determining the state of the program at the time of failure can be difficult; understanding why a particular state is troublesome can be even more difficult. Multi-threaded programs often fail in unexpected ways, and often in a nondeterministic fashion. Bugs may manifest themselves in a sporadic fashion, frustrating developers who are accustomed to troubleshooting issues that are consistently reproducible and predictable. Finally, multi-threaded applications can fail in a drastic fashion— deadlocks cause an application or worse yet, the entire system, to hang. Users tend to find these types of failures to be unacceptable.

This chapter examines general purpose techniques that are useful when debugging multi-threaded applications. Intel has developed a number of tools, including the Intel® Thread Checker, the Intel Thread Profiler, and the Intel Debugger that help debug and profile multi-threaded applications. These tools are discussed in Chapter 11.

General Debug Techniques

Regardless of which library or platform that you are developing on, several general principles can be applied to debugging multi-threaded software applications.

215

Designing with Debugging in Mind

The first technique for eliminating bugs in multi-threaded code is to avoid introducing the bug in the first place. Many software defects can be prevented by using proper software development practices.[1] The later a problem is found in the product development lifecycle, the more expensive it is to fix. Given the complexity of multi-threaded programs, it is critical that multi-threaded applications are properly designed up front.

How often have you, as a software developer, experienced the following situation? Someone on the team that you're working on gets a great idea for a new product or feature. A quick prototype that illustrates the idea is implemented and a quick demo, using a trivial use-case, is presented to management. Management loves the idea and immediately informs sales and marketing of the new product or feature. Marketing then informs the customer of the feature, and in order to make a sale, promises the customer the feature in the next release. Meanwhile, the engineering team, whose original intent of presenting the idea was to get resources to properly implement the product or feature sometime in the future, is now faced with the task of delivering on a customer commitment immediately. As a result of time constraints, it is often the case that the only option is to take the prototype, and try to turn it into production code.

While this example illustrates a case where marketing and management may be to blame for the lack of following an appropriate process, software developers are often at fault in this regard as well. For many developers, writing software is the most interesting part of the job. There's a sense of instant gratification when you finish writing your application and press the run button. The results of all the effort and hard work appear instantly. In addition, modern debuggers provide a wide range of tools that allow developers to quickly identify and fix simple bugs. As a result, many programmers fall into the trap of coding now, deferring design and testing work to a later time. Taking this approach on a multi-threaded application is a recipe for disaster for several reasons:

- *Multi-threaded applications are inherently more complicated than single-threaded applications.* Hacking out a reliable, scalable implementation of a multi-threaded application is hard;

---

[1] There are a number of different software development methodologies that are applicable to parallel programming. For example, parallel programming can be done using traditional or rapid prototyping (Extreme Programming) techniques.

even for experienced parallel programmers. The primary reason for this is the large number of corner cases that can occur and the wide range of possible paths of the application. Another consideration is the type of run-time environment the application is running on. The access patterns may vary wildly depending on whether or not the application is running on a single-core or multi-core platform, and whether or not the platform supports simultaneous multithreading hardware. These different run-time scenarios need to be thoroughly thought out and handled to guarantee reliability in a wide range of environments and use cases.

■ *Multi-threaded bugs may not surface when running under the debugger.* Multi-threading bugs are very sensitive to the timing of events in an application. Running the application under the debugger changes the timing, and as a result, may mask problems. When your application fails in a test or worse, the customer environment, but runs reliably under the debugger, it is almost certainly a timing issue in the code.

While following a software process can feel like a nuisance at times, taking the wrong approach and not following any process at all is a perilous path when writing all but the most trivial applications. This holds true for parallel programs.

While designing your multi-threaded applications, you should keep these points in mind.

■ *Design the application so that it can run sequentially.* An application should always have a valid means of sequential execution. The application should be validated in this run mode first. This allows developers to eliminate bugs in the code that are not related to threading. If a problem is still present in this mode of execution, then the task of debugging reduces to single-threaded debugging.

In many circumstances, it is very easy to generate a sequential version of an application. For example, an OpenMP application compiled with one of the Intel compilers can use the openmp-stubs option to tell the compiler to generate sequential OpenMP code.

■ *Use established parallel programming patterns.* The best defense against defects is to use parallel patterns that are known to be safe. Established patterns solve many of the common parallel programming problems in a robust manner. Reinventing the wheel is not necessary in many cases.

■ *Include built-in debug support in the application.* When trying to root cause an application fault, it is often useful for programmers to be able to examine the state of the system at any arbitrary point in time. Consider adding functions that display the state of a thread—or all active threads. Trace buffers, described in the next section, may be used to record the sequence of accesses to a shared resource. Many modern debuggers support the capability of calling a function while stopped at a breakpoint. This mechanism allows developers to extend the capabilities of the debugger to suit their particular application's needs.

Code Reviews

Many software processes suggest frequent code reviews as a means of improving software quality. The complexity of parallel programming makes this task challenging. While not a replacement for using well established parallel programming design patterns, code reviews may, in many cases, help catch bugs in the early stages of development.

One technique for these types of code reviews is to have individual reviewers examine the code from the perspective of one of the threads in the system. During the review, each reviewer steps through the sequence of events as the actual thread would. Have objects that represent the shared resources of the system available and have the individual reviewers (threads) take and release these resources. This technique will help you visualize the interaction between different threads in your system and hopefully help you find bugs before they manifest themselves in code.

As a developer, when you get the urge to immediately jump into coding and disregard any preplanning or preparation, you should consider the following scenarios and ask yourself which situation you'd rather be in. Would you rather spend a few weeks of work up front to validate and verify the design and architecture of your application, or would you rather deal with having to redesign your product when you find it doesn't scale? Would you rather hold code reviews during development or deal with the stress of trying to solve mysterious, unpredictable showstopper bugs a week before your scheduled ship date? Good software engineering practices are the key to writing reliable software applications. Nothing is new, mysterious, or magical about writing multi-threaded applications. The complexity of this class of applications means that developers must be conscious of these fundamental software engineering principles and be diligent in following them.

Extending your Application—Using Trace Buffers

Chapter 7 identified two categories of bugs found in multi-threaded applications: synchronization bugs and performance bugs. Synchronization bugs include race conditions and deadlocks that cause unexpected and incorrect behavior. Performance bugs arise from unnecessary thread overhead due to thread creation or context switch overhead, and memory access patterns that are suboptimal for a given processor's memory hierarchy. The application returns the correct results, but often takes too long to be usable. This chapter focuses on debugging synchronization bugs that cause applications to fail.

In order to find the cause of these types of bugs, two pieces of information are needed:

1. Which threads are accessing the shared resource at the time of the failure.

2. When the access to the shared resource took place.

In many cases, finding and fixing synchronization bugs involves code inspection. A log or trace of the different threads in the application and the pattern in which they accessed the shared resources of the code helps narrow down the problematic code sections. One simple data structure that collects this information is the trace buffer.

A trace buffer is simply a mechanism for logging events that the developer is interested in monitoring. It uses an atomic counter that keeps track of the current empty slot in the array of event records. The type of information that each event can store is largely up to the developer. A sample implementation of a trace buffer, using the Win32 threading APIs, is shown in Listing 8.1.[2]

---

[2] In the interest of making the code more readable, Listing 8.1 uses the `time()` system call to record system time. Due to the coarse granularity of this timer, most applications should use a high performance counter instead to keep track of the time in which events occurred.

```
1    // Circular 1K Trace buffer
2    #define TRACE_BUFFER_SIZE 1024
3
4    typedef struct traceBufferElement
5    {
6        DWORD threadId;
7        time_t timestamp;
8        const char *msg;
9    } traceBufferElement;
10
11   static LONG m_TraceBufferIdx = -1;
12   static traceBufferElement traceBuffer[TRACE_BUFFER_SIZE];
13
14   void InitializeTraceBuffer()
15   {
16       m_TraceBufferIdx = -1;
17
18       /* initialize all entries to {0, 0, NULL} */
19       memset(traceBuffer, 0,
20               TRACE_BUFFER_SIZE*sizeof(traceBufferElement));
21   }
22
23   void AddEntryToTraceBuffer(const char *msg)
24   {
25       LONG idx = 0;
26
27       // Get the index into the trace buffer that this
28       // thread should use
29       idx = InterlockedIncrement(&m_TraceBufferIdx) %
30                                   TRACE_BUFFER_SIZE;
31
32       // Enter the data into the Trace Buffer
33       traceBuffer[idx].threadId = GetCurrentThreadId();
34       traceBuffer[idx].timestamp = time(NULL);
35       traceBuffer[idx].msg = msg;
36   }
37
38   void PrintTraceBuffer()
39   {
40       int i;
41       printf("Thread ID  Timestamp   Msg\n");
42       printf("----------|----------|--------------------"
43               "----------------\n");
44
45       // sort by timestamp before printing
46       SortTraceBufferByTimestamp();
```

```
47      for (i = 0; i < TRACE_BUFFER_SIZE; i++)
48      {
49          if (traceBuffer[i].timestamp == 0)
50          {
51              break;
52          }
53          printf("0x%8.8x|0x%8.8x| %s\n",
54                  traceBuffer[i].threadId,
55                  traceBuffer[i].timestamp,
56                  traceBuffer[i].msg);
57      }
58  }
```

Listing 8.1   Sample Implementation of a Trace Buffer

Listing 8.1, creates a trace buffer that can store 1,024 events. It stores these events in a circular buffer. As you'll see shortly, once the circular buffer is full, your atomic index will wrap around and replace the oldest event. This simplifies your implementation as it doesn't require dynamically resizing the trace buffer or storing the data to disk. In some instances, these operations may be desirable, but in general, a circular buffer should suffice.

Lines 1–13 define the data structures used in this implementation. The event descriptor traceBufferElement is defined in lines 4–9. It contains three fields: a field to store the thread ID, a timestamp value that indicates when the event occurred, and a generic message string that is associated with the event. This structure could include a number of additional parameters, including the name of the thread.

The trace buffer in Listing 8.1 defines three operations. The first method, InitializeTraceBuffer(), initializes the resources used by the trace buffer. The initialization of the atomic counter occurs on line 16. The atomic counter is initialized to –1. The initial value of this counter is –1 because adding a new entry in the trace buffer requires us to first increment (line 29) the atomic counter. The first entry should be stored in slot 0. Once the trace buffer is initialized, threads may call AddEntryToTraceBuffer() to update the trace buffers with events as they occur. PrintTraceBuffer() dumps a listing of all the events that the trace buffer has logged to the screen. This function is very useful when combined with a debugger that allows users to execute code at a breakpoint. Both Microsoft Visual Studio[†] and GDB support this capability. With a single command, the developer can see a log of all the recent events being monitored, without having to parse a data structure using the command line or a watch window.

Note that the implementation of the trace buffer in Listing 8.1 logs events as they are passed into the buffer. This doesn't necessarily guarantee that the trace buffer will log events exactly as they occur in time. To illustrate this point, consider the two threads shown in Listing 8.2.

```
unsigned __stdcall Thread1(void *)
{
    // ... thread initialization
    // write global data
    m_global = do_work();
    AddEntryToTraceBuffer(msg);
    // ... finish thread
}

unsigned __stdcall Thread2(void *)
{
    // ... thread initialization
    // read global data
    Thread_local_data = m_global;
    AddEntryToTraceBuffer(msg);
    // ... finish thread
}
```

Listing 8.2   Two Threads Logging Events to a Trace Buffer

By now it should be clear what the problem is. A race condition exists between the two threads and the access to the trace buffer. Thread1 may write to the global data value and then start logging that write event in the trace buffer. Meanwhile, Thread2 may read that same global value after the write, but log this read event before the write event. Thus, the data in the buffer may not be an accurate reflection of the actual sequence of events as they occurred in the system.

One potential solution to this problem is to protect the operation that you want to log and the subsequent trace buffer access with a synchronization object. A thread, when logging the event, could request exclusive access to the trace buffer. Once the thread has completed logging the event, it would then unlock the trace buffer, allowing other threads to access the buffer. This is shown in Listing 8.3.

```
// This is NOT RECOMMENDED
unsigned __stdcall Thread1(void *)
{
   // ... thread initialization
   // write global data

   LockTraceBuffer();

   m_global = do_work();
   AddEntryToTraceBuffer(msg);

   UnlockTraceBuffer();

   // ... finish thread
}

unsigned __stdcall Thread2(void *)
{
   // ... thread initialization
   // read global data
   LockTraceBuffer();

   Thread_local_data = m_global;
   AddEntryToTraceBuffer(msg);

   UnlockTraceBuffer();
   // ... finish thread
}
```

Listing 8.3   Incorrectly Synchronizing Access to the Trace Buffer

There are a number of drawbacks to this technique. Using a synchronization primitive to protect access to a trace buffer may actually mask bugs in the code, defeating the purpose of using the trace buffer for debug. Assume that the bug the developer is tracking down is related to a missing lock around the read or write access in the thread. By locking access to the trace buffer, the developer is protecting a critical section of code that may be incorrectly unprotected. Generally speaking, when tracking down a race condition, the programmer should avoid synchronizing access to the trace buffer. If you synchronize access and your application works, it's a clue that there may be a problem in the synchronization mechanism between those threads.

The preferred method to overcoming this limitation is to log a message before and after the event occurs. This is demonstrated in Listing 8.4.

```
unsigned __stdcall Thread1(void *)
{
   // ... thread initialization
   // write global data
   AddEntryToTraceBuffer(before_msg);
   m_global = do_work();
   AddEntryToTraceBuffer(after_msg);
   // ... finish thread
}

unsigned __stdcall Thread2(void *)
{
   // ... thread initialization
   // read global data
   AddEntryToTraceBuffer(before_msg2);
   Thread_local_data = m_global;
   AddEntryToTraceBuffer(after_msg2);
   // ... finish thread
}
```

Listing 8.4   Preferred Method of Logging Messages with a Trace buffer

By logging a before and after message, a programmer can determine whether or not the events occurred as expected. If the before and after messages between the two threads occur in sequence, then the developer can safely assume that the event was ordered. If the before and after messages are interleaved, then the order of events is indeterminate; the events may have happened in either order.

A trace buffer can be used to gather useful data about the sequence of operations occurring in a multi-threaded application. For other more difficult problems, more advanced threading debug tools may be required. These tools are discussed in Chapter 11.

Debugging Multi-threaded Applications in Windows

Most Windows programmers use Microsoft Visual Studio as their primary integrated development environment (IDE). As part of the IDE, Microsoft includes a debugger with multi-threaded debug support. This section examines the different multi-threaded debug capabilities of Visual Studio, and then demonstrates how they are used.

Threads Window

As part of the debugger, Visual Studio provides a "Threads" window that lists all of the current threads in the system. From this window, you can:

- *Freeze (suspend) or thaw (resume) a thread.* This is useful when you want to observe the behavior of your application without a certain thread running.

- *Switch the current active thread.* This allows you to manually perform a context switch and make another thread active in the application.

- *Examine thread state.* When you double-click an entry in the Threads window, the source window jumps to the source line that the thread is currently executing. This tells you the thread's current program counter. You will be able to examine the state of local variables within the thread.

The Threads window acts as the command center for examining and controlling the different threads in an application.

Tracepoints

As previously discussed, determining the sequence of events that lead to a race condition or deadlock situation is critical in determining the root cause of any multi-thread related bug. In order to facilitate the logging of events, Microsoft has implemented *tracepoints* as part of the debugger for Visual Studio 2005.

Most developers are familiar with the concept of a breakpoint. A tracepoint is similar to a breakpoint except that instead of stopping program execution when the applications program counter reaches that point, the debugger takes some other action. This action can be printing a message or running a Visual Studio macro.

Enabling tracepoints can be done in one of two ways. To create a new tracepoint, set the cursor to the source line of code and select "Insert Tracepoint." If you want to convert an existing breakpoint to a tracepoint, simply select the breakpoint and pick the "When Hit" option from the Breakpoint submenu. At this point, the tracepoint dialog appears.

When a tracepoint is hit, one of two actions is taken based on the information specified by the user. The simplest action is to print a message. The programmer may customize the message based on a set of predefined keywords. These keywords, along with a synopsis of what gets printed, are shown in Table 8.1. All values are taken at the time the tracepoint is hit.

Table 8.1   Tracepoint Keywords

Keyword	Evaluates to
$ADDRESS	The address of the instruction
$CALLER	The name of the function that called this function
$CALLSTACK	The state of the callstack
$FUNCTION	The name of the current function
$PID	The ID of the process
$PNAME	The name of the process
$TID	The ID of the thread
$TNAME	The name of the thread

In addition to the predefined values in Table 8.1, tracepoints also give you the ability to evaluate expressions inside the message. In order to do this, simply enclose the variable or expression in curly braces. For example, assume your thread has a local variable `threadLocalVar` that you'd like to have displayed when a tracepoint is hit. The expression you'd use might look something like this:

```
Thread: $TNAME local variables value is {threadLocalVar}.
```

Breakpoint Filters

Breakpoint filters allow developers to trigger breakpoints only when certain conditions are triggered. Breakpoints may be filtered by machine name, process, and thread. The list of different breakpoint filters is shown in Table 8.2.

Table 8.2   Breakpoint Filter Options

Filter	Description
MachineName	Specifies that the breakpoint should only be triggered on certain machines
ProcessId	Limit breakpoint to process with the matching ID
ProcessName	Limit breakpoint to process with matching name
ThreadId	Limit breakpoint to thread with matching ID
ThreadName	Limit breakpoint to thread with matching name

Breakpoint filters can be combined to form compound statements. Three logic operators are supported: `!` (NOT), `&` (AND), and `||` (OR).

Naming Threads

When debugging a multi-threaded application, it is often useful to assign unique names to the threads that are used in the application. In Chapter 5, you learned that assigning a name to a thread in a managed application was as simple as setting a property on the thread object. In this environment, it is highly recommended that you set the name field when creating the thread, because managed code provides no way to identify a thread by its ID.

In native Windows code, a thread ID can be directly matched to an individual thread. Nonetheless, keeping track of different thread IDs makes the job of debugging more difficult; it can be hard to keep track of individual thread IDs. An astute reader might have noticed in Chapter 5 the conspicuous absence of any sort of name parameter in the methods used to create threads. In addition, there was no function provided to get or set a thread name. It turns out that the standard thread APIs in Win32 lack the ability to associate a name with a thread. As a result, this association must be made by an external debugging tool.

Microsoft has enabled this capability through predefined exceptions built into their debugging tools. Applications that want to see a thread referred to by name need to implement a small function that raises an exception. The exception is caught by the debugger, which then takes the specified name and assigns it to the associated ID. Once the exception handler completes, the debugger will use the user-supplied name from then on.

The implementation of this function can be found on the Microsoft Developer Network† (MSDN) Web site at msdn.microsoft.com by searching for: "setting a thread name (unmanaged)." The function, named `SetThreadName()`, takes two arguments. The first argument is the thread ID. The recommended way of specifying the thread ID is to send the value -1, indicating that the ID of the calling thread should be used. The second parameter is the name of the thread. The `SetThreadName()` function calls `RaiseException()`, passing in a special 'thread exception' code and a structure that includes the thread ID and name parameters specified by the programmer.

Once the application has the `SetThreadName()` function defined, the developer may call the function to name a thread. This is shown in

Listing 8.5. The function `Thread1` is given the name `Producer`,[3] indicating that it is producing data for a consumer. Note that the function is called at the start of the thread, and that the thread ID is specified as -1. This indicates to the debugger that it should associate the calling thread with the associated ID.

```
unsigned __stdcall Thread1(void *)
{
    int i, x = 0; // arbitrary local variable declarations
    SetThreadName(-1, "Producer");

    // Thread logic follows
}
```

Listing 8.5   Using SetThreadName to Name a Thread

Naming a thread in this fashion has a couple of limitations. This technique is a debugger construct; the OS is not in any way aware of the name of the thread. Therefore, the thread name is not available to anyone other than the debugger. You cannot programmatically query a thread for its name using this mechanism. Assigning a name to a thread using this technique requires a debugger that supports exception number 0x406D1388. Both Microsoft's Visual Studio and WinDbg debuggers support this exception. Despite these limitations, it is generally advisable to use this technique where supported as it makes using the debugger and tracking down multi-threaded bugs much easier.

Putting It All Together

Let's stop for a minute and take a look at applying the previously discussed principles to a simplified real-world example. Assume that you are writing a data acquisition application. Your design calls for a producer thread that samples data from a device every second and stores the reading in a global variable for subsequent processing. A consumer thread periodically runs and processes the data from the producer. In order to prevent data corruption, the global variable shared by the producer and consumer is protected with a Critical Section. An example of a simple implementation of the producer and consumer threads is shown in Listing 8.6. Note that error handling is omitted for readability.

---

[3] Admittedly the function name `Thread1` should be renamed to `Producer` as well, but is left somewhat ambiguous for illustration purposes.

```
1  static int m_global = 0;
2  static CRITICAL_SECTION hLock; // protect m_global
3
4     // Simple simulation of data acquisition
5  void sample_data()
6  {
7     EnterCriticalSection(&hLock);
8     m_global = rand();
9     LeaveCriticalSection(&hLock);
10 }
11
12    // This function is an example
13    // of what can be done to data
14    // after collection
15    // In this case, you update the display
16    // in real time
17 void process_data()
18 {
19    EnterCriticalSection(&hLock);
20    printf("m_global = 0x%x\n", m_global);
21    LeaveCriticalSection(&hLock);
22 }
23
24    // Producer thread to simulate real time
25    // data acquisition. Collect 30 s
26    // worth of data
27    unsigned __stdcall Thread1(void *)
28    {
29       int count = 0;
30       SetThreadName(-1, "Producer");
31       while (1)
32       {
33          // update the data
34          sample_data();
35
36          Sleep(1000);
37          count++;
38          if (count > 30)
39             break;
40       }
41       return 0;
42    }
43
44    // Consumer thread
45    // Collect data when scheduled and
46    // process it. Read 30 s worth of data
47    unsigned __stdcall Thread2(void *)
48    {
49       int count = 0;
```

```
50          SetThreadName(-1, "Consumer");
51          while (1)
52          {
53              process_data();
54
55              Sleep(1000);
56              count++;
57              if (count > 30)
58                  break;
59          }
60          return 0;
61      }
```

Listing 8.6   Simple Data Acquisition Device

The producer samples data on line 34 and the consumer processes the data in line 53. Given this relatively simple situation, it is easy to verify that the program is correct and free of race conditions and deadlocks. Now assume that the programmer wants to take advantage of an error detection mechanism on the data acquisition device that indicates to the user that the data sample collected has a problem. The changes made to the producer thread by the programmer are shown in Listing 8.7.

```
void sample_data()
{
   EnterCriticalSection(&hLock);
   m_global = rand();
   if ((m_global % 0xC5F) == 0)
   {
      // handle error
      return;
   }
   LeaveCriticalSection(&hLock);
}
```

Listing 8.7   Sampling Data with Error Checking

After making these changes and rebuilding, the application becomes unstable. In most instances, the application runs without any problems. However, in certain circumstances, the application stops printing data. How do you determine what's going on?

The key to isolating the problem is capturing a trace of the sequence of events that occurred prior to the system hanging. This can be done with a custom trace buffer manager or with tracepoints. This example uses the trace buffer implemented in Listing 8.1.

Now armed with a logging mechanism, you are ready to run the program until the error case is triggered. Once the system fails, you can stop the debugger and examine the state of the system. To do this, run the application until the point of failure. Then, using the debugger, stop the program from executing. At this point, you'll be able bring up the Threads window to see the state information for each thread, such as the one shown in Figure 8.1.

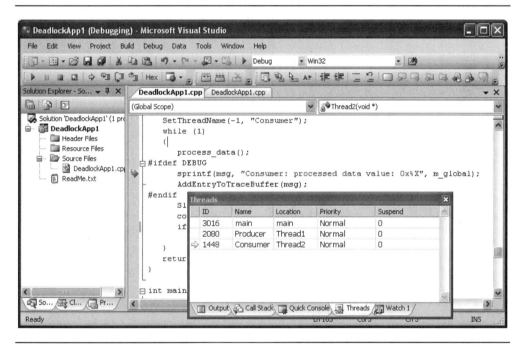

Figure 8.1   Examining Thread State Information Using Visual Studio 2005

When you examine the state of the application, you can see that the consumer thread is blocked, waiting for the `process_data()` call to return. To see what occurred prior to this failure, access the trace buffer. With the application stopped, call the `PrintTraceBuffer()` method directly from Visual Studio's debugger. The output of this call in this sample run is shown in Figure 8.2.

```
1      Thread ID |Timestamp    Msg
2      --------- |---------    |------------------------------------
3      0x0000728|1137395188|Producer: sampled data value: 0x29
4      0x00005a8|1137395188|Consumer: processed data value: 0x29
5      0x0000728|1137395189|Producer: sampled data value: 0x78
6      0x00005a8|1137395189|Consumer: processed data value: 0x78
7      0x0000728|1137395190|Producer: sampled data value: 0x18BE
8      0x0000728|1137395190|Producer: sampled data value: 0x6784
9      0x0000728|1137395190|Producer: sampled data value: 0x4AE1
10     0x0000728|1137395191|Producer: sampled data value: 0x3D6C
```

Figure 8.2   Output from trace buffer after Error Condition Occurs

Examination of the trace buffer log shows that the producer thread is still making forward progress. However, no data values after the first two make it to the consumer. This coupled with the fact that the thread state for the consumer thread indicates that the thread is stuck, points to an error where the critical section is not properly released. Upon closer inspection, it appears that the data value in line 7 of the trace buffer log is an error value. This leads up back to your new handling code, which handles the error but forgets to release the mutex. This causes the consumer thread to be blocked indefinitely, which leads to the consumer thread being starved. Technically this isn't a deadlock situation, as the producer thread is not waiting on a resource that the consumer thread holds.

The complete data acquisition sample application is provided on this book's Web site, www.intel.com/intelpress/mcp.

Multi-threaded Debugging Using GDB

For POSIX threads, debugging is generally accomplished using the GNU Project Debugger (GDB). GDB provides a number of capabilities for debugging threads, including:

■ Automatic notification when new threads are created

■ Listing of all threads in the system

■ Thread-specific breakpoints

■ The ability to switch between threads

■ The ability to apply commands to a group of threads

Not all GDB implementations support all of the features outlined here. Please refer to your system's manual pages for a complete list of supported features.

Notification on Thread Creation

When GDB detects that a new thread is created, it displays a message specifying the thread's identification on the current system. This identification, known as the *systag*, varies from platform to platform. Here is an example of this notification:

```
Starting program: /home/user/threads
[Thread debugging using libthread_db enabled]
[New Thread -151132480 (LWP 4445)]
[New Thread -151135312 (LWP 4446)]
```

Keep in mind that the systag is the operating system's identification for a thread, not GDB's. GDB assigns each thread a unique number that identifies it for debugging purposes.

Getting a List of All Threads in the Application

GDB provides the generic *info* command to get a wide variety of information about the program being debugged. It is no surprise that a subcommand of info would be *info threads*. This command prints a list of threads running in the system:

```
(gdb) info threads
2 Thread -151135312 (LWP 4448)  0x00905f80 in vfprintf ()
from /lib/tls/libc.so.6
* 1 Thread -151132480 (LWP 4447)  main () at threads.c:27
```

The info threads command displays a table that lists three properties of the threads in the system: the thread number attached to the thread by GDB, the systag value, and the current stack frame for the current thread. The currently active thread is denoted by GDB with the * symbol. The thread number is used in all other commands in GDB.

Setting Thread-specific Breakpoints

GDB allows users that are debugging multi-threaded applications to choose whether or not to set a breakpoint on all threads or on a particular thread. The much like the info command, this capability is enabled via an extended parameter that's specified in the *break* command. The general form of this instruction is:

```
break linespec thread threadnum
```

where *linespec* is the standard gdb syntax for specifying a breakpoint, and *threadnum* is the thread number obtained from the info threads command. If the `thread` *threadnum* arguments are omitted, the breakpoint applies to all threads in your program. Thread-specific breakpoints can be combined with conditional breakpoints:

```
(gdb) break buffer.c:33 thread 7 if level > watermark
```

Note that stopping on a breakpoint stops all threads in your program. Generally speaking this is a desirable effect—it allows a developer to examine the entire state of an application, and the ability to switch the current thread. These are good things.

Developers should keep certain behaviors in mind, however, when using breakpoints from within GDB. The first issue is related to how system calls behave when they are interrupted by the debugger. To illustrate this point, consider a system with two threads. The first thread is in the middle of a system call when the second thread reaches a breakpoint. When the breakpoint is triggered, the system call may return early. The reason—GDB uses signals to manage breakpoints. The signal may cause a system call to return prematurely. To illustrate this point, let's say that thread 1 was executing the system call `sleep(30)`. When the breakpoint in thread 2 is hit, the sleep call will return, regardless of how long the thread has actually slept. To avoid unexpected behavior due to system calls returning prematurely, it is advisable that you check the return values of all system calls and handle this case. In this example, `sleep()` returns the number of seconds left to sleep. This call can be placed inside of a loop to guarantee that the sleep has occurred for the amount of time specified. This is shown in Listing 8.8.

```
int sleep_duration = 30;
do
{
    sleep_duration = sleep(sleep_duration);
} while (sleep_duration > 0);
```

Listing 8.8   Proper Error Handling of System Calls

The second point to keep in mind is that GDB does not single step all threads in lockstep. Therefore, when single-stepping a line of code in one thread, you may end up executing a lot of code in other threads prior to returning to the thread that you are debugging. If you have breakpoints in other threads, you may suddenly jump to those code sections. On some OSs, GDB supports a scheduler locking mode via the set scheduler-locking command. This allows a developer to specify that the current thread is the only thread that should be allowed to run.

Switching between Threads

In GDB, the *thread* command may be used to switch between threads. It takes a single parameter, the thread number returned by the info threads command. Here is an example of the thread command:

```
(gdb) thread 2
[Switching to thread 2 (Thread -151135312 (LWP 4549))]#0
PrintThreads (num=0xf6fddbb0) at threads.c:39
39          {
(gdb) info threads
* 2 Thread -151135312 (LWP 4549)   PrintThreads (num=0xf6fddbb0)
at threads.c:39
  1 Thread -151132480 (LWP 4548)   main () at threads.c:27
(gdb)
```

In this example, the thread command makes thread number 2 the active thread.

Applying a Command to a Group of Threads

The thread command supports a single subcommand *apply* that can be used to apply a command to one or more threads in the application. The thread numbers can be supplied individually, or the special keyword *all* may be used to apply the command to all threads in the process, as illustrated in the following example:

```
(gdb) thread apply all bt
Thread 2 (Thread -151135312 (LWP 4549)):
#0  PrintThreads (num=0xf6fddbb0) at threads.c:39
#1  0x00b001d5 in start_thread () from
/lib/tls/libpthread.so.0
#2  0x009912da in clone () from /lib/tls/libc.so.6

Thread 1 (Thread -151132480 (LWP 4548)):
#0  main () at threads.c:27
39          {
(gdb)
```

The GDB backtrace (*bt*) command is applied to all threads in the system. In this scenario, this command is functionally equivalent to: thread apply 2 1 bt.

Key Points

This chapter described a number of general purpose debugging techniques for multi-threaded applications. The important points to remember from this chapter are:

■ Proper software engineering principles should be followed when writing and developing robust multi-threaded applications.

■ When trying to isolate a bug in a multi-threaded application, it is useful to have a log of the different sequence of events that led up to failure. A trace buffer is a simple mechanism that allows programmers to store this event information.

■ Bracket events that are logged in the trace buffer with "before" and "after" messages to determine the order in which the events occurred.

■ Running the application in the debugger may alter the timing conditions of your runtime application, masking potential race conditions in your application.

■ Tracepoints can be a useful way to log or record the sequence of events as they occur.

■ For advanced debugging, consider using the Intel software tools, specifically, the Intel Debugger, the Intel Thread Checker, and the Intel Thread Profiler.

Chapter 9

Single-Core Processor Fundamentals

To gain a better understanding of threading in multi-core hardware, it is best to review the fundamentals of how single-core processors operate. During the debugging, tracing, and performance analysis of some types of programs, knowing a processor's details is a necessity rather than an option. This chapter and Chapter 10 provide the architectural concepts of processors that are pertinent to an understanding of multi-threaded programming. For internal instruction-level details, you should consult Intel Software Developers Guides at Intel's Web site.

This chapter discusses single-core processors as a basis for understanding processor architecture. If you are already familiar with the basics of processors and chipsets, you might skip this chapter and move directly to Chapter 10.

Processor Architecture Fundamentals

The term *processor* has become loosely defined. A more precise definition is developed in the following sections. A *chipset* is the set of chips that helps processors interact with physical memory and other components. Here, the *chip* is actually a processor but without centralized main processing capability. A block diagram with all the basic components in a computer system is represented in Figure 9.1.

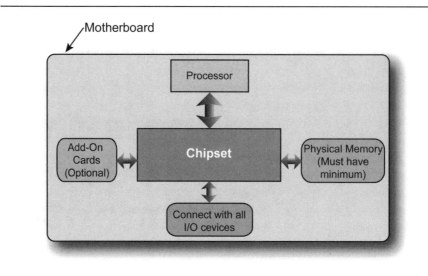

Figure 9.1   Basic Components in a Computer System

You might be familiar with two chips in the chipset. Previously these chips were known as the *Northbridge* and *Southbridge* and they were connected by a shared PCI bus. Intel changed the implementation and started using dedicated point-to-point connections or direct media interface (DMI) between these two chips and introduced Intel Hub Architecture (IHA), as shown in Figure 9.2. IHA replaced the Northbridge and Southbridge with the Memory Controller Hub (MCH) and the I/O Controller Hub (ICH). When graphics and video features are built into the MCH, it is called the Graphics Memory Controller Hub (GMCH). A front side bus (FSB) attaches the chipset to the main processor.

To understand the impact of the hardware platform on an application, the questions to pose are which processor is being used, how much memory is present, what is the FSB of the system, what is the cache size, and how the I/O operations take place? The answer to most of these questions is dictated by the processor.

The smallest unit of work in a processor is handled by a single transistor. A combination of transistors forms a *logic block* and a set of logic blocks create a *functional unit*—some examples are the Arithmetic Logic Unit (ALU), Control Units, and Prefetch Units. These functional units receive instructions to carry out operations. Some functional units are more influential than others and some remain auxiliary. The functional units, or blocks, form a *microprocessor* or *Central Processing Unit (CPU)*. A high-level block diagram of a microprocessor is shown in Figure 9.3(a). The manufacturing process of a microprocessor produces a physical *die* and the packaged die is called the *processor*. Figure 9.3(b) shows a photo of a die. Inside a computer system, the processor sits on a socket. To show the physical entity of processor and socket, see Figure 9.3(c). Sometimes the processor is referred to as the CPU. For simplicity's sake, this book refers to processor and microprocessor interchangeably. Different processors usually have a different number of functional units.

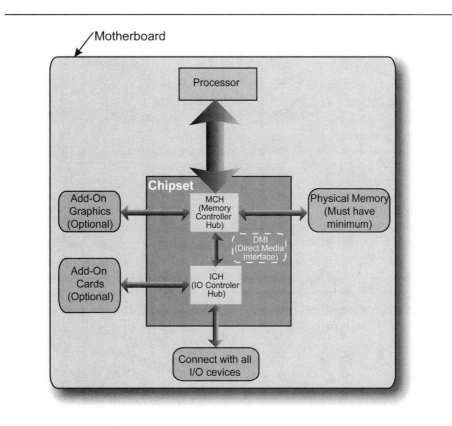

Figure 9.2   A System Showing MCH, ICH, and FSB

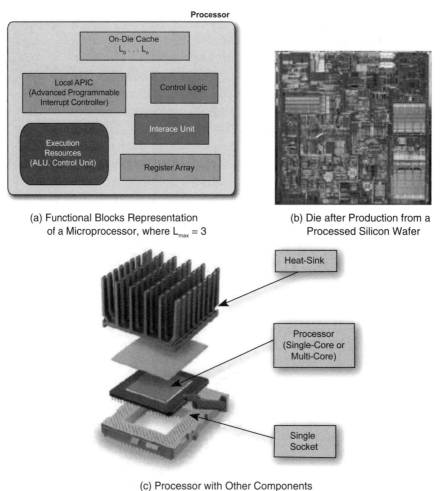

(a) Functional Blocks Representation of a Microprocessor, where $L_{max} = 3$

(b) Die after Production from a Processed Silicon Wafer

(c) Processor with Other Components

Figure 9.3 Processor, Die, and Socket

A processor fetches software instructions as input, performs instruction decode operations to make instructions understood by the processor, does some specific tasks, and finally produces the output, as illustrated in Figure 9.4. All these operations are done through the functional blocks inside a processor and all of the pipeline stages are within the boundary of a processor.

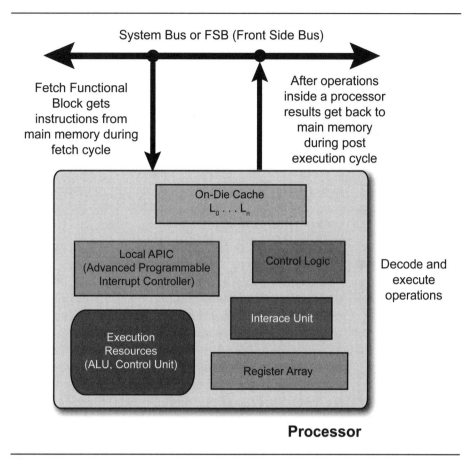

Figure 9.4 Processor Attached with the System Bus Showing Basic Operational Steps

Now let's review the internals of a processor.

■ The on-die caches are usually referred to as levels: L1, L2, and L3. L1 is the smallest and L3 is the largest. Most of the 32-bit processors do not yet have an L3 cache, whereas the currently available Intel® Itanium® processors have large L3 caches, such as the 6-megabyte L3 cache in the Itanium 2 processor.

■ The Local Advanced Programmable Interrupt Controller (Local APIC) unit is specific to a processor and provides interrupt handling capability to a specific processor. This is not the I/O APIC. The I/O APIC is a part of the chipset that supports interrupt handling of different I/O devices through the Local APIC. The I/O APIC is an off-chip unit and usually a part of a multi-processor-based chipset.

■ The interface unit is the functional block that helps to interface a processor with the system bus or front side bus (FSB).

■ The register array is the set of registers present in a processor. The number of registers can vary significantly from one generation of processor to another: 32-bit processors without Intel Extended Memory 64 Technology (Intel EM64T) have only eight integer registers, whereas 64-bit Itanium® processors have 128 integer registers.

■ The execution resources include the integer ALU, Floating-Point execution, and branch units. The number of execution units and the number of active execution units per cycle—referred to as the number of issue ports—vary from processor to processor. The execution speed of functional blocks varies as well and these implementations get improved from generation to generation. The number of execution units is sometimes referred to as the machine width. For example, if the processor has six execution units, the processor is said to be a six-wide machine.

Other types of functional blocks are available in the processor and they vary with respect to the type of processor as well. There are areas in a processor referred to as queues that temporarily retain instructions prior to going into the next phase of operation through the pipeline stages. The scheduler is another functional block. It determines when micro-operations are ready to execute based on the readiness of their dependent input register operand sources and the availability of the execution resources the micro-operations need to complete their operation.

The execution flow of operations in a processor is shown in Figures 9.5 and 9.6. These figures depict the basic four steps of the pipeline: fetch, decode, execute, and write. In reality the process is somewhat more complicated.

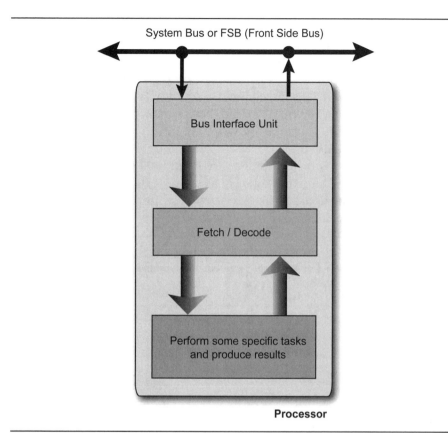

Figure 9.5   Basic Execution Flow in a Processor

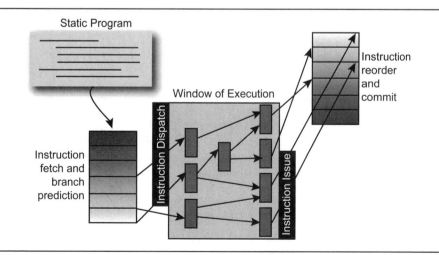

Figure 9.6   Basic Execution Flow in a Superscalar Processor

Different types of Instruction Set Architecture (ISA) processors exist, but in reality the basic aspects of a processor core remain the same. Intel technology can be divided into two primary types of cores: superscalar[1] and Explicitly Parallel Instruction Computing (EPIC). All the processors discussed here are based on these two types. You might already be familiar with a superscalar core. Intel's mainstream superscalar processor architecture began in 1993 with the introduction of the Intel Pentium® processor. This superscalar architecture evolved into the Intel NetBurst® microarchitecture, as found in the Pentium 4 processor.

Figure 9.7 provides a block diagram of the Intel Pentium 4 processor. Here the functional blocks are partitioned into three distinctive segments, front end, back end or execution core, and memory subsystem.

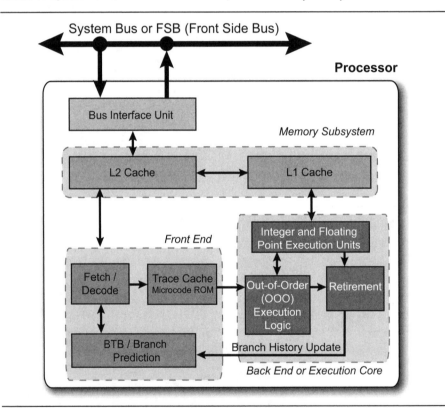

Figure 9.7   Execution Flow inside Intel® Pentium® 4 Processor

---

[1] A processor with a single pipeline is called a scalar processor and a CPU with multiple pipelines is called a superscalar processor.

Comparing Superscalar and EPIC Architecture

Intel recently started developing multi-core processors for both superscalar and EPIC architectures. The superscalar architecture is commonly referred to as wide, speculative, and dynamic in nature. To provide a better understanding of differences between these two architectures, Table 9.1 compares superscalar and EPIC architecture and Figure 9.8 shows the operational flow in these two architectures.

Table 9.1   Comparison of Superscalar and EPIC Architecture

Superscalar	EPIC
Supports 32-bit and 64-bit (Intel EM64T)	Supports 64-bit (Intel® Itanium® Architecture)
Effective resource utilization with minimum number of registers array	Massive resources with large number of registers array
RISC-like instructions	RISC-like instructions bundled into groups of three
Has multiple parallel execution units	Has multiple parallel execution units
Runtime scheduling	Mostly static scheduling with the help of compiler
Single path speculative execution with branch prediction	Both paths of speculative execution with branch prediction
Loads data from memory only when needed, and tries to find the data in the caches first	Speculatively loads data before its needed, and still tries to find data in the caches first

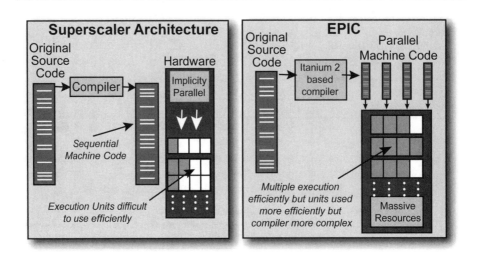

Figure 9.8   Operational Comparison between Superscalar and EPIC

Key Points

Understanding the basics of a single-core processor is essential to comprehend how threading works on a multi-core processor. The important concepts and terms to keep in mind are:

- There are different functional blocks that form a microprocessor such as, Arithmetic Logic Unit, Control Units, and Prefetch Units.

- A chipset is used to interface the processor to physical memory and other components.

- A processor is the container of the dies, and the die is the microprocessor or CPU. In loose terms, processor and microprocessor get used interchangeably.

- The high-level operations for multi-core processors remain the same as for single-core processors.

- Two fundamentally different generic architectures are available from Intel: wide superscalar and EPIC.

Now that the basic building blocks of a processor have been covered, the following chapter explores multi-core processor architecture from a hardware perspective, focusing on the Pentium 4 processor and Itanium architecture.

Chapter 10

Threading on Intel® Multi-Core Processors

The concepts of threading from a software perspective were covered in previous chapters. Chapter 2 also touched briefly on threading inside hardware and Chapter 9 covered the concepts of single-core processors. This chapter describes in more detail what threading inside hardware really means, specifically inside the processor. Understanding hardware threading is important for those developers whose software implementation closely interacts with hardware and who have control over the execution flow of the underlying instructions. The degree to which a developer must understand hardware details varies. This chapter covers the details of the multi-core architecture on Intel processors for software developers, providing the details of hardware internals from a threading point of view.

Hardware-based Threading

Chapter 9 describes the basics of the single-core processor. In most cases, threaded applications use this single-core multiple-issue superscalar processor. The "threading illusion" materializes from the processor and that is called instruction level parallelism (ILP). This is done through a context-switch operation. The operational overhead of context switching should be limited to a few processor cycles. To perform a context switch operation, the processor must preserve the current processor state of the current instruction before switching to other instruction. A processor keeps ongoing operational information mainly in registers and a policy dictates this context switch operation.

The simplest class of processor is single-issue, single-thread (SIST) or single-threaded scalar-based processor. For SIST, the OS handles multiple threads. In terms of hardware resource sharing and the level of granularity of resource hold time, there are two types of processors available: coarse-grained multi-threading (CGMT) and fine-grained multi-threading (FGMT). Each maintains a policy of sharing resources among threads.

For coarse-grained multi-threading, or switch-on-event multi-threading, a thread has full control over processor resources for a specified quantum of time or number of processor cycles. In fine-grained multi-threading, the thread switching takes place at an instruction-cycle boundary. That means the overhead associated with thread switching is higher for a coarse-grained than for a fine-grained implementation. To reflect the policy associated with these processors, coarse-grained multi-threading is also referred to as blocked multi-threading scalar, and fine-grained multi-threading as interleaved multi-threading scalar, illustrated in Figure 10.1. Both fine- and coarse-grained multi-threading are sometimes referred to as temporal multi-threading (TMT).

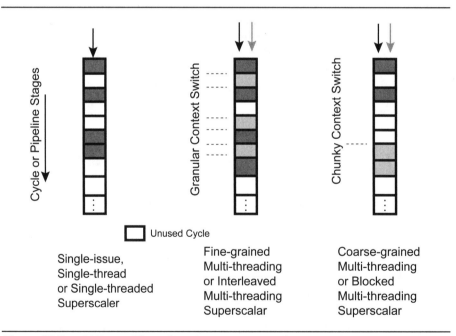

Figure 10.1   Different Threading Scenarios on Multi-issue Processors

From an application level, it appears that multiple threads run at the same time, but in reality the system does not have enough resources to support those threads simultaneously. The OS scheduler, in combination with the hardware scheduler and execution core, gives the impression of threading.

For systems with multiple processors or symmetric multi-processor (SMP) systems with shared memory, the scenario is different. In an SMP environment, the system can utilize thread-level parallelism (TLP) as well by running different threads in parallel on different processors. The OS scheduler is also responsible for handling this thread balancing act on the system. The use of ILP and TLP lack the benefit of resource utilization. To address the issue of processor resource utilization, the introduction of simultaneous multi-threading (SMT) allows multiple threads to compete for shared available resources, shown in Figure 10.2.

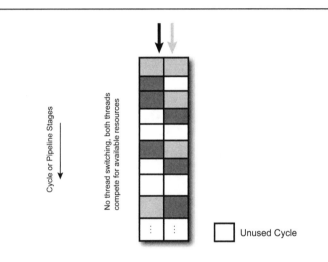

Figure 10.2   SMT Handles Multiple Threads

SMT hardware is effective for those applications that require complementary hardware resources during runtime. A multi-threaded singleton application—an application that has dependency on a specific functional unit of the CPU, such as integer or floating point functional units—might suffer a performance penalty on an SMT platform. In an SMT processor, TLP gets converted into ILP and accommodates variations among ILP and TLP. In terms of granularity, to utilize resources effectively an SMT processor exploits both coarse-grained and fine-granted parallelism.

When a processor has two or more cores, then that processor is referred to as *chip multiprocessing* (CMP). Here, each core executes hardware threads independently of other hardware threads, and shared memory helps to maintain inter-thread communication, shown in Figure 10.3. This independent thread execution on a multi-core processor is referred as *chip multi-threading* (CMT).

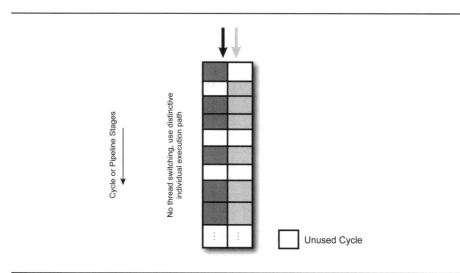

Figure 10.3   CMP Handles Multiple Threads

The concept of CMP has been around for a while in the specialized processor domain, in areas like communication and DSP. In CMP technology, multiple processors reside on a single die. To extend the usability of the CMP in the general processor domain, the industry introduced the concept of multi-core processors, which are slightly different than CMPs even though many publications started using CMP as a generic description of multi-core processors. In CMPs, multiple processors get packed on a single die, whereas for multi-core processors, a single die contains multiple cores rather than multiple processors. The concept of CMP can be confused with the existence of multiprocessor systems-on-chip (MPSoC). CMP and MPSoC are two different types of processors used for two different purposes. CMP is for general-purpose ISA hardware solutions, whereas MPSoC is used in custom architectures. In simple terms, the CMP is the one that has two or more conventional processors on a single die, as shown in Figure 10.4.

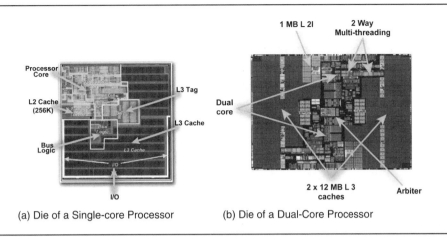

(a) Die of a Single-core Processor   (b) Die of a Dual-Core Processor

Figure 10.4   Single-core and Dual-Core Processor Dies

Several dimensions of technological evolution influenced the development of hardware threading. Process technology helps to manufacture smaller transistors and accommodates more transistors in a smaller package and keeps everything within the *thermal envelope*—the amount of heat allowed for a single processor. When you think of a processor, you must realize that there can be a good number of instructions in flight at operational time. In the Intel NetBurst® microarchitecture as many as 126 instructions remain in flight at any one time, positioned in various stages of execution and ready to execute simultaneously. To handle these many instructions and utilize processor resources, it is essential to incorporate parallelism effectively in a processor. This is one of the major reasons for the evolution of processors from superscalar to SMT to multi-core architecture.

Threading from Intel

Now that you have an idea what hardware threading means, you can easily guess that Intel has been implementing threading in processors for some time—in fact with the introduction of the Intel Pentium® superscalar processor in 1993. The performance was not impressive compared to the current standard, but was just a beginning of threading-based solutions on a processor. The progress continued and the next shift took place in 2000 with the introduction of Hyper-Threading Technology (HT Technology) for the 32-bit world and by the addition of Explicit Parallel Instruction Computing (EPIC) architecture with the launch of 64-bit Itanium® processors. The next wave from Intel came with the addition of dual-core processors in 2005, and further developments are in the works. To understand Intel threading solutions from the processor level and the availability of systems based on these processors, review the features of brands like Intel® Core™ Duo, Intel Pentium Processor Extreme Edition, Intel Pentium D, Intel Xeon®, Intel Pentium 4, and Intel Itanium 2. As stated before, when you are going to select different types of processor for your solution, you have to make sure the processor is compatible with the chipset. To learn more details on processors and compatibility, visit the Intel Web site.

Hyper-Threading Technology

Hyper-Threading Technology (HT Technology) is a hardware mechanism where multiple independent hardware threads get to execute in a single cycle on a single superscalar processor core, as shown in Figure 10.5. The implementation of HT Technology was the first SMT solution for general processors from Intel. In the current generation of Pentium 4 processors, only two threads run on a single-core by sharing, and replicating processor resources.

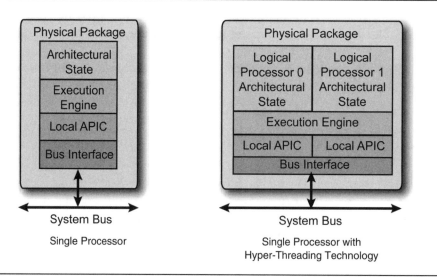

Figure 10.5   Single Processor System without Hyper-Threading Technology and Single Processor System with Hyper-Threading Technology

Inside a processor with HT Technology, two threads share resources from a single core, and that is why these threads are referred to as logical processors. In terms of physical processor core resources, a Pentium 4 processor with HT Technology and one without are almost the same. Only the die size is increased for the additional logic on the processor with HT Technology. The number of registers on processors with and without HT Technology remains the same. Obviously only one of these two threads can use a shared resource at a time.

From the OS perspective, the system represents two logical processors. This configuration allows a thread to be executed on each logical processor. Instructions from both threads are simultaneously dispatched for execution by the processor core. The processor core executes these two threads concurrently, using out-of-order instruction scheduling to keep execution units as busy as possible during each clock cycle. Figure 10.6 shows that the time taken to process *n* threads on a single processor is significantly more than a single-processor system with HT Technology enabled. This is because with HT Technology enabled, two logical processors process two threads concurrently on one physical processor.

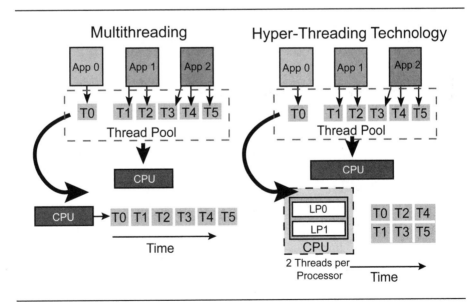

Figure 10.6 Multi-threaded Processing using Hyper-Threading Technology

Difference between Multiprocessor and Hyper-Threading Technology

Multiprocessor technology is referred to as MP. In MP multiple physical processors exist, whereas HT Technology relates to only one physical processor. In an MP environment, each processor could be enabled with HT Technology as well, as shown in Figure 10.7. For an MP environment without HT Technology, each thread dynamically gets a fixed number of devoted functional blocks in a processor, whereas with HT Technology the resources get shared among threads and a thread assignment policy determines the resource utilization.

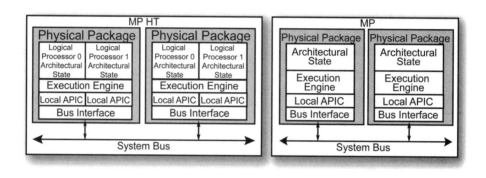

Figure 10.7   Multiprocessor with and without Hyper-Threading Technology

Hyper-Threading Technology Architecture

HT Technology is integrated into the Intel NetBurst microarchitecture using 90nm technology. The operational protocols and algorithms are improved to accommodate two execution flows of hardware threads. The various generations of processors with HT Technology are enhanced by additional features, whereas the architectural core remains the same. Figure 10.8 shows the different functional blocks in the architecture of the Pentium 4 processor with HT Technology.

The instruction decoding phase is independent of the execution phase. This separation helps to maintain the flow of the two threads. The instruction fetch logic keeps two streaming buffers for use with both threads and two instruction pointers (IP) to track the progress of instruction fetches for the two logical processors. In the case of branch prediction, branch prediction structures return a stack buffer and branch history buffer that get duplicated, and a large global history array is shared with entries that are tagged with logical processor IDs. The decode logic preserves two copies of all the necessary states required to perform an instruction decode, even though the decoding operations are done through a coarse-grained scheme in a single cycle.

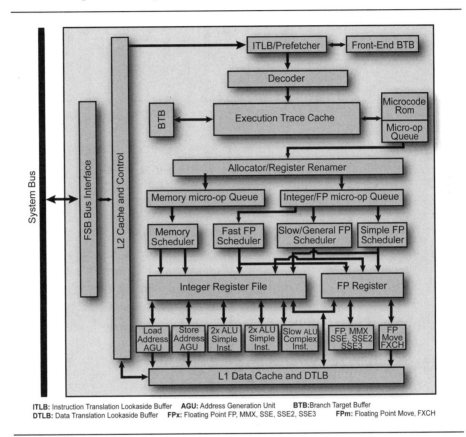

Figure 10.8   Pentium® 4 Processor Architecture with Queue and Scheduler Splits

The decode logic passes decoded instructions to the trace cache, also referred to as the advanced instruction cache. In reality, this is somewhat different than the conventional instruction cache. The trace cache stores already-decoded instructions in the form of micro-ops and maintains data integrity by associating a logical processor ID. The inclusion of the trace cache helps to remove the complicated decodes logic from the main execution phase. The trace cache orders the decoded micro-ops into program-ordered sequences or traces. If both hardware threads need access to the trace cache, the trace cache provides access with a fine-grained approach rather than coarse-grained. The trace cache can hold up to 12K micro-ops, but not every required instruction can reside in the trace cache. That is why, when the requested instruction micro-op is not available in the trace cache, the instruction needs to bring it from L2 cache—this event is called a *Trace Cache Miss*. On the other hand, when the instruction micro-ops remain available in trace cache and instruction flow does not need to take extra steps to get required instructions from L2, the event is referred to as a *Trace Cache Hit*.

In the front end of a processor with HT Technology, both hardware threads make independent progress and keep data association. The micro-op queues decouple the front end from the execution core and have a hard partition to accommodate two hardware threads. Once the front end is ready to prepare the microcode, the operational phase gets transferred to the backend out-of-order execution core, where appropriate execution parallelism takes place among microcode streams. This is done with the help of distributor micro-op queues and schedulers which keep the correct execution semantics of the program. To maintain the two hardware threads' register resource allocation, two Register Allocation Tables (RATs) support two threads. The register renaming operation is done in parallel to allocator logic. The execution is done by the advanced dynamic execution engine (DEE) and the rapid execution engine (REE). Six micro-ops get dispatched in each cycle through DEE and certain instructions are executed in each half cycle by REE. When two hardware threads want to utilize back-end, each thread gets allocation through a fine-grained scheme and a policy is established to limit the number of active entries each hardware thread can have in each scheduler queue. To provide ready micro-ops for different ports, the collective dispatch bandwidth across all of the schedulers is twice the number of micro-ops received by the out-of-order core.

Once the out-of-order execution core allows instructions from both threads interleaved in an arbitrary fashion to complete execution, it places issued micro-ops in the reorder buffer by alternating between two hardware threads. If for some instruction, one hardware thread is not ready to retire micro-ops, other threads can utilize the full retirement bandwidth.

In the memory subsystem, the Data Translation Lookaside Buffer (DTLB) is a shared resource but maintains hardware thread tags or logical processor tags to maintain data integrity. The rest of the cache hierarchies get shared by hardware threads. Inside the bus, no priority is assigned to logical processors or hardware threads, even though the distinction between requests from two logical processors is maintained reliably. The interrupt maintenance is done through local APICs, which are unique to each logical processor.

Multi-Core Processors

To understand multi-core processors, this section extends the concepts of single core and differentiates the meaning of *core* from that of *processor*. The following sections also cover the basics of the multi-core architecture, what is available today, and what may be available beyond multi-core architecture.

Architectural Details

Chapter 9 reviewed how a single-core processor contains functional blocks, where most of the functional blocks perform some specific operations to execute instructions. The core in this case is a combination of all of the functional blocks that directly participate in executing instructions. The unified on-die Last Level Cache (LLC) and Front Side Bus (FSB) interface unit could be either part of the core or not, depending on the configuration of the processor.

Some documents exclusively differentiate between *core* and *execution core*. The only difference is that an execution core is the main set of functional blocks that directly participate in an execution, whereas *core* encompasses all available functional blocks. To remain consistent, this book tries to distinguish the differences. In Figure 10.9, different core configurations are shown. Using shared LLC in a multi-core processor, the cache coherency complexity is reduced, but there needs to be a mechanism by which the cache line keeps some identifying tag for core association or dynamically splits the cache for all cores. Also, when the FSB interface gets shared, this helps to minimize FSB traffic. Proper utilization of a multi-core processor also comes from a compatible chipset.

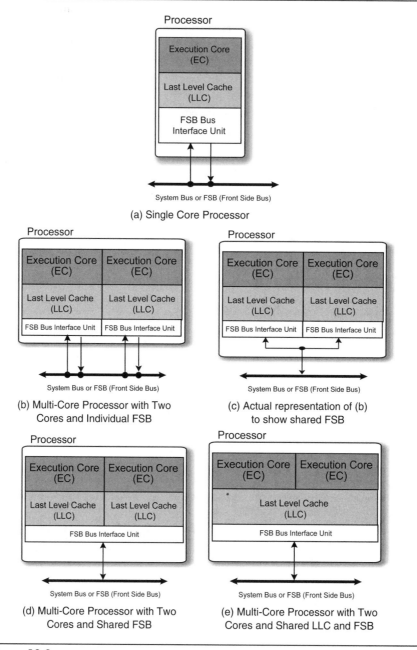

(a) Single Core Processor

(b) Multi-Core Processor with Two
Cores and Individual FSB

(c) Actual representation of (b)
to show shared FSB

(d) Multi-Core Processor with Two
Cores and Shared FSB

(e) Multi-Core Processor with Two
Cores and Shared LLC and FSB

Figure 10.9   Processor Core Configurations

The number of cores can vary, but the cores remain symmetrical; that is why you see product announcements for two, four, eight, or more cores in processors. You will be seeing the representation of the number of cores by 2^n (where, in theory, $0 < n < \infty$). Projected theoretical representations always remain blocked by available technologies. With the constraint in current technology, the proposed geometry of current and upcoming multi-core processors is shown in Table 10.2.

Table 10.2 Disclosed Multi-Core Processors with Specific Features

Processor Brand or Code Name	Number of Cores	LLC Size	HT Technology Present	FSB Interface Unit (Shared or Independent)
Intel® Core™ Duo	2	1×2 MB	No	Shared
Intel® Pentium® D	2	2×1 MB	No	Independent
Intel® Pentium® Processor Extreme Edition	2	2×1 MB	Yes	Independent
Intel codename Presler	2	2×2 MB	No	Independent
Intel codename Dempsey	2	2×2 MB	Yes	Independent
Intel codename Paxville	2	2×2 MB	Yes	Shared
Intel® Itanium® processor codenamed Montecito	2	2×12 MB	Yes	Shared

Table 10.3 shows only two physical cores. The number of threads supported by these processors is currently limited to two cores, but with respect to the platform, the number of threads varies with respect to the chipset where these processors are being used. If the chipset supports $\mathcal{N}$ number of processors, then the number of hardware threads for that platform can be as high as $\mathcal{N} \times 2 \times 2$. For the latest updates about available processors, visit the Intel Web site.

Networking Model of Multi-Core Processors

How do multiple cores communicate with each other and how are these cores positioned inside a die? These concerns are similar to network topology issues. The interconnection could be bus, mesh, ring, cross-bar, and so on. Different vendors utilize different topologies for these interconnections. Currently from Intel, the interconnection follows the existing FSB-based connection scheme. This approach has some important legacy aspects associated with it. Remember, auxiliary and required components must support multi-core processors and for that, all these components must support and have cohesive features to handle multi-core processors. The core of a multi-core processor does the same things that a single core based processor does except that with a multi-core processor, cores have to operate in a concerted way.

How about threads on these multi-core processors? What will happen with your application as the number of cores increase? The more cores that processors support, the more hardware threads you get to utilize. The multi-core processor hardware is evolving with updated protocols and improved logic. To implement threading in software, you need to use a methodology for synchronization. If you have ever performed operations to handle hardware threads directly, you know the level of synchronization that needs to be done. The layer above the hardware needs to support proper synchronization of the processors. Otherwise, an application might not get the expected performance gain. You also need to understand which operating systems support these multi-core processors and which compilers generate better code to deal with these many hardware threads.

Comparison between Multiprocessors and Multi-Core Processors

A multiprocessor represents multiple physical processors, whereas a multi-core processor represents multiple cores in a single physical processor, as shown in Figure 10.10. That means a multiprocessor can be built from a number of multi-core processors. Think of a multiprocessor environment as containing multiple sockets where you can plug in multiple processors. A multi-core processor resides on a single socket.

(a) Multiprocessor with Single-Core Processors

(b) Multiprocessor with Multi-Core Processors

Figure 10.10   Multiprocessor with Single-Core and Multi-Core processors

Multi-Core for Itanium® Architecture

The evolution of multi-core processors is not bounded by superscalar architecture. Intel announced a next-generation multi-core processor into the Explicitly Parallel Instruction Computing (EPIC) architecture domain code-named Montecito. Montecito introduces two cores in a single die, as shown in Figure 10.11 Even though the Itanium processor is an explicitly parallel instruction computing processor which provides exclusive instruction-level parallelism, to utilize resources and reduce miss penalties, Montecito incorporates both ILP and TLP. The implementation of ILP is similar to the implementation concepts of HT Technology, where resources get shared by fine-grained and coarse-grained parallelism, as well as SMT. In the current Itanium architecture, the concept of HT Technology blends Switch-on Event Multi-threading (SoEMT) for the cores and SMT for the memory hierarchy. The SoEMT is a form of coarse-grained parallelism where the time constants are varied based on dynamic behaviors of the instruction stream or events. Don't confuse this term with Intel EM64T.

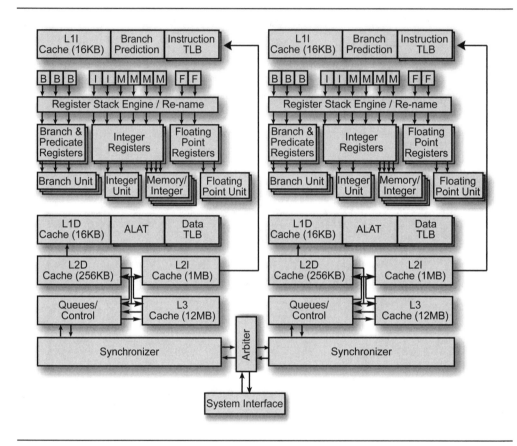

Figure 10.11   Multi-Core Architecture of Intel Itanium® Processor code-named Montecito

The FSB interface is shared among the cores. Montecito supports two cores in each socket and two hardware threads on each core. So, one socket has four contexts. This can be seen as comparable to a dual-core platform with HT Technology.

In Montecito, each core attaches to the FSB interface through the arbiter, which provides a low-latency path for a core to initiate and respond to system events while ensuring fairness and forward progress.

The arbiter maintains communication with the core through a synchronization functional block, as shown in Figure 10.12. The arbiter maintains each core's unique identity to the FSB interface and operates at a fixed ratio to the FSB interface frequency.

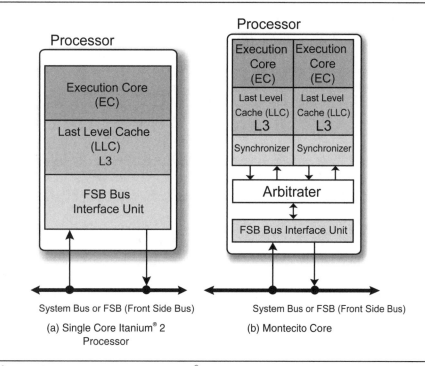

Figure 10.12   Single Core Itanium® 2 Processor and Montecito Core

An asynchronous interface between the arbiter and each core enables the core and cache frequency to vary as needed. This arbiter and the synchronizers add a small amount of latency to transactions both from a core to the system interface and from the system interface to a core.

The arbiter consists of a set of address queues, data queues, synchronizers, control logic for core and FSB interface arbitration, error-correction code (ECC) encoders/decoders, and parity generators. The arbiter interleaves core requests on a one-to-one basis when both cores have transactions to issue. When only one core has requests, it can issue its requests without waiting for the other core to issue a transaction. Because read latency is the greatest concern, the read requests are typically the highest priority, followed by writes, and finally clean victim notifications from the LLC.

Each core tracks the occupancy of the arbiter's queues using a credit system for flow control. As requests complete, the arbiter informs the appropriate core of the type and number of de-allocated queue entries. The cores use this information to determine which, if any, transaction to issue to the arbiter. The arbiter manages the system interface protocols while the cores track individual requests. The arbiter tracks all in-order requests and maintains the system interface protocol. Deferred or out-of-order transactions are tracked by the core with the arbiter simply passing the appropriate system interface events on to the appropriate core. The arbiter has the ability to support various legacy configurations by adjusting where the agent identifier—socket, core, and/or thread—is driven on the system interface. The assignment of socket and core must be made at power on and cannot be changed dynamically. The assignment of a thread is fixed, but the driving of the thread identifier is under Processor Abstraction Layer (PAL) control since it is for information purposes only and is not needed for correctness or forward progress.

In the core, one thread has exclusive access to the execution resources (foreground thread) for a period of time while the other thread is suspended (background thread). Thread control logic evaluates the thread's ability to make progress and may dynamically decrease the foreground thread's time quantum if it appears that it will make less effective use of the core than the background thread. This ensures better overall utilization of the core resources over strict temporal multi-threading (TMT) and effectively hides the cost of long latency operations such as memory accesses, especially the on-die LLC cache misses, which has latency of 14 cycles. Other events, such as the time-out and forward progress event, provide fairness, and switch hint events provide paths for the software to influence thread switches. These events have an impact on a thread's urgency that indicates a thread's ability to effectively use core resources. Many switch events change a thread's urgency, or the prediction that a thread is likely to make good use of the core resources.

Each thread has an urgency value that is used as an indication of a thread's ability to make effective use of the core execution resources. The urgency of the foreground thread is compared against the background thread at every LLC event. If the urgency of the foreground thread is lower than the background thread then the LLC event may initiate a thread switch. Thread switches may be delayed from when the control logic requests a switch to when the actual switch occurs. The reasons for delay include serialization operations and long latency accesses. Urgency can take on values from 0 to 7. An urgency of 0 denotes that a thread has no useful work to perform. An urgency of 7 is only used for a thread that is switched due to a time-out event when its current urgency is 5. An external interrupt directed at the background thread sets the urgency for the background thread at 6 to provide a reasonable response time for interrupt servicing, but the urgency for the current thread that receives an interrupt is not changed. The nominal urgency is 5 and indicates that a thread is effectively using (or would effectively use) the core execution resources (no LLC misses outstanding). The urgency is reset to 5 when the background thread with urgency above 5 becomes the foreground thread. Every LLC miss event decrements the urgency by 1 after the urgency is compared, eventually saturating at 0. Similarly, every LLC return event increments the urgency by 1 before the urgency is compared saturating at 5.

Though most of the hardware threads are controlled by a processor control functional block, in Montecito you would be able to control threads using the hint@pause instruction. The hint@pause instruction is used by software to initiate a thread switch. The intent is to allow code to indicate that it does not have any useful work to do and that its execution resources should be given to the other thread. Some later event may change the work for the thread and should awaken the thread such as an interrupt.

The hint@pause instruction forces a switch from the foreground thread to the background thread. This instruction can be predicated to conditionally initiate a thread switch. The current issue group retires before the switch is initiated. Consequently, the following code sequences are equivalent:

Hint at beginning of issue group:

```
hint@pause
add         r1 = r2, r3
add         r4 = r2, r0
```

Hint at end of issue group:

```
add         r1 = r2, r3
add         r4 = r2, r0
hint@pause
```

Having all these changes in Montecito does not affect legacy software.

Multiple Processor Interaction

Up to this point, the book has covered hardware, architecture, and the impact of software on a multi-core environment. As yet no detailed information has been offered about the concepts of communication among processors or cores. This section discusses details about multiple processor intercommunication. It is impossible to organize a parallel computational system without establishing communication channels or other means of interaction between different parts of such a system. Thus, completely isolating processors and preventing them from exchanging information would not constitute a good approach to parallel computations. Moreover, establishing a dedicated resource to be shared between multiple processors, like shared memory in symmetric multiprocessing, is generally not enough for an efficient parallel operation. Additional means must be provided to facilitate interaction among multiple processors. The following section covers how this communication usually gets done in a multi-threaded environment.

Inter-Processor Communication and Multi-threaded Programming

The APIC plays a major role in communication among cores or processors using the interprocessor interrupt (IPI). To illustrate interprocessor communication for multi-threaded programming, Figure 10.13 depicts how the IPI scheme is used in a parallel programming environment.

One of the most important reasons an operating system uses IPIs is to schedule the execution of threads on multiple processors. Normally, the system may reschedule threads upon each timer or similar periodic external interrupt. But, once a thread triggers a synchronization object— and this may happen at an unpredictable moment in time, not at all periodically—other threads waiting on that object need to be executed. Of course, they may be queued and run at the next periodic interruption signal, though in this case a considerable amount of time is wasted, from the processor's point of view, Another approach is to program the threads in a manner that allows them to check the state of the other threads they depend on, but such a programming scheme sometimes cannot even be called parallel. Figure 10.14 illustrates these statements: since all threads are executed in a preemptive environment, the model of polling a state variable in memory does not always work well—threads may get preempted and the actual execution may be shifted in time with regard to the moment when the state change occurred.

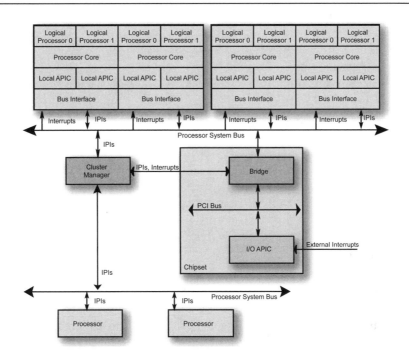

Figure 10.13 Relationship of Each Processor's Local APIC, I/O APIC, and System Bus in a Multiprocessor System

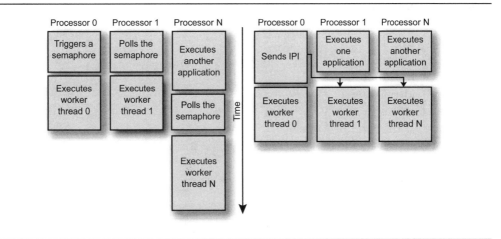

Figure 10.14 Use of Interprocessor Interrupts in Parallel Programming

Again, by employing the IPI scheme, the system ensures that all waiting threads are executed immediately after the synchronization object has been triggered, and executed with a predictable delay time, much less than the normal rescheduling period.

But in some situations a thread's wait time does not exceed the time quantum granted to the thread by the operating system. In this case it would be inefficient to reschedule the thread's execution by returning control to the OS or by making other threads issue an IPI to wake up your waiting thread, since the interrupt delivery delay may be much greater than the actual wait interval. The only solution would be to keep control and wait for other threads in a loop. This is where the hardware monitor/wait approach yields the best benefit to a programmer, because one can boost the performance by providing a hint to the processor that the current thread does not need any computational resources since all it does is wait for a variable to change.

Power Consumption

You might be surprised to find this section in a software book. You might know that you can control your system power by using available system level APIs such as GetSystemPowerStatus and GetDevicePowerState. Mobile application developers understand the issue with power more than others. Traditionally, systems and applications have been designed for high performance. In fact, our entire discussion up to this point has been concerned with architectural and programming innovations to increase performance of applications and systems. However, recently the power consumption of the platform has become a critical characteristic of a computing system.

Power Metrics

Increases in power consumption have occurred despite dramatic and revolutionary improvements in process technology and circuit design. The primary reason behind the increase in power has been the continued emphasis on higher performance. As complexity and frequency of processors has increased over the years to provide unprecedented levels of performance the power required to supply these processors has increased steadily too. A simplified equation that demonstrates power-performance relationship for the CMOS circuits on which all modern processors are based is:

$$P \cong ACV^2 f$$

The first component in the equation captures the dynamic power of charging and discharging transistor circuits from which basic functional blocks of processors are built. The power is directly proportional to switching frequency (f), square of the supply voltage (V) and total capacitance (C). Since not all functional blocks are used at any given time by a processor workload and not all gates are switched, A represents activity factor or the number of switched transistors on a die.

The equation above demonstrates the trade-off between performance and power. As processor frequency increases so does power consumption. As processor architecture becomes more complex to support greater levels of instruction level parallelism and increased performance, capacitance of system increases and so does dynamic power.

Another and more subtle point is that concurrent processing can also lead to significant power reduction. Splitting the workload into multiple threads and running them in parallel can significantly increase processor power efficiency. Multi-threading attacks two primary sources of energy inefficiency that is related to activity factor A and total processor capacitance C: unutilized resources and wasted resources due to aggressive speculation in modern processors. Multi-threaded processors rely much less on speculation and provide better resource utilization leading to improved power efficiency.

The processor's power efficiency can be measured and quantified in a variety of ways. One common metric is peak power or Thermal Design Power (TDP). This is the maximum power at which the processor can run without exceeding thermal solution capabilities and damaging the part. Another common metric used to quantify processor power consumption is average power. It is usually computed as an average of instantaneous power readings over execution of a certain benchmark. A more accurate measurement of power efficiency is performance per watt. It may be expressed in a variety of ways such as energy per instruction, MIPS/watts, or benchmark performance score per average processor power consumption. All these metrics reflect a fundamental interplay between performance and power, and demonstrate the interdependency between the two. The power efficiency metric is the fact that processors must be efficient both in active and idle states. In reality, processors in mobile, desktop, and server platforms spend a significant amount of time doing nothing or being idle. Ensuring that processor power consumption is minimal in this state is critical for the overall power efficiency. Note that a processor with higher TDP or active power consumption will be more energy efficient and potentially have lower average power if it provides a very low power idle state. While it may be beneficial to expand power for active workload for performance reasons, there is no benefit to wasting power when you are doing nothing!

Reducing Power Consumption

The discussion so far has focused on the fundamental aspects and importance of processor power consumption. It should be clear that reducing processor power has become an overriding design goal. Achieving low power processor operation is a complex task that requires effort at multiple layers of hardware and software infrastructure. At the silicon level, designers have developed advanced techniques such as strained silicon and sleep transistors to reduce leakage and idle power. At the logic level, extensive clock gating allows to turn off tree branches to latches and flip-flops when they are not used saving considerable amount of power.

At the architecture level processors expose different frequency and voltage settings that allow operating systems to adjust processor performance to current workload demand. As the equation shows, processor power is proportional to its frequency and square of the voltage. Adjusting these two parameters to workload demand can lead to significant power benefits without impacting perceived system performance. In fact, frequency and voltage scaling is a feature in almost all Intel processors today and is better known as Enhanced Intel SpeedStep® Technology. In addition, Intel processors support highly efficient frequency and voltage transitions with rapid frequency scaling and no-stall voltage changes. Since reaching low power state might not be worthwhile if it takes a long time these capabilities are essential to maintaining system performance and reducing dynamic power consumption.

When available, operating systems use Enhanced Intel SpeedStep Technology to reduce platform power during operation. Both Linux and Windows implement similar algorithms. Operating systems determine the right frequency setting by measuring the time they spend in idle loop. Whenever the processor is underutilized the OS determines the frequency that will increase processor utilization to a certain level. On the other hand, if processor utilization becomes higher than a certain threshold, the OS will increase processor frequency to meet higher demand. In today's operating system, power management is governed by Advance Configuration and Power Interface (ACPI). ACPI is part of BIOS and exposes power management features and details to the operating system. All Intel processors today provide support for a variety of idle and performance states enabling operating systems to take advantage of these features for power efficient operation.

Finally, in addition to processors and operating systems, applications have a responsibility to reduce power consumption of computing devices. With the proliferation of multi-core processors, application developers have a great opportunity to decrease system power consumption by writing efficient and optimized multi-threaded applications. Multi-core processors offer clear performance benefits with close to linear speedup as you add cores. With the performance advantage coming from parallelism and not from an increase in frequency and voltage, multi-core processors can be very energy-efficient. By writing multi-threaded applications that take full advantage of parallelism provided by the cores, developers can cause processor throughput to be dramatically increased, more than making up for greater power dissipation due to a larger number of cores, and resulting in significant net gain in power efficiency.

Beyond Multi-Core Processor Architecture

Every technology has a next step. Things go from conception to research and move on to development. The progression continues to evolve. You now know that having more than a single core is referred to as multi-core. In theory, the number of cores is only limited by the availability of supporting technologies. Over time we can anticipate processors with more and more cores as we continue to innovate. Intel is working to deliver innovative processor technology on a roadmap as proposed in Figure 10.15.

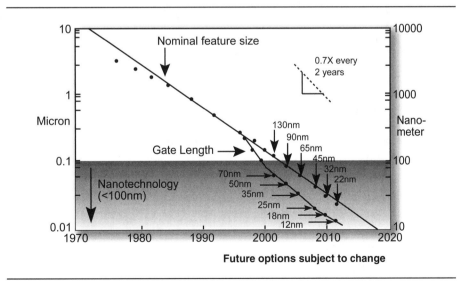

Figure 10.15 Progression of Silicon Technology towards Nanoscale

The silicon technology is also approaching the nanoscale domain to enhance transistor density as well, as shown in Figure 10.16.

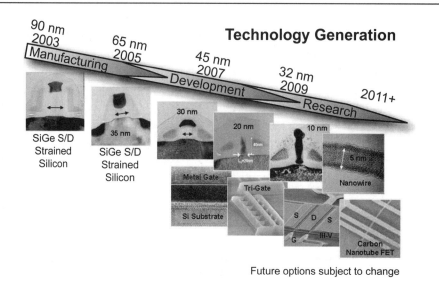

Figure 10.16 Innovation-enabled Technology Pipeline

Beyond nanoscale, the technology proposes to drive transistors to the quantum level. If the progress continues, you can expect processors with many cores before the end of this decade. As the number of cores increases, the processor architecture will provide significant hardware-based, thread-level, parallel capability on a single processor. With these levels of compaction and multiplicity, just imagine the possibilities for the future of multi-core processors.

Key Points

When developing a software application, the focus usually remains on the implementation layer and the layer below. Several layers separate the abstracted application and the hardware. With the recent development of more than one core in a single package, developers have to consider every component in the solution domain to optimize the capabilities of these new processors.

Key concepts to remember about threading on multi-core processors:

■ There are four types of threading models used in a processor: fine-grained, coarse-grained, SMT, and CMT.

■ For the fine-grained threading model, context switching occurs in every cycle and for the coarse-grained threading model, context switching occurs when a pipeline gets stalled. On the other hand, there is no context switching required for true SMP or multi-core processors.

■ Processors have enough resources to handle a good number of instructions in flight during full operation.

■ Intel has two types of general processor architecture: wide speculative superscalar and EPIC. Superscalar processors are used for Intel 32-bit processors and Intel EM64T. EPIC is used for Itanium processors.

■ Recently, an implementation of HT Technology was introduced in the Itanium processor as well.

■ Interprocessor or intercore communication is done by inter-processor interrupt (IPI) with the help of Advanced Programmable Interrupt Controller (APIC) features in the processors.

■ Advance Configuration and Power Interface (ACPI) exposes processor frequency and voltage levels as performance states.

■ The power factors can be controlled through software APIs.

■ Enhanced Intel SpeedStep Technology is available on platforms to improve power-based performance.

Chapter **11**

Intel® Software Development Products

Writing a threaded application requires the same create, debug, and tuning steps needed to make a working application that is not threaded. While so much is the same, it is most interesting to look at what is different.

This chapter takes a look at Intel's suite of software and focuses on the aspects of these products that Intel has included for threaded applications. Intel's suite of products is arguably the most comprehensive available today for threaded programming for C++ or Fortran developers, including a few tools that are currently unique or leading examples.

Most of the tools are focused on threading. A section in this chapter also describes Message Passing Interface (MPI) programming and the tools to support it. MPI programming is an important programming method to consider when you are trying to make highly scalable code that might even run on a very large supercomputer.

Overview

Intel has been working with multiprocessor designs and the tools to support them for well over a decade. In order to assist programmers, Intel has made available a number of tools for creating, debugging, and tuning parallel programs.

Investigate

Most programming work begins with an existing application. It often begins with a prototype of a framework or critical elements of the application, for those working to program something entirely new. Whether a prototype or a preexisting application, some initial investigation plays a critical role in guiding future work. Tools such as the Intel® VTune™ Performance Analyzer and the Intel Thread Profiler are extremely useful. The Intel compilers can play a strong role in "what if" experiments by simply throwing some switches, or inserting a few directives in the code, and doing a recompile to see what happens.

Create/Express

Applications are written in a programming language, so a compiler is a natural place to help exploit parallelism. No programming languages in wide usage were designed specifically with parallelism in mind. This creates challenges for the compiler writer to automatically find and exploit parallelism. The Intel compilers do a great deal to find parallelism automatically. Despite this great technology, there are too many limitations in widely used programming languages, and limitations in the way code has been written for decades, for this to create a lot of success. Automatic parallelization by the compiler is nevertheless a cheap and easy way to get *some* help— all automatically. Auto-parallelization is limited by all popular programming languages because the languages were designed without regard to expressing parallelism. This is why extensions like OpenMP are needed, but they are still limited by the programming languages they extend. There is no cheap and easy way to achieve parallelism using these languages.

To overcome limitations imposed by conventional programming languages, the Intel compilers support OpenMP, which allows a developer to add directives to the code base that specify how different code segments may be parallelized. This allows programs to get significant performance gains in a simple, easy-to-maintain fashion. The OpenMP extensions have been covered in some detail in Chapter 6. Intel libraries also help make the production of threaded applications easier. In this case, Intel engineers have done the work for you and buried it in the implementation of the libraries. These may be the very same libraries you were using before threading.

Debugging

Having multiple threads combine to get the work of an application done gives rise to new types of programming errors usually not possible with single threaded applications. Up until recently, these threading errors were simply bugs that needed to be debugged the old fashion way—seek and find. With the Intel Thread Checker, developers can directly locate threading errors. It can detect the potential for these errors even if the error does not occur during an analysis session. This is because a well-behaved threaded application needs to coordinate the sharing of memory between threads in order to avoid race conditions and deadlock. The Intel Thread Checker is able to locate examples of poor behavior that should be removed by the programmer to create a stable threaded application.

Tuning

Performance tuning of any application is best done with non-intrusive tools that supply an accurate picture of what is actually happening on a system. Threaded applications are no exception to this. A programmer, armed with an accurate picture of what is happening, is able to locate suboptimal behavior and opportunities for improvement. The Intel Thread Profiler and the Intel VTune Performance Analyzer help tune a threaded application by making it easy to see and probe the activities of all threads on a system.

Intel® Thread Checker

The Intel Thread Checker is all about checking to see that a threaded program is not plagued by coding errors in how threads interoperate that can cause the program to fail. It is an outstanding debugging tool, even for programs that seem to be functioning properly. Just knowing that such a tool exists is a big step since this is such a new area for most programmers. Finding this class of programming error is especially difficult and frustrating because the errors manifest themselves as nondeterministic failures that often change from run to run of a program and most often change behavior when being examined using a debugger.

Developers use the Intel Thread Checker to locate a special class of threading coding errors in multi-threaded programs that may or may not be causing the program to fail. The Intel Thread Checker creates diagnostic messages for places in a program where its behavior in a multi-threaded environment is potentially nondeterministic. The Intel Thread Checker identifies issues including data races, deadlocks, stalled threads, lost signals and abandoned locks. The Intel Thread Checker supports analysis of threaded programs that use OpenMP, POSIX, and the Windows API.

Chapter 7 explained *data races* and *deadlocks* which are the two programming errors that can occur because of threading. These are difficult to debug as they can cause results to be indeterminate and to differ from the output that a non-threaded version of the program would produce. Deadlock causes a program, or a subset of threads, to not be able to continue executing at all because of errors in the way it was programmed.

The process of finding critical multi-threading programming issues like data races and deadlocks starts with running a program with the Intel Thread Checker to collect data. Once this data collection has occurred, the Intel Thread Checker is used to view the results of the program execution. These results are shown in a prioritized list of diagnostic and warning messages based on the trace data. Sorting and organizing the Diagnostics list in various ways helps focus on the most important issues. This tool isolates threading bugs to the source code line where the bug occurs. It shows exactly where in a program threading errors are likely to happen. When the Intel Thread Checker detects an issue, it reports the function, context, line, variable, and call stack to aid in analysis and repair. It also provides a suggestion of possible causes for the threading errors and suggested solutions with one-click diagnostic help.

The Intel Thread Checker suggests all necessary warnings for effective threaded application diagnosis, while allowing you to choose which warnings to display at different points in the product development cycle.

How It Works

The Intel Thread Checker can do its analysis using built-in binary instrumentation and therefore can be used regardless of which compiler is used. This is particularly important with modern applications that rely on dynamically linked libraries (DLLs) for which the source code is often unavailable. The Intel Thread Checker is able to instrument an application and the shared libraries, such as DLLs, that the application utilizes.

When combined with the Intel compiler and its compiler-inserted instrumentation functionality, Intel Thread Checker gives an even better understanding by making it possible to drill down to specific variables on each line. Figure 11.1 shows the diagnostic view and Figure 11.2 shows the source view of the Intel Thread Checker.

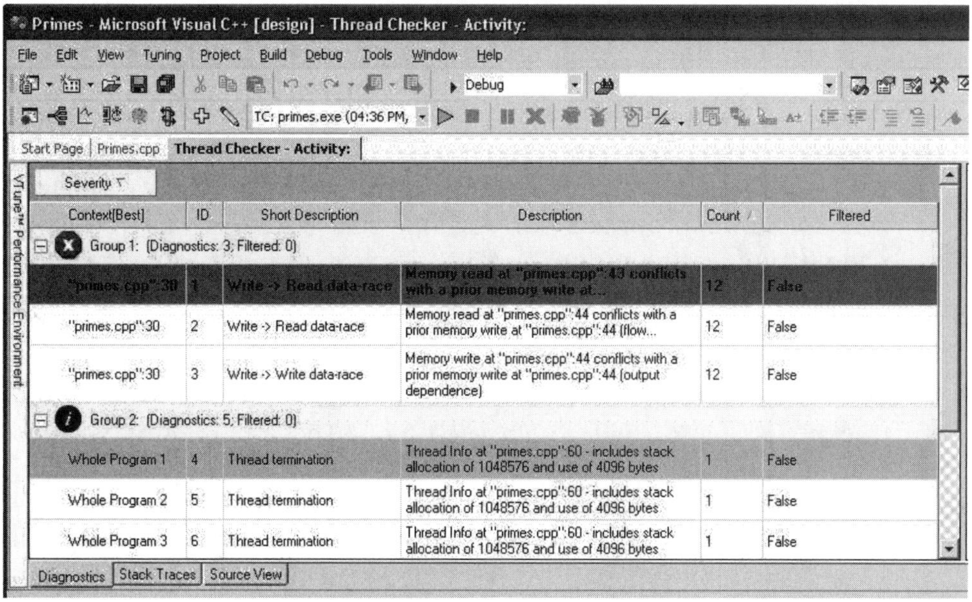

Figure 11.1 Intel® Thread Checker Diagnostic View

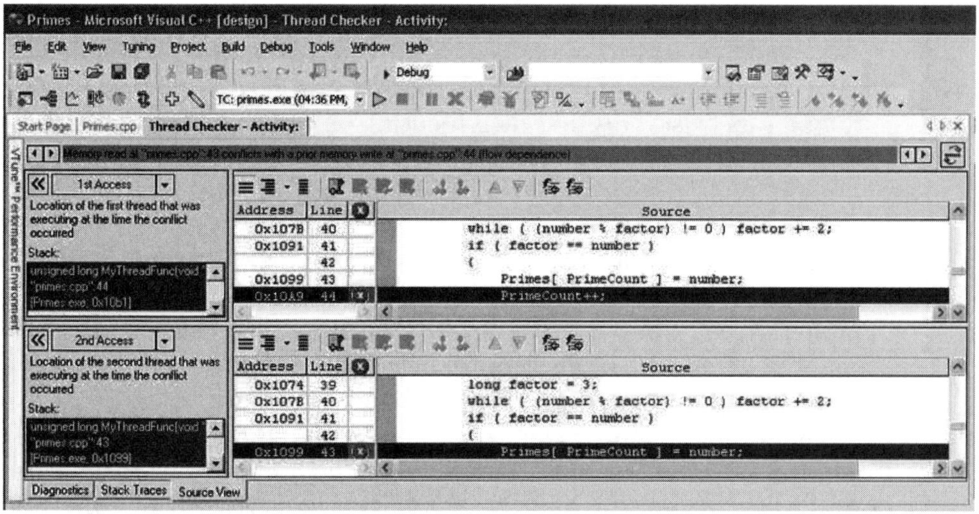

Figure 11.2 Intel® Thread Checker Source View

Usage Tips

Because the Intel Thread Checker relies on instrumentation, a program under test will run slower than it does without instrumentation due to the amount of data being collected. Therefore, the most important usage tip is to find the smallest data set that will thoroughly exercise the program under analysis. Selecting an appropriate data set, one that is representative of your code without extra information, is critical so as not to slow execution unnecessarily. It is generally not practical to analyze a long program or run an extensive test suite using this tool.

In practice, three iterations of a loop—first, middle, and last—are usually sufficient to uncover all the problems that the Intel Thread Checker is able to find within each loop. The exception is when `if` conditions within the loop do different things for specific iterations. Because of the overhead involved in the Intel Thread Checker operation, you should choose a data set for testing purposes that operates all the loops that you are trying to make run in parallel, but has the smallest amount of data possible so that the parallel loops are only executed a small number of iterations. Extra iterations only serve to increase the execution time. If you have a particular section of code you would like to focus on, you can either craft your data and test case to exercise just that part, or you can use the Pause/Resume capabilities of the Intel Thread Checker.

The Intel Thread Checker prioritizes each issue it sees as an error, warning, caution, information, or remark, as shown in Figure 11.3. Sorting errors by severity and then focusing on the most important issues first is the best way to use the tool.

Before you prepare your code for use with the Intel Thread Checker, you should ensure that your code is safe for parallel execution by verifying that it is sequentially correct. That is, debug it sequentially before trying to run in parallel. Also, if your language or compiler needs special switches to produce thread-safe code, use them. This comes up in the context of languages like Fortran, where use of stack (automatic) variables is usually necessary, and not always the default for a compiler. The appropriate switch on the Intel Fortran Compiler is `-Qauto`. Use of this option on older code may cause issues, and the use of a SAVE statement in select places may be required for subroutines that expect variables to be persistent from invocation to invocation.

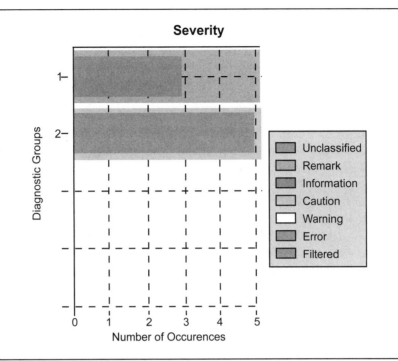

Figure 11.3   Intel® Thread Checker Bar Chart with Error Categories

Using Intel® Thread Checker with OpenMP

OpenMP programs are threaded programs and can suffer from the same errors and performance problems as explicitly threaded applications. OpenMP is discussed in detail in Chapter 6. Using Intel Thread Checker, you can avoid the standard task of identifying storage conflicts in previously threaded code. With OpenMP, the diagnostic output of Intel Thread Checker identifies and allows the categorizing of the scope of variables within parallel regions. This allows a programmer using OpenMP to try a directive that is close to correct and fine tune it using Intel Thread Checker. Intel has provided a whitepaper on this exact topic on their developer web site, www.intel.com/software, titled *Intel® Threading Tools and OpenMP* by Clay P. Breshears.

Intel Compilers

Just as with previous hardware technologies, the compiler can play a central or supporting role in taking advantages the multi-processor/multi-core/multi-threading capabilities of your shared memory platform. Intel Corporation has been supporting multi-threading capabilities in its compilers for many years now. This section explores those technologies.

OpenMP†

In Chapter 6, you learned how OpenMP can be used as a portable parallel solution and that Intel compilers have support for OpenMP within the Windows and Linux environments. Intel compilers support all the implementation methodologies discussed in Chapter 6. At the time of this writing, Version 9.1 of the Intel compilers support the OpenMP API 2.5 specification as well as the workqueuing extension, a feature proposed by Intel for OpenMP 3.0. To get the Intel compiler to recognize your OpenMP constructs, compile with the following switch:

- Windows: `/Qopenmp`
- Linux: `-openmp`

Some of the many advantages of using OpenMP to thread software are:

- It is intuitive and comparatively easy to introduce into your application.
- It is portable across operating systems, architectures, and compilers.
- The compiler has the opportunity to make architecture-specific optimizations.

OpenMP API achieves these goals by leaving the implementation up to the compiler.

Atomic

The OpenMP Atomic directive is probably the most obvious example of a feature where the compiler is able to provide a fast implementation. The atomic directive is similar to a critical section—in that only one thread may enter the atomic section of code at a time—but it places the limitation on the developer that only very simplistic and specific statements can follow it.

When you use the atomic directive as follows:

```
#pragma omp atomic
     workunitdone++;
```

The compiler can issue the following instructions that allow the hardware to atomically add one to the variable

```
mov        eax, 0x1h
lock xadd  DWORD PTR [rcx], eax
```

This is much more efficient than locking the code using a critical section or a mutex, then updating the variable, and finally releasing the lock, which can take hundreds or thousands of cycles, depending on the implementation. This could be created using inline assembly or compiler intrinsics, except that then the code would not be portable to other architectures or OS environments.

The Intel compilers will perform other optimization algorithms when compiling OpenMP code. The atomic example was chosen due to its simplicity. As optimization techniques are developed by Intel's compiler developers, those techniques usually get added in the compiler so that everyone who uses OpenMP with the Intel compiler benefits, whether they are aware of it or not.

Auto-Parallel

The Intel compilers have another feature to help facilitate threading. The auto-parallelization feature automatically translates serial source code into equivalent multi-threaded code. The resulting binary behaves as if the user inserted OpenMP pragmas around various loops within their code. The switch to do this follows:

- Windows: /Qparallel
- Linux: -parallel

For some programs this can yield a "free" performance gain on SMP systems. For many programs the resulting performance is less than expected, but don't give up on the technology immediately. There are several things that can be done to increase the probability of performance for this auto-parallel switch.

Increasing or decreasing the threshold for which loops will be made parallel might guide the compiler in creating a more successful binary. The following switch guides the compiler heuristics for loops:

- Windows: /Qpar_threshold[:n]
- Linux: -par_threshold[n]

where the condition 0 <= n <= 100 holds and represents the threshold for the auto-parallelization of loops. If n=0, then loops get auto-parallelized always, regardless of computation work volume. If n=100, then loops get auto-parallelized when performance gains are predicted based on the compiler analysis data. Loops get auto-parallelized only if profitable parallel execution is almost certain. The intermediate values 1 through 99 represent the percentage probability for profitable speed-up. For example, n=50 directs the compiler to parallelize only if there is a 50 percent probability of the code speeding up if executed in parallel.

Using auto-parallelization in combination with other switches like Inter-Procedural Optimizations (IPO), Profile Guided Optimizations (PGO) and High Level Optimizations (HLO) aids the compiler in making more correct choices while threading the code.

If auto-parallelization does not help directly, it can perhaps help indirectly. The Intel compilers also support a compiler reporting feature and the switch is:

- Windows: `/Qpar_report[n]`
- Linux: `-par_report[n]`

where 0 <= n <= 3. If n=3, then the report gives diagnostic information about the loops it analyzed. The following demonstrates the use of this report on a simplistic example. Given the following source:

```
1    #define NUM 1024
2    #define NUMIJK 1024
3    void multiply_d( double a[][NUM], double b[][NUM],
4                     double c[][NUM] )
5    {
6        int i,j,k;
7        double temp;
8        for(i=0; i<NUMIJK; i++) {
9            for(j=0; j<NUMIJK; j++) {
10               for(k=0; k<NUMIJK; k++) {
11                   c[i][j] = c[i][j] + a[i][k] * b[k][j];
12               }
13           }
14       }
15   }
```

The compiler produces the following report:

```
$ icc multiply_d.c -c -parallel -par_report3
    procedure: multiply_d
    serial loop: line 10: not a parallel candidate due to insufficient
work
    serial loop: line 8
        anti data dependence assumed from line 11 to line 11, due to "b"
        anti data dependence assumed from line 11 to line 11, due to "a"
```

```
flow data dependence assumed from line 11 to line 11, due to "c"
flow data dependence assumed from line 11 to line 11, due to "c"
serial loop: line 9
  anti data dependence assumed from line 11 to line 11, due to "b"
  anti data dependence assumed from line 11 to line 11, due to "a"
  flow data dependence assumed from line 11 to line 11, due to "c"
  flow data dependence assumed from line 11 to line 11, due to "c"
```

Based on this report, you can see the compiler thinks a dependency exists between iterations of the loop on the a, b, and c arrays. This dependency is due to an aliasing possibility—basically, it is possible that the a or b array points to a memory location within the c array. It is easy to notify the compiler that this is not possible[1]. To handle such instances, any of the following techniques can be used:

■ Inter-Procedural Optimization (IPO)

  – Windows: /Qipo

  – Linux: -ipo

■ Restrict keyword

■ Aliasing switches: /Oa, /Ow, /Qansi_alias

■ #pragma ivdep

After modifying the code as follows:

...

```
void multiply_d(double a[][NUM], double  b[][NUM], double  c[restrict][NUM])
```

...

the following report is produced:

```
$ icc multiply_d.c -c -parallel -par_report3 -c99
procedure: multiply_d
  serial loop: line 10: not a parallel candidate due to insufficent work
multiply_d.c(8) : (col. 2) remark: LOOP WAS AUTO-PARALLELIZED.
  parallel loop: line 8
    shared      : { "c" "b" "a" }
    private     : { "i" "j" "k" }
    first priv.: { }
    reductions  : { }
```

---

[1] In this case, the programmer assumes the responsibility of ensuring that this aliasing doesn't occur. If the programmer is wrong, unpredictable results will occur.

This technique can also be used as a guide in adding OpenMP pragmas to the source. For the above example, the following OpenMP changes are easy to identify:

```
1   #define NUM 1024
2   #define NUMIJK 1024
3   void multiply_d( double a[][NUM], double b[][NUM],
4                    double c[][NUM] )
5   {
6       int i,j,k;
7       double temp;
8   #pragma omp parallel for shared(a,b,c) private(i,j,k)
9       for(i=0; i<NUMIJK; i++) {
10          for(j=0; j<NUMIJK; j++) {
11              for(k=0; k<NUMIJK; k++) {
12                  c[i][j] = c[i][j] + a[i][k] * b[k][j];
13              }
14          }
15      }
16  }
```

The auto-parallelization feature of the Intel compilers may provide an easy performance gain in your source. If it doesn't, you can increase its probability of helping you guide it with other switches, aliasing techniques, or by using it to guide the insertion of OpenMP pragmas. If a specific portion of the application does not thread through auto-parallelization—or if it does thread the code, but it does so inefficiently—report this to Intel through Intel Premier Support Web site. It is possible that the compiler developers can add that optimization to the compiler, thereby making the application run faster, as well as improving the compiler for the overall community.

Software-based Speculative Precomputation

Version 9.0 of the Intel compilers introduced a "preview" feature called Software-based Speculative Precomputation (SSP), also known as Helper Threads. The goal of SSP is to hide memory latencies associated with single-threaded applications by utilizing idle or unused multi-threading hardware resources to prefetch data from memory into the cache. In order to do the prefetch, the compiler creates secondary thread(s) that run on behalf of the main thread. The secondary thread or threads try to access data in memory that will soon be needed by the main thread. If the needed data is not currently in the cache, a cache miss occurs and the data is loaded into the cache. In the ideal case, the data will be in the cache before the main thread needs the data. Since the hardware threading resources would have been idle otherwise, this technique effectively eliminates performance penalties associated with memory latencies. This technique will work for any system that can execute threads simultaneously and includes a shared cache that multiple threads can access directly.

In order for this technique to yield a performance gain the compiler needs detailed data about cache misses within your application. The compiler needs to gather an execution profile of your application and data on cache misses from the Performance Monitoring Unit (PMU) in order to identify where cache misses are occurring in your application.

Compiler Optimization and Cache Optimization

In order to achieve the maximum benefit from threading, it is also important to make sure your application is optimized for the underlying hardware platform. Two aspects that are relevant to threading should be considered:

- Increasing cache usage (thereby decreasing bus bandwidth)
- Increasing the performance of every thread

One of the performance-limiting factors on a parallel processing capable system is the memory subsystem bottleneck. The Intel compiler can help avoid main memory accesses by performing optimizations within the compiler to maximize the use of the caches— which ultimately decreases the amount of data that needs to pass through the memory bus.

On some architectures it is often optimal to reduce the use of prefetching, as this can cause unnecessary accesses to memory. When the Intel compiler uses OpenMP or Auto-Parallelization, the compiler may reduce using prefetches on architectures where this is relevant.

The default switches in the Intel compiler may not yield the optimal performance or the best cache optimizations. The compiler has several features that can increase the probability that your application will perform better:

- Higher Optimization Levels (/O1,/O2,/O3)
- Vectorization (/Q[a]xP, /Q[a]xN, Q[a]xW, /Q[a]xB, /Q[a]xK)
- Inter-Procedural Optimizations (/Qipo)
- Profile Guided Optimizations (/Qprof_gen -> /Qprof_use)

Intel® Debugger

Chapter 8 covered a number of general purpose debugging techniques for multi-threaded applications. In order to provide additional help to developers Intel has developed a debugging tool appropriately named the Intel Debugger (IDB). The Intel Debugger is shipped as part of the Intel compilers. It is a full-featured symbolic source-code application debugger that helps programmers to locate software defects that result in run-time errors in their code. It provides extensive debugging support for C, C++ and Fortran, including Fortran 90. It also provides a choice of control from the command line, including both dbx and gdb modes, or from a graphical user interface, including a built-in GUI, ddd, Eclipse CDT, and Allinea DDT.

The Intel compilers enable effective debugging on the platforms they support. Intel compilers are "debugger-agnostic" and work well with native debuggers, the Intel Debugger, and selected third-party debuggers. By the same token, the Intel Debugger is compiler-agnostic and works well with native compilers, the Intel compilers, and selected third-party compilers. This results in a great deal of flexibility when it comes to mixing and matching development tools to suite a specific environment.

In addition, the Intel Debugger provides excellent support for the latest Intel processors, robust performance, superior language-feature support, including C++ templates, user-defined operators, and modern Fortran dialects (with Fortran module support); and support for Intel Compiler features not yet thoroughly supported by other debuggers.

The Intel Debugger is a comprehensive tool in general and also supports extensively for threaded applications as well. Some of the advanced capabilities of the Intel Debugger for threaded applications are:

■ Includes native threads and OpenMP threads

■ Provides an "all threads stop" / "all threads go" execution model

■ Acquires thread control on attach and at thread creation

■ Ability to list all threads and show indication of thread currently in focus

■ Set focus to a specific thread

■ Sets breakpoints and watchpoints for all threads or for a subset of all threads (including a specific thread)

■ Most commands apply to thread currently in focus or to any/all threads as appropriate

- Optional thread-specific qualifier for many commands
- Access to Thread Local Storage and Shared Local Variables

For the cluster-parallel applications, the Intel Debugger makes use of MPI including a proprietary cluster aggregation network and support for user-defined process sets that can be stopped or moved forward independently of one another.

Even though the Intel Debugger does not support examining the content of mutexes and condition variables, it can be used from the command line to call directly into native thread libraries and OpenMP libraries for more detailed information.

Intel Libraries

Libraries are an ideal way to utilize parallelism. The library writer can hide all the parallelism and the programmer can call the routines without needing to write parallel code. Intel has two libraries that implement functions that have been popular for many years, and which Intel has gradually made more and more parallel leading up to today when they are parallelized to a great extent. Both of Intel's libraries are programmed using OpenMP for their threading, and are pre-built with the Intel compilers. This is a great testimonial to the power of OpenMP, since these libraries produce exceptional performance using this important programming method.

Intel® Math Kernel Library

The Intel Math Kernel Library (Intel MKL) is a set of highly optimized routines used for mathematical problem solving. The routine are used for solving problems of computational linear algebra, performing the discrete Fourier transforms, and solving some other computation-intensive problems. The library includes routines of the BLAS, Sparse BLAS, LAPACK and ScaLAPACK packages (Fortran interfaces), sparse solver, interval linear solvers, CBLAS (C interface to BLAS routines), as well as discrete Fourier (with Cluster DFTI) and fast Fourier transform routines, vector mathematical functions, and the Vector Statistical Library (Fortran and C interfaces for random number generators and convolution/correlation mathematical operations). The library functions ensure high performance when run on Intel processors or compatible processors. Level 3 BLAS and most LAPACK routines, in particular, take advantage of multiprocessor computation through threading.

Intel MKL is threaded in a number of places: sparse solver, LAPACK (*GETRF, *POTRF, *GBTRF, *GEQRF, *ORMQR, *STEQR, *BDSQR routines), all Level 3 BLAS, Sparse BLAS matrix-vector and matrix-matrix multiply routines for the compressed sparse row and diagonal formats, and all discrete Fourier transform (DFT) routines—except 1D transformations when DFTI_NUMBER_OF_TRANSFORMS=1 and sizes are not a power-of-two, and all fast Fourier transform (FFT) routines.

Intel® Integrated Performance Primitives

The Intel Integrated Performance Primitives (Intel IPP) are a set of highly optimized routines used as the basis for much multimedia encode/decode work as well as a variety of other nonscientific problems. The routines are used for image processing, audio coding, speech coding, JPEG, video coding, speech recognition, color conversion, computer vision, data compression, signal processing, cryptography, string processing, matrix processing and vector math. The library functions ensure high performance when run on Intel processors or compatible processors. Higher level routines take advantage of multiprocessor computation through threading. Each release has a list of functions that take advantage of threading; the IPP 5.0 release, for instance, lists 563 routines that use OpenMP to offer parallelism.

Parallel Program Issues When Using Parallel Libraries

Using a parallel library from a program that expresses some parallelism itself creates a situation where some thought is required. Running a four-processor machine is most efficient if a program uses four active threads. However, if the program is actively running four threads in a parallel region, and each thread calls a library routine that in turn tries to spawn four threads, the elegance disappears and conflict arises. Therefore, it is critical that a developer understand not only the parallel nature of their application, but the underlying parallel implementation of any external libraries used in implementing that application.

If the user threads the program using OpenMP directives and uses the Intel compilers to compile the program, Intel Math Kernel Library (Intel MKL) and the user program will both use the same threading library. This solves many potential issues automatically for the user. Intel's libraries will determine if the function is called while in a parallel region in the program, and if it is, it does not spread its operations over multiple threads. However, the Intel libraries can be aware that the function is in a parallel region only if the threaded program and the library are using the same threading library. If the user program is threaded by some other means, the library may operate in multi-threaded mode and the computations may be slow or possibly corrupted. This implies that the programmer should take the following into consideration:

- If the user threads the program using OS threads (pthreads on Linux, Win32 threads on Windows), and if more than one thread calls the library, and the function being called is threaded, it is important that threading in Intel MKL be turned off. Set OMP_NUM_THREADS=1 in the environment. This is the default with Intel MKL except for sparse solver.

- If the user threads the program using OpenMP and compiles the program using a compiler other than a compiler from Intel, then the best approach is to force the library to run in serial. This case is more problematic than the previous one in that setting OMP_NUM_THREADS in the environment affects both the compiler's threading library and the threading library used by the Intel libraries. For Intel's Math Kernel Library, you set MKL_SERIAL=YES, which forces Intel MKL to serial mode regardless of OMP_NUM_THREADS value.

- If multiple programs are running on a multiple-CPU system, as in the case of a parallelized program running using MPI for communication in which each processor is treated as a node, then the threading software will see multiple processors on the system even though each processor has a separate process running on it. In this case, OMP_NUM_THREADS should be set to 1 to force serial use of the libraries and defer to the wisdom of the programmer to orchestra the system usage at a higher level.

The Future

Libraries will expand as a popular method for achieving parallelism. The need for more standardization—for compilers, users, and libraries to cooperate with regards to the creation and activation of threads—will grow. Right now, a careful programmer can pour through the documentation for libraries and compilers and sort out how to resolve potential conflicts. As time passes, we hope to see some consensus on how to solve this problem and make programming a little easier. We will see the emergence of more domain specific parallel libraries, as well as some general frameworks built around libraries.

Intel® Threading Building Blocks

Intel is developing a new approach to help developers with libraries. The Intel Threading Building Blocks are a higher-level abstraction for threaded applications that will also be understandable by analysis tools. Since the project is currently in development, consult the Intel Web site for more information on features and availability.

Intel® VTune™ Performance Analyzer

The Intel VTune Performance Analyzer is a system-wide analysis tool that offers event sampling and call graphs that include all information available broken down not only by processes/tasks, but also by the threads running within the processes. Intel Press offers a whole book on the Analyzer, which dives into its numerous capabilities. This section gives you just a flavor for the features, and highlights some of the ways the Analyzer feature can be used in the tuning of threaded applications.

Users have summed up the tool by saying that the VTune analyzer "finds things in unexpected places." Users of the VTune analyzer are enthusiastic about this tool largely because of this remarkable capability. Threading adds a dimension to already complex modern computer systems. It is no surprise when things happen on a system that cannot be easily anticipated. When you seek to refine a computer system, the best place to start is with a tool that can find these hidden problems by giving a comprehensive performance exam.

Measurements are the key to refinement. The Intel VTune Performance Analyzer is a tool to make measurements. It also has wonderful features to help you understand those measurements, and even advises you on what exceptional values may mean and what you can do about them.

Taking a close look at the execution characteristics of an application can guide decisions in terms of how to thread an application. Starting with the hotspots—the main performance bottlenecks—in the application, one can see if threading can be applied to that section of code. Hotspots are found using the event sampling features in the VTune analyzer. If the hotspot is in a location with little opportunity for parallelism, a hunt up the calling sequence will likely find better opportunities. The calling sequence can be traced back using the call-graph capability of the analyzer. Implementations of threads can be refined by looking at balance using the Samples Over Time feature and the Intel Thread Profiler in the analyzer.

Find the Hotspot

The VTune analyzer can find the modules, functions, threads and even the line of source code that consume most of the CPU cycles without requiring a special build of the application. Source code displays require a version with symbol information not stripped out—the default on Linux, and needs a special option on Windows.

Shown here in Figure 11.4 is the module view in the analyzer for Windows after collecting sampling data on the platform. It shows the majority of CPU being spent in our program. Additional mouse clicks will reveal functions and even the source code lines.

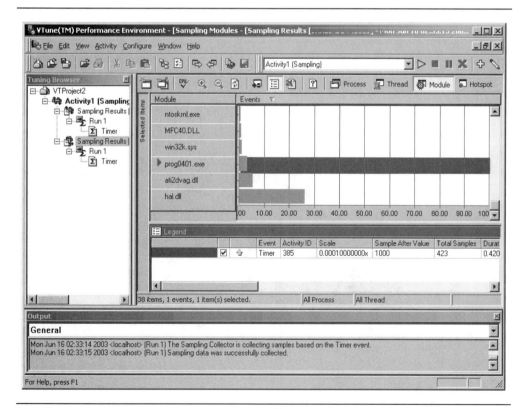

Figure 11.4   Sampling Results Using the Intel® VTune™ Performance Analyzer

If you can distribute the work currently done on one processor onto two processors, you can theoretically double the performance of an application. Amdahl's law reminds us that we cannot make a program run faster than the sequential—not written to run in parallel—portion of the application, so don't expect to leap to doubled performance every time.

Using Call Graph for Finding a Threading Point

The VTune analyzer includes a Call Graph feature to create a call graph of an application. By looking at the call graph as shown in Figure 11.5, you can find places farther up in the call tree from the hotspot in a function where it could make sense to create a thread. By rewriting a higher level location in a program to partition the work among several threads, parallel processing should improve the performance of the application.

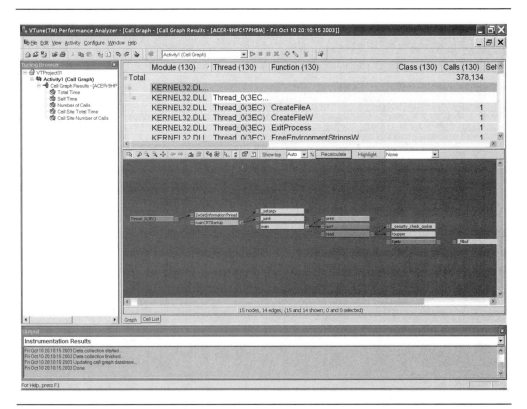

Figure 11.5 Call Graph Results, Viewed by Thread

Check the Load Balancing

How well distributed and parallelized the workload is can be examined using the VTune analyzer's Samples Over Time feature. The Samples Over Time display shows how, for a particular application, module, or thread, the time data was collected, as shown in Figure 11.6. Looking at the thread sampling data over time shows if the CPU time consumed by each thread was about the same, providing evidence of whether the workload was evenly distributed. You can also look to see if the number of samples taken by each thread was significant and in the same range.

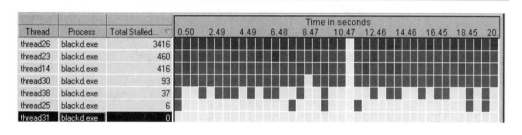

Figure 11.6   Example of a Sampling Over Time View

Intel® Thread Profiler

The Intel Thread Profiler is implemented as a view within the VTune Performance Analyzer, but it is so significant that it should be discussed as if it were an entirely separate product. Unlike the rest of the VTune analyzer, the Intel Thread Profiler is aware of synchronization objects used to coordinate threads. Coordination can require that a thread wait, so knowing about the synchronization objects allows Intel Thread Profiler to display information about wait time, or wasted time. The Intel Thread Profiler helps a developer tune for optimal performance by providing insights into synchronization objects and thread workload imbalances that cause delays along the longest flows of execution.

The Intel Thread Profiler shows an application's critical path as it moves from thread to thread, helping a developer decide how to use threads more efficiently, shown in Figure 11.7. It is able to identify synchronization issues and excessive blocking time that cause delays for Win32, POSIX threaded and OpenMP code. It can show thread workload imbalances so a developer can work to maximizes threaded application performance by maximizing application time spent in parallel regions doing real work. Intel Thread Profiler has special knowledge of OpenMP, and can graphically display the performance results of a parallel application that has been instrumented with calls to the OpenMP statistics-gathering run-time engine.

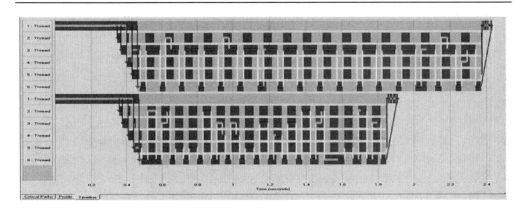

Figure 11.7 The Intel® Thread Profiler Critical Path—Timeline View

The Timeline view shows the contribution of each thread to the total program, whether on the critical path or not. The Thread Profilers also has the ability to zero in on the critical path: the Critical Paths view shows how time was spent on your program's critical path, the Profile view displays a high-level summary of the time spent on the critical path.

Using the VTune Performance Analyzer and the Intel Thread Profiler together, provide insights for a developer about threading in their applications and on their systems. Together, these analysis tools help the developer avoid searching for opportunities through trial and error by providing direct feedback.

MPI Programming

Threading is a convenient model where each thread has access to the memory of the other thread. This is portable only between shared memory machines. In general, parallel machines may not share memory between processors. While this is not the case with multi-core processors, it is important to point out that parallel programs need not be written assuming shared memory.

When shared memory is not assumed, the parts of a program communicate by passing messages back and forth. It is not important how the messages are passed; the details of the interconnect are hidden in a library. On a shared memory machine, such as a multi-core processor, this is done through shared memory. On a supercomputer with thousands of processors, it may be done through an expensive and very high speed special network. On other machines, it may be done via the local area network or even a wide area network.

In order for a message-passing program to be portable, a standard for the message passing library was needed. This formed the motivation behind the Message Passing Interface (MPI), which is the widely used standard for message passing. Many implementations exist including vendor-specific versions for their machines or interconnects. The two most widely used versions of MPI are MPICH, with roots from the earliest days of UNIX and now hosted by Argonne National Lab, and LAM/MPI, an open-source implementation hosted by Indiana University.

MPI makes possible source-code portability of message-passing programs written in C, C++, or Fortran. This has many benefits, including protecting investments in a program, and allowing development of the code on one machine such as a desktop computer, before running it on the target machine, which might be an expensive supercomputer with limited availability.

MPI enables developers to create portable and efficient programs using tightly coupled algorithms that require nodes to communicate during the course of a computation. MPI consists of a standard set of API calls that manage all aspects of communication and data transfer between processors/nodes. MPI allows the coordination of a program running as multiple processes in a distributed (not shared) memory environment, yet is flexible enough to also be used in a shared memory system such as a multi-core system.

Intel Support for MPI

Intel has both performance tuning software and its own MPI library. The library is known as the Intel MPI Library, and is not specifically for any brand of machine, or for that matter any particular interconnect. The performance tuning tool that Intel developed to support optimized MPI performance analysis is called the Intel Trace Analyzer and Collector.

Intel® MPI Library

Intel created a version of MPI that eliminates a key drawback of MPI libraries—the need to build a version of a program for each different interconnect. The Intel MPI Library is possible because the library uses the Direct Access Programming Library (DAPL) supplied by virtually every interconnect vendor, plus Intel supplies its own library for generic methods such as shared memory. This library allows a developer to create an efficient program for all platforms in a single binary by linking with one MPI that can automatically configure for the interconnect present at run time. This changes MPI from its traditional source-level compatibility only to also offer binary-level compatibility. This opens up application developers to create executables of their programs that can run on a dual-core processor desktop or a 4,096-node supercomputer, while maintaining competitive performance with the old methods of producing a separate build for each fabric.

The library offers a great deal of flexibility by allowing both users and developers to select fabrics at run time. The library supports all MPI-1 features plus many MPI-2 features, including file I/O, generalized requests, and preliminary thread support. The library is based on Argonne National Laboratory's MPICH-2 release of the MPI-2 specification.

Intel offers this library for Linux. Microsoft recently started to offer a version of an MPI library for Windows that also gives developers the ability to have a single efficient binary as well. Figure 11.8 shows how an application is linked with the Intel MPI library, which in turn accesses the DAPL layer.

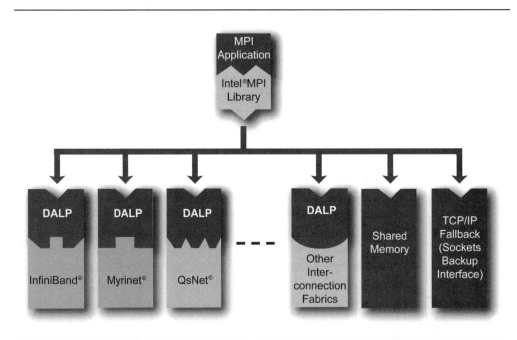

Figure 11.8　Intel® MPI Library Abstracts the DAPL-based Interconnects

Intel® Trace Analyzer and Collector

The Intel Trace Analyzer and Collector allows a developer to analyze, optimize, and deploy high-performance applications on clusters. The collector interacts with an MPI application to collect information at run time, and the analyzer is used to display the collected traces after the run to allow analysis of the information. A developer can see concurrent behavior of parallel applications through Timeline Views and Parallelism Displays, as shown in Figure 11.9. The analyzer calculates statistics for specific time intervals, processes, or functions. It also displays application activities, event source code locations, and message passing along a time axis.

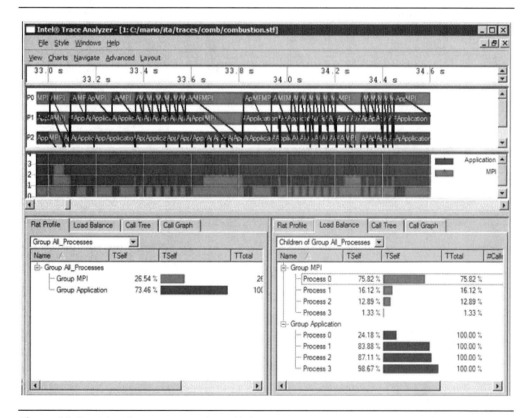

Figure 11.9   Timeline Views and Parallel Displays

Scalability is a key concern with any parallel program, and the analyzer provides views that are particularly useful for a developer seeking to enhance scalability. A user can navigate through trace data levels of abstraction: cluster, node, process, thread, and function. The Detailed and

Aggregate Views, shown in Figure 11.10, allow examination of aspects of application run-time behavior, grouped by functions or processes.

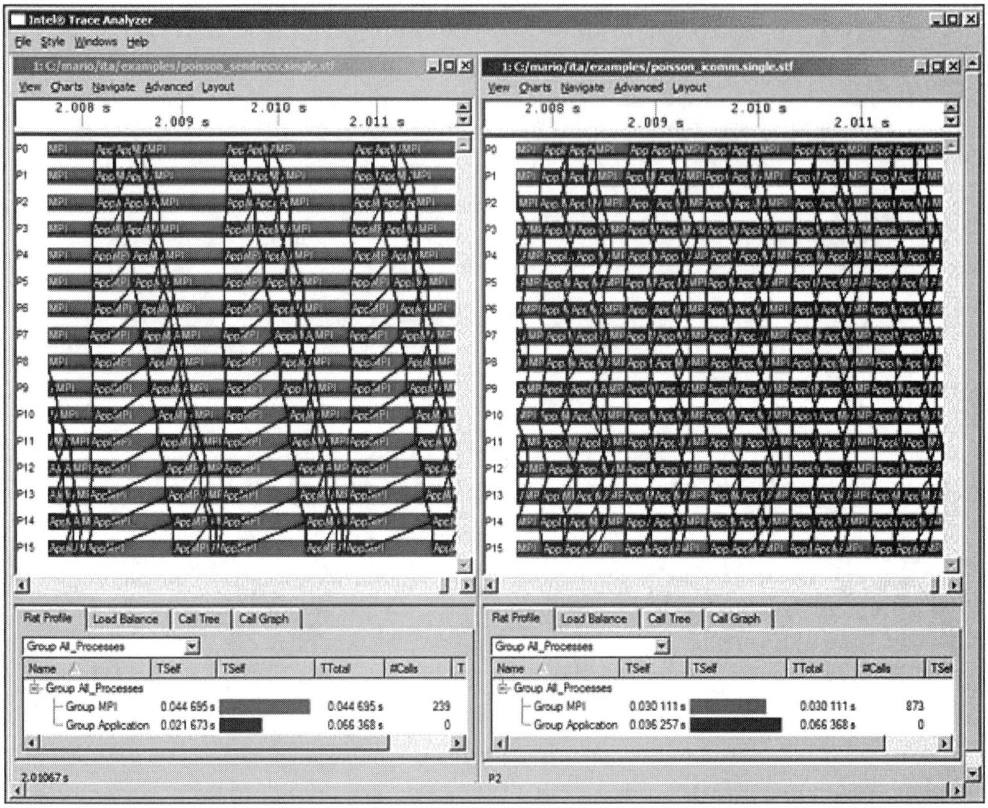

Figure 11.10   Detailed and Aggregate Views

For parallel application development on cluster systems, these offer powerful capabilities and belong in any MPI developer's toolkit. They offer a great opportunity to understand MPI application behavior, which in turns helps achieve high execution performance.

Key Points

Parallel programming is more natural than forcing our thinking into sequential code streams. Yet, the change from this type of thinking that developers have all been trained on means we all need to think differently than we have for decades.

Assistance from the makers of developer tools can help us with coding/expressing, debugging, tuning, and testing our parallel applications.

Keep the following points in mind when using Intel software development products:

- Automatic parallelization by the compiler is cheap and easy to try, and generally limited in how much it is likely to help.

- Software-based Speculative Precomputation (SSP), also known as Helper Threads, is a "preview" feature in Intel's latest compilers. SSP uses additional threads to hide memory latencies by prefetching data into cache.

- Intel Thread Checker can find errors in parallel programming even when the errors are not causing the program to fail during testing.

- Gaining insight into the actual operation of an application may be the most important way to help developers. The Intel VTune Performance Analyzer with the Intel Thread Profiler are powerful tools for gaining such insights.

- The Intel VTune Performance Analyzer provides a non-intrusive way of analyzing the performance of your application. The Intel Thread Profiler is a view within the VTune tool that allows programmers to profile multi-threaded programs.

- The Intel Math Kernel Library and the Intel Integrated Performance Primitives provide developers with high-performance routines for math and multimedia routines, respectively. Developers need to pay careful attention to the interaction between threads in their local application and how the libraries create and use threads.

- Programming using message passing, such as with MPI, can lead to highly scalable programs that can run on the largest computers as well as new multi-core processors. Support for using MPI in an application is provided by the Intel MPI Library. MPI-based applications can be optimized using the Intel Trace Analyzer and Collector.

- The Intel Debugger, included as part of the Intel compiler software distribution, provides multi-threading debugging capabilities, including support for OpenMP.

These are complex and powerful tools. Describing all the features and capabilities is beyond the scope of the book. For a more complete discussion of all the different features and capabilities please refer to the documentation included with the programs and stay up to date with the latest information, which can be found at the Intel Software Network Web site at www.intel.com/software.

Glossary

64-bit mode The mode in which 64-bit applications run on platforms with Intel® Extended Memory 64 Technology (Intel® EM64T). *See* **compatibility mode**.

advanced programmable interrupt controller (APIC) The hardware unit responsible for managing hardware interrupts on a computing platform.

aliasing A situation in which two or more distinct references map to the same address in memory or in cache.

alignment The need for data items to be located on specific boundaries in memory. Misaligned data can cause the system to hang in certain cases, but mostly it detrimentally affects performance. Padding helps keep data items aligned within aggregate data types.

architecture state The physical resources required by a **logical processor** to provide software with the ability to share a single set of physical execution resources. The architecture state consists of the general purpose CPU registers, the control registers, and the **advanced programmable interrupt controller (APIC)**. Each copy of the architecture state appears to software as a separate physical processor.

associativity The means by which a memory cache maps the main RAM to the smaller cache. It defines the way cache entries are looked up and found in a processor.

atomic Operations that are indivisible (hence, the reference to the atom), meaning that all the operations must be completed or none of them can be. Example atomic operations relevant to multi-core programming include access to shared (global) memory locations, database transactions, and any sequence of operations that, if interrupted, would leave the software or the system in an unstable or corrupted state.

barrier A synchronization mechanism that prevents forward progress by a group of threads until all threads, or in some implementations, a certain number of threads, reach the same point in their execution. Threads will block until all threads in the group, or the threshold level has been reached. Through this method, a thread from an operational set has to wait for all or some number of other threads in that set to complete in order to be able to proceed to the next execution step.

base address The starting address of a segment.

big-endian A way of storing values in memory that is favored by RISC processors. In this scheme, for example, a two-byte integer whose value is 0x0123 is stored in consecutive bytes in memory as 01 23. The big-end (the most significant bits) are stored in the lower addressed-byte, hence the name. *See* **little endian**.

cache coherency The need for caches on separate processors to contain the same values with respect to a data item that is held in the cache of more than one processor.

cache line The minimum amount of memory read by a processor from RAM into its caches. The size of a cache line can be determined by processor-specific calls. On recent IA-32 processors and those with Intel EM64T, the cache line is 128 bytes.

canonical address A memory address that uses a special format and is required for memory references. *See* **effective address**.

chip multiprocessing (CMP) A technology in which multiple processors reside on a single die, are singly packaged, and utilize a single socket of the platform.

Common Language Runtime (CLR) The virtual machine and execution layer in Microsoft's .NET environment.

coarse-grained multi-threading (Also referred to as switch-on-event multi-threading) a type of threading in which the thread has full control over processor resources for a specified threshold of timing windows or number of processor cycles.

compatibility mode The operating mode in which 32-bit applications can run on a 64-bit operating system on platforms with Intel EM64T.

concurrency The operational and execution methodology by which common resources or CPUs simultaneously execute parallel tasks or threads.

condition variable A mechanism that allows a thread to wait on some condition or event to occur. Another thread will signal the waiting thread once the condition occurs. Condition variables are almost always used in conjunction with a mutex and a Boolean expression that indicates whether or not the condition is met.

context switch The event that occurs when one thread stops executing on a given CPU and yields control of the CPU to another thread. During this event, the thread-specific state, including CPU registers, instruction pointer, and stack pointer must be saved so that the thread being evicted from the CPU may eventually be restored. This event allows multiple processes to share a single CPU resource.

control registers Registers that are used to configure hardware to operate in certain modes and perform specific actions. These registers can be read and modified only by software at the highest privilege levels, such as the operating system and device drivers.

convoying A common problem in lock-based synchronization where multiple threads are blocked from executing while waiting to acquire a shared **lock**. Convoys reduce concurrency and hence the overall performance of multi-threaded programs

core The instruction execution portion of the processor, plus the caches and interfaces to system buses.

cooperative multi-threading A form of multitasking where threads of control voluntarily give up control of the CPU to other threads. In a cooperative multi-threading scheme, threads are not pre-empted by an external entity such as the operating system.

CPUID An assembly instruction that returns information on the runtime processor. The information that it provides depends on the values of parameters passed to it in various registers. The available data is extended each time Intel modifies the processor architecture in an important way.

critical section The part of a process where multiple threads overlap, and that contains at least one shared resource that the various threads may access. Only one thread is allowed to access the critical section at any given time.

data decomposition The process of breaking down program tasks by the data they work on rather than by the nature of the task.

data-level parallelism *see* **data decomposition**.

data race A condition where multiple threads attempt to access the same memory location at the same time. In a data race, the value of the memory location is undefined and generally incorrect. Data races are generally avoided by synchronizing access to the shared memory location.

deadlock A situation in which one thread (Thread A) is waiting for a resource held by another thread (Thread B), while holding a resource that is needed by Thread B. Since Thread A and Thread B are blocked waiting for resources held by the other thread, the threads are locked and no forward progress is made.

decomposition The process of breaking programs down into a series of discrete tasks. There are three types of decomposition: functional, data, and a variant of functional decomposition, called producer/consumer.

Dekker's Algorithm A technique used in multi-threaded programming for mutual exclusion that allows two threads to share a single resource using shared memory.

double word On x86 architectures, a 32-bit data item.

dual-core is a term that describes a processor architecture in which two processor cores are placed on the same physical die.

effective address A memory address that consists of two parts: a base address and a displacement from that base address.

EM64T *See* **Intel Extended Memory 64 Technology**.

endian How numerical values are stored in bytes. *See* **big-endian** and **little-endian**.

false sharing A problem that occurs when threads on two different chips are both accessing the data item that are in the same cache line. Each access requires both processors to update their caches. If the updated item is used only by a single processor, all other processors are still forced to update their caches despite the fact they don't need to know about the change in data; hence the term, false sharing.

fence A restraining mechanism, usually an instruction, that allows synchronization among multiple attributes or actions in a system, and ensures proper memory mapping from software to hardware memory models. The fence instruction guarantees completeness of all pre-fence memory operations and halts all post-fence memory operations until the completion of fence instruction cycles.

fiber A thread that is scheduled and managed in user space. Also known as green threads, or user-level threads.

fine-grained locking An operational locking mechanism where the protection boundary is attributed to a single shared resource. Multiprocessor and real-time kernels utilize fine-grained locking. This increases concurrency in a system.

fine-grained multi-threading A type of threading in which the thread switching takes place at an instruction cycle boundary.

flow dependence A type of data dependency in which one statement depends on the value of a variable of the previous statement and there is no redefinition of the variable between these two statements, such as if a variable V is defined in statement S1 and later used at statement S2 with no redefinition of V, then there exists a flow dependency between S1 and S2.

functional decomposition A partitioning technique that subdivides a program into different tasks based on the different independent operations that it performs..

GDB (Gnu Debugger) A debugger that provides a number of capabilities for debugging POSIX threads (**Pthreads**).

GDT *See* **global descriptor table**.

general-purpose register (GPR) A register that has no function pre-assigned by the processor or the operating system. As such, GPRs can be used for whatever purpose the software needs.

global descriptor table (GDT) A system table that can hold up to 8,192 entries that describe data items, such as segments, procedure entry points, LDTs and the like. A given system must have a GDT.

GPR *See* **general-purpose register**.

hazard pointer A miniature garbage collector that handles pointers involved in compare-exchange operations; called a hazard pointer, because it presents a hazard to lockless algorithms.

horizontal multi-threading *See* **simultaneous multi-threading (SMT)**.

Hyper-Threading Technology (HT Technology) Intel's implementation of simultaneous multi-threading, in which multiple threads execute simultaneously on the same processor core.

IA (Intel architecture) The family of Intel processors to which a given chip belongs.

IA-32 (Intel architecture, 32 bits) The Intel architecture for processors whose ILP is all 32-bits. It includes Intel Pentium® 4 and Xeon® processors prior to the advent of Intel EM64T.

IA-32e (Intel architecture 32-bit extended) Shorthand for the Intel architecture mode in which the instructions for Intel EM64T are in use. It supports 32-bit software via compatibility mode and 64-bit software via 64-bit mode.

IA-32 EL (Emulation Layer) A means of executing 32-bit IA-32 code on an Intel Itanium® processor.

IA-64 (Intel architecture, 64 bits) Shorthand for the 64-bit architecture used in Intel Itanium processors.

inline C++ keyword that suggests to the compiler that it replace calls to a function with the actual executable code for the function. This step increases performance by eliminating the overhead of the function call, but it can also detrimentally affect performance if overused by increasing code size excessively.

ILP (integer-long-pointer) The programming model used by an operating system on a specific processor platform. It refers to the size in bits of the integer, long integer, and pointer data types.

Intel EM64T *See* Intel Extended Memory 64 Technology.

Intel Extended Memory 64 Technology Provides 64-bit extensions to the processor instruction set that enables IA-32e processors to execute 64-bit operating systems and applications.

IPC (inter-process communication) The methodology by which processes or computers exchange data with other processes or computers using standard protocols.

Java Virtual Machine (JVM) A software interpreter that translates precompiled Java bytecodes into machine instructions and executes them on a hardware platform.

kernel thread A thread that is managed and scheduled by the kernel. Kernel threads relieve the burden of scheduling and managing threads from the programmer; however, kernel threads may require additional overhead as they are managed by the operating system. As a result, operations on them may require a system call. Most modern operating systems have very efficient implementations that minimize this overhead, making kernel threads the preferred threading technique in most cases.

latency The preferred term for delay in the semiconductor industry.

LDT *See* **local descriptor table**

linear address An address that points to a byte in the system's linear address space. On systems that don't use paging, the linear address is the same as the physical address of the byte in RAM. On systems that do use paging, this address must be converted to an actual physical address by a series of lookups.

linear address space The memory that is addressable directly by the processor. Under normal circumstances, this space would correspond with 4 gigabytes of memory on 32-bit systems. This address space is different from the physical address space, in that an IA-32 system could be configured with less than 4 gigabytes of RAM. In such a case, its linear address space remains 4 gigabytes, but its physical address space is the lower number that corresponds to the amount of RAM physically present.

little endian A way of storing values in memory that is favored by CISC architectures, such as IA-32 processors. In this scheme, for example, a two-byte integer whose value is 0x0123 is stored in consecutive bytes in memory as 23 01 The little-end (the least important bits) are stored in the lower addressed-byte, hence the name. *See* **big endian**.

live lock The hazard status that occurs when threads continually conflict with each other and back off.

load balancing The distribution of work across multiple threads so that they all perform roughly the same amount of work.

local descriptor table A system table that can hold up to 8,192 entries. These entries describe system data items, such as segments, procedure entry points, and the like. A system can have zero or more Local Descriptor Tables.

lock A mechanism for enforcing limits on access to a shared resource in an environment that has many threads of execution. Locks are one way of enforcing concurrency control policies.

logical processor The hardware interface exposed by processors with Hyper-Threading Technology that makes it appear, from software's perspective, that multiple processors are available. This is accomplished by duplicating the **architecture state** of the processor, including the CPU register set and interrupt control logic. Logical processors share a single set of physical execution resources.

loop scheduling In OpenMP, a method of partitioning work done in a loop between multiple threads. There are four loop scheduling types, including static, dynamic, guided, and runtime.

memory cage A relaxed memory model idiom that starts with an acquire **fence** and ends in a release fence. Memory cages keep things that are inside from getting out, and not vice versa.

memory latency The delay caused by accessing RAM memory. This delay arises in large part because RAM chips run at one tenth the clock speed of most modern processors.

message A special method of communication to transfer information or a signal from one domain to another.

micro-ops The smallest executable unit of code that a processor can run. IA-32 instructions are translated into micro-ops before they are executed.

MMX™ Technology An extended instruction set introduced by Intel to improve performance in multimedia applications.

model-specific register (MSR) Special registers that vary from one processor generation to the next. They contain data items that are used by the operating system and the processor for memory management, performance monitoring, and other system functions.

monitor A simplistic, abstracted synchronization methodology that guarantees mutual exclusion of internal data and has thread synchronization capabilities. A **critical section** gets included in a monitor to allow a thread exclusive access to internal data without interference from other threads.

MSR *See* **model-specific register**.

multi-core is a term that describes a processor architecture in which two or more processor cores are placed on the same physical die.

multiple-processor system-on-a-chip *See* **chip multiprocessing (CMP)**.

multitasking A technique used by operating systems that allow users to run multiple processes, or applications, simultaneously.

multi-threading A technique used to run multiple threads of execution in a single process or application.

mutex The mechanism by which threads acquire control of shared resources. A mutex is also referred to as mutual-exclusion semaphore. A mutex has two states, locked and unlocked.

mutual exclusion A technique for synchronization among threads that limits execution in a particular **critical section** of code to a single **thread** of execution.

mutual exclusion semaphore *See* **mutex**.

.NET Microsoft's managed execution environment.

non-blocking algorithm An algorithm designed not to use locks. The defining characteristic of a non-blocking algorithm is that stopping a thread does not prevent the rest of the system from making progress.

Non-Uniform Memory Access (NUMA) An architecture that physically links two or more SMPs, where one SMP can access memory of another SMP. As the name NUMA suggests, not all processors have equal access time to the memory. When cache coherency is preserved for NUMA architecture, it is called cc-NUMA.

NUMA *See* **Non-Uniform Memory Access**.

on-chip multiprocessing *See* **chip multiprocessing (CMP)**.

OpenMP An application programming interface that provides a platform-independent set of compiler pragmas, directives, function calls, and environment variables that explicitly instruct the compiler how and where to use parallelism in an application.

padding Unused bytes placed in a structure or other aggregate data object to assure that all fields are properly aligned.

PAE *See* **physical address extensions**.

page directory base register A register that contains the base address of the system page directory. This register is generally collocated in control register CR3.

page directory entry An entry in the system's page directory table that contains detailed data about the status of a given memory page, such as whether it's present in memory, and about what access rights can be granted to it.

page directory pointer table In 64-bit mode, this second look-up table is consulted during resolution of linear addresses to physical addresses. It occurs after the PML4 and before the page directory table.

page map level 4 table The first look-up table used in resolving linear addresses in 64-bit mode to physical addresses.

page size extensions Technology that enables page sizes beyond the default 4 kilobytes. Using page size extensions, pages can be 2 megabytes or 4 megabytes.

page size extensions (36-bits) An alternative to PAE for extending addresses to 36-bits on IA-32 architectures.

parallelism The operational and execution methodology by which different resources or CPUs execute the same task simultaneously.

PDBR *See* **page directory base register**.

physical address The actual location of an item in the physical address space.

physical address extensions A method of extending 32-bit addresses to 36 bits on IA-32 architectures. On platforms with Intel EM64T, PAE enables similar extensions that are implemented differently.

physical address space The range of addresses that the processor can generate on the memory bus. Hence, it reflects the total amount of addressable physical memory on a given system.

PML4 *See* **page map level 4 table**.

POSIX thread (Pthread) A portable, standard threading API that is supported on a number of different operating systems, including many different flavors of Unix, MacOS, and Microsoft Windows.

priority ceilings A method for raising the priority of a **thread** when it acquires a lock. A priority ceiling is the maximum priority level of any thread that needs to access a **critical section** of code. The thread that acquires a lock that has a priority ceiling value immediately runs at that priority level. This technique is used to avoid the problem of **priority inversion**.

priority inheritance A method of allowing a lower priority thread to inherit the priority of a high priority thread when the low priority thread holds a lock that is needed by the high priority thread. This is commonly used to avoid the problem of **priority inversion**.

priority inversion A threading problem observed in priority based schedulers where a low priority thread holds a lock that is required by a high priority thread. Meanwhile, a medium priority thread is running, preventing the low priority thread from releasing the lock, thus starving the high priority thread. This bug was encountered on the Mars Pathfinder mission.

privilege level The level of permissible activities as enforced by the processor. Privilege level 0 is the highest level of privilege—all processor instructions can be executed at this privilege level. Most applications running on IA-32 architectures run at privilege level 3.

Certain instructions that change the way the processor functions cannot be executed from this privilege level.

preemptive multi-threading A thread-based scheduling technique where the currently running thread is stopped by an external entity, usually the operating system. The current thread loses control of the CPU, and another thread is allowed to execute. The process of switching between threads is known as a **context switching**.

prefetching Loading data items or instructions into cache prior to the processor's need for them. Prefetching prevents processor stalls by making sure that needed data is always in cache. Modern Intel IA-32 processors support prefetching in hardware and software.

process A process is a program in execution. It contains a main thread of execution, as well as an address space, and other resources allocated to it by the operating system. Processes are sometimes referred to as heavy-weight processes.

processor affinity The preference for a thread to run on a given processor.

processor order A semi-relaxed memory consistency model. This method maintains the correctness of consistency of memory read-write sequences.

producer/consumer (P/C) decomposition A common form of **functional decomposition** where the output of one task, the producer, becomes the input to another, the consumer..

PSE *See* **page size extensions**

PSE-36 *See* **page size extensions (36-bits)**

Pthread *See* **POSIX thread**

read-write lock A lock that allows simultaneous read access to multiple threads but limits the write access to only one thread.

recursive lock A lock that is called recursively by the thread that currently owns the lock.

register Registers are special, high-speed locations in the processor where data items and addresses are placed for use by the processor in executing a specific instruction.

register file The collection of all the registers available on a specific processor.

relaxed consistency A memory consistency model that maintains memory to be consistent only at certain synchronization events and ensures maintenance of memory write operations by following consistency constraints. Relaxed consistency helps reduce the cost of memory access by hiding the latency of write operations.

quadword On IA-32 architectures, a 64-bit data item.

register pressure A situation in which software requires more registers than are presently available, which leads to excess swapping of data in and out of registers, thereby reducing performance.

Savage benchmark A Fortran benchmark designed by Bill Savage to exercise a system's floating-point arithmetical capabilities.

segment A block of memory used for a discrete task by a program or the operating system.

segment descriptor An entry in a descriptor table that contains important data regarding a specific segment.

segment selector The part of a logical address that serves as a reference to a segment descriptor in a descriptor table.

serializing event An instruction or action that causes the processor to cease all speculative and out-of-order execution and discard the results of any instruction executed but not retired. The processor then resumes processing at the current instruction. These events occur because certain execution aspects, such as precision of floating-point calculations, have changed, generally at the request of the running program.

segment override The act of loading a specific value in a segment base register, rather than employing the default value. In 64-bit mode, segment overrides can be performed on the FS and GS segment registers only.

semaphore A special type of variable used for synchronization. Semaphores can only be accessed by two operations, wait and signal. A semaphore is an extension of a **mutex**, and allows more than one thread in a **critical section**.

sequential consistency When, at any given instant in time in a sequential program, memory has a well defined state.

single-issue, single-thread A baseline processor threading model that does not exploit any parallelism.

SIMD The acronym stands for "single instruction, multiple data items," a technology in which a single arithmetic operation is performed on multiple data items at one time. It is frequently useful for the arithmetic performed in multimedia and imaging applications. Intel's

Streaming SIMD Extensions (SSE) family of technologies uses SIMD extensively.

simultaneous multi-threading (SMT) A processor multi-threading model that allows threads to compete for shared available resources and enhance processor utilization.

soft affinity The policy used by Microsoft Windows to select a processor for execution of a thread. This policy suggests to the Windows scheduler that threads should, as much as possible, run on the processor on which they ran previously.

spin wait A tight or time-delayed loop-based locking mechanism used for synchronization. Spin waits allow a thread to wait for something else to happen instead of calling an interrupt.

SSE (Streaming SIMD Extensions) Extensions to IA-32 processors designed for fast performance of routine tasks, especially in multimedia and imaging applications. SSE makes extensive use of **SIMD**.

SSE2 (Streaming SIMD Extensions 2) The second generation of **SSE** instructions introduced by Intel with the Pentium 4 processor in 2001. It added support for 64-bit double-precision arithmetic and included cache management instructions, among other features.

SSE3 (Streaming SIMD Extensions 3) The third generation of **SSE** instructions introduced with the Prescott generation of Pentium 4 processors in 2004. Among other features, these 13 instructions add capabilities for performing arithmetic within a single XMM register and efficiently converting floating-point numbers to integers.

synchronization The process by which two or more threads coordinate their activities and allow threads to coexist efficiently. There are four distinct means available for synchronizing threads: mutexes, condition variables, read/write locks, and semaphores.

taskqueuing An extension to OpenMP by Intel that allows programmers to parallelize special control functions such as recursive functions, dynamic tree searches, and pointer chasing while loops.

task state segment All the data the processor needs to manage a task is stored in a special of segment, known as the task state segment.

thread The minimal schedulable execution entity. Threads contain an instruction pointer to the instruction stream that the thread executes, CPU state information, and a stack pointer. Depending on the platform, additional information may be kept by the operating system or hardware platform. Threads are sometimes called "lightweight processes."

thread pool A collection of worker **threads** that are used to perform independent units of work on demand. Thread pools reduce the overhead of thread creation/destruction.

thread safe A property of a section of code that determines whether or not multiple **threads** may simultaneously execute that block of code. A function is considered to be thread safe if and only if the function returns the proper results when multiple threads are calling the function at the same time.

thunking A form of backwards-compatibility mechanism used by Microsoft in Windows to enable older binaries to run on modern versions of Windows.

translation look-aside buffer (TLB) An on-chip cache that holds page-lookup information.

TSS *See* **task state segment**.

uniform memory access (UMA) UMA is also referred to as symmetric multiprocessor (SMP) or cache coherent UMA (CC-UMA) architecture. With UMA, all the processors are identical and have equal access time to memory. Cache Coherent means, if one processor updates a location in shared memory, all the other processors know about the update.

virtual 8086 A method of executing 16-bit programs on IA-32 processors. No longer used today, but supported on IA-32 processors for backward compatibility. It is not supported in IA-32e Compatibility mode.

virtual machine monitor (VMM) A virtualization layer between a host system and virtual machines, where the virtual machine is the container of operating systems. VMM is also referred to as a hypervisor.

word The basic, default amount of data that a given architecture uses. It is generally as wide as an integer and the size of the default address.

References

Books and Articles

Abrams, Brad. 2004. *.NET Framework Standard Library Annotated Reference, Volume 1: Base Class Library and Extended Numerics Library*. Redmond, WA: Microsoft Press.

Alagarsamy, K. 2003. Some Myths About Famous Mutual Exclusion Algorithms, *ACM SIGACT News*, Vol. 34, No. 3, September, 2003.

Andrews, Gregory R. 2000. *Foundations of Multithreaded, Parallel, and Distributed Programming*. Boston, MA: Addison-Wesley.

Ang, Boon, Derek Chiou, Larry Rudolph, and Arvind. 1996. Message Passing Support for Multi-grained, Multi-threading, and Multi-tasking Environments. MIT Laboratory for Computer Science, Computation Structures Group, Memo 394.

Barham, Paul, Boris Dragovic, Keir Fraser, Steven Hand, Tim Harris, Alex Ho, Rolf Neugebauery, Ian Pratt, and Andrew Warfield. 2003. Xen and the Art of Virtualization. University of Cambridge Computer Laboratory, 15 JJ Thomson Avenue, Cambridge, UK, CB3 0FD, SOSP'03, October 19–22, 2003, Bolton Landing, New York, USA.

Barney, Blaise. Introduction to Parallel Computing. Lawrence Livermore National Laboratory, Livermore Computing. Available at: http://www.llnl.gov/computing/tutorials/parallel_comp/.

Barney, Blaise. 2006. POSIX Threads Programming. Lawrence Livermore National Laboratory. Available at: http://www.llnl.gov/computing/tutorials/pthreads/

Blumofe, Robert D., Christopher F. Joerg, Bradley C. Kuszmaul, Charles E. Leiserson, Keith H. Randall, and Yuli Zhou. 1995. Cilk: An Efficient Multithreaded Runtime System. *Proceedings of the 5th ACM SIGPLAN Symposium on Principles and Practice of Parallel Programming* (July):207–216.

Brinch Hansen, Per. 1972. Structured Multiprogramming. *Communications of the ACM*, 15(7):574–578.

Bulpin, James Roy. 2004. Operating System Support for Simultaneous Multithreaded Processors. PhD thesis, King's College, University of Cambridge, September.

Butenhof, David R. 1997. *Programming with POSIX^t Threads.* Boston, MA: Addison-Wesley Professional.

Chandra, Rohit, Leonardo Dagum, Dave Kohr, Dror Maydan, Jeff McDonald, and Ramesh Menon. 2001. *Parallel Programming in OpenMP.* San Francisco, CA: Morgan Kaufmann Publishers.

Culler, David E., Jaswinder Pal Singh. 1999. *Parallel Computer Architecture – A Hardware/Software Approach.* San Francisco, CA: Morgan Kaufmann.

Dijkstra, Edsger W. 1968. The Structure of the "THE" Multiprogramming System. *Communications of the ACM*, 11(5):341–346.

Frigo, Matteo and Steven G. Johnson. 1997. Fastest Fourier Transform in the West. Massachusetts Institute of Technology. Technical Report MIT-LCS-TR-728 (September).

Garcia-Rosello, Emilio, Jose Ayude, J. Baltasar Garcia Perez-Schofield, and Manuel Perez-Cota. 2002. Design Principles for Highly Reusable Concurrent Object-Oriented Systems. Computer Sciences Department, University of Vigo, Spain. Vol. 1, No. 1, May-June.

Gerber, Richard, Aart J. C. Bik, Kevin B. Smith, and Xinmin Tian. 2006. *The Software Optimization Cookbook, Second Edition.* Hillsboro, OR: Intel Press.

Goodman, James R., Mary K. Vernon, and Philip J. Woest. 1989. Efficient Synchronization Primitives for Large-Scale Cache-Coherent Multiprocessors. ACM, 1989 0-89791-300-0/89/0004/0064

Grama, Ananth, Anshul Gupta, George Karypis, and Vipin Kumar. 2003. *Introduction to Parallel Computing.* Boston, MA: Addison-Wesley.

Hennessy, John L. and David A. Patterson. 2003 *Computer Architecture – A Quantitative Approach.* San Francisco, CA: Morgan Kaufmann.

Hill, Mark D. 1998. Multiprocessors Should Support Simple Memory Consistency Models. *IEEE Computer* (August), 31(8):28–34.

Hoare, C.A.R. 1974. Monitors: An Operating System Structuring Concept. *Communications of the ACM*, 17(10):549–557.

Holt, Bill. 2005. Moore's Law, 40 years and Counting – Future Directions of Silicon and Packaging. InterPACK '05, Heat Transfer Conference.

Holub, Allen. 2000. *Taming Java Threads.* Berkeley, CA: Apress.

Hughes, Cameron and Tracey Hughes. 2004. *Dividing C++ Programs into Multiple Threads.* Boston, MA: Addison Wesley.

Intel Corporation. 2003. *Intel® Hyper-Threading Technology, Technical User's Guide.* Santa Clara, CA: Intel Corporation.

_____. 2005. IA-32 *Intel Architecture Optimization Reference Manual.* Available at: http://www.intel.com/

_____. 2006a. *Intel Itanium Architecture Software Developer's Manual, Volume 1: Application Architecture, Volume 2: System Architecture, Volume 3: Instruction Set Reference.* Available at: http://www.intel.com/

_____. 2006b. *IA-32 Intel Architecture Software Developers' Manual, Volume 1: Basic Architecture, Volume 2A-2B: Instruction Set Reference, Volume 3: System Programming Guide.* Available at: http://www.intel.com/

_____. 2006c. Intel Processor Identification and the CPUID Instruction, Application Note 485. Available at: http://www.intel.com/

Kleiman, Steve, Devang Shah, and Bart Smaalders. 1996. *Programming with Threads.* Upper Saddle River, NJ: Prentice Hall.

Kongetira, Poonacha, Kathirgamar Aingaran, and Kunle Olukotun. 2005. Niagara: A 32-way Multithreaded SPARC Processor. *IEEE Micro* (March/April), 25(2):21–29.

Kubiatowicz, John David. 1998. Integrated Shared-Memory and Message-Passing Communication in the Alewife Multiprocessor. PhD Thesis, Massachusetts Institute of Technology, February.

Lea, Doug. 1997. *Concurrent Programming in Java – Design Principles and Patterns*. Boston, MA: Addison-Wesley.

Lo, Jack L., Susan J. Eggers, Joel S. Emer, Henry M. Levy, Rebecca L. Stamm, and Dean M. Tullsen. 1997. Converting Thread-Level Parallelism to Instruction-Level Parallelism via Simultaneous Multithreading. *ACM Transactions on Computer Systems*, Vol. 15, No. 3, August,

Mattson, Tim. Nuts and Bolts of Multithreaded Programming. Santa Clara, CA: Intel Corporation. Available at: http://www.intel.com.

Mattson, Tim, Beverly Sanders, and Berna Massingill. 2004. *Patterns for Parallel Programming*. Boston, MA: Addison-Wesley Professional.

Michael, Maged. 2004. Hazard Pointers: Safe Memory Reclamation for Lock-Free Objects. *IEEE Transactions on Parallel and Distributed Systems* (June), 15(6):491–504.

Nutt, Gary J. 2000. *Operating Systems – A Modern Perspective*. Boston, MA: Addison-Wesley.

Redstone, Joshua A., Susan J. Eggers, and Henry M. Levy. 2000. An Analysis of Operating System Behavior on a Simultaneous Multithreaded Architecture. *Proceedings of the 9th International Conference on Architectural Support for Programming Languages and Operating Systems,* November.

Reek, Kenneth A. 2002. The Well-Tempered Semaphore: Theme with Variations. *ACM SIGCSE Bulletin* (March), 34(1):356–359.

Reeves, Glenn E. 1998. "Re: What Really Happened on Mars?" *Risks-Forum Digest* (January), 19(58).

Seng, John S., Dean M. Tullsen, and George Z. N. Cai. 2000. Power-Sensitive Multithreaded Architecture. *IEEE*, 0-7695-0801-4/00

Shen, John Paul and Mikko H. Lipasti. 2005. Modern Microprocessor Design – Fundamentals of Superscalar Processors. New York: McGraw-Hill.

Smith, James E. and Ravi Nair. 2005. *Virtual Machines – Versatile Platforms for Systems and Processes*. San Francisco, CA: Morgan Kaufmann.

Stokes, Jon. 2002. Introduction to Multithreading, Superthreading and Hyperthreading. *Ars Technica*, October.

Sutter, Herb and James Larus. 2005. Software and the Concurrency Revolution. *Microprocessor*, Vol. 3, No. 7, September.

Ungerer, Theo, Borut Robič, and Jurij Šilc. 2003. A Survey of Processors with Explicit Multithreading. *ACM Computing Surveys*, Vol. 35, No. 1, March.

Vahalia, Uresh. 1995. *UNIX Internals: The New Frontiers*. Upper Saddle River, NJ: Prentice Hall.

Wadleigh, Kevin R. and Isom L. Crawford. 2000. *Software Optimization for High Performance Computing*. Indianapolis, IN: Prentice Hall PTR.

Wisniewski, Robert W., Leonidas I. Kortothanassis, and Michael L. Scott. 1995. High Performance Synchronization Algorithms for Multiprogrammed Multiprocessors. Department of Computer Science, University of Rochester, Rochester, NY.

Tools and Web Sites

Cluster computing resources: http://www.buyya.com/cluster/

Intel Software Web site: http://www.intel.com/software/

Message Passing Interface (MPI) Forum: http://www.mpi-forum.org

Message Passing Interface (MPI) training: http://www.mhpcc.edu/training/workshop/mpi/

POSIX Threads Programming. Lawrence Livermore National Laboratory: http://www.llnl.gov/computing/hpc/training/

pthreads-win32. An open source version of Pthreads for Windows. The library is actively maintained and is under the stewardship of Red Hat, Inc: http://sourceware.org/pthreads-win32/

Index

66 *As the pace of technology introduction increases, it's difficult to keep up. Intel Press has established an impressive portfolio. The breadth of topics is a reflection of both Intel's diversity as well as our commitment to serve a broad technical community.*

I hope you will take advantage of these products to further your technical education. **99**

Patrick Gelsinger
Senior Vice President
Intel Corporation

**Turn the page to learn about titles
from Intel Press for system developers**

Get the most out of IA-32 platforms

The Software Optimization Cookbook, Second Edition

High-Performance Recipes for IA-32 Platforms

By Richard Gerber, Aart J.C. Bik, Kevin B. Smith, and Xinmin Tian

ISBN 0-9764832-1-1

The Software Optimization Cookbook

Optimization Cookbook

High-Performance Recipes for IA-32 Platforms

Richard Gerber, Aart J.C. Bik, Kevin B. Smith, and Xinmin Tian

Second Edition

Intel PRESS

Books by Engineers, for Engineers

(intel)

The Software Optimization Cookbook, Second Edition, provides updated recipes for high-performance applications on Intel platforms. Through simple explanations and examples, four experts show you how to address performance issues with algorithms, memory access, branch prediction, automatic vectorization, SIMD instructions, multiple threads, and floating-point calculations.

Software developers learn how to take advantage of Intel® Extended Memory 64 Technology (Intel® EM64T), multi-core processing, Hyper-Threading Technology, OpenMP†, and multimedia extensions. This book guides you through the growing collection of software tools, compiler switches, and coding optimizations, showing you efficient ways to improve the performance of software applications for Intel platforms.

❝ This book simplifies the task for engineers who strive to develop high-performance software...❞

Lars Petter Endresen,
Doctor of Engineering, Physics,
Scandpower Petroleum Technology

Highlights include:

- Automatic vectorization and hints on how to guide the compiler
- Compiler support for multi-threading
- The performance impacts of shared L2 and L3 caches
- Loop optimizations and when to use the compiler for performance gain
- Use of intrinsics to exploit SIMD

Software developers who want to understand the latest techniques for delivering more performance and to fine-tune their coding skills will benefit from this book.

● Programming with Intel® Extended Memory 64 Technology
Migrating Software for Optimal 64-bit Performance

By Andrew Binstock

ISBN 0-9764832-0-3

A veteran technology analyst helps programmers fully capitalize on 64-bit processing capabilities for the desktop while ensuring full compatibility with current 32-bit operating systems and applications. Through examples written in C, this concise book explains how you can enjoy the flexibility to move to 64-bit computing and achieve better performance when working with large datasets.

❝ This book is really practical and useful. It thoroughly covers the depth of the technology...❞

*Oleksiy Danikhno,
Director, Application
Development and Architecture
A4Vision, Inc.*

● VTune™ Performance Analyzer Essentials
Measurement and Tuning Techniques for Software Developers

By James Reinders

ISBN 0-9743649-5-9

The Intel® VTune™ Performance Analyzer "illuminates" your system and everything running on it. This book is a guide for software application developers, software architects, quality assurance testers, and system integrators who wish to use the VTune analyzer to take the guesswork out of software tuning.

❝ A comprehensive approach to increasing software productivity...❞

*Malik S. Maxutov,
Professor and Senior Lecturer,
Moscow State Geological
Prospecting University*

Intel® Integrated Performance Primitives

*How to Optimize Software Applications
Using Intel® IPP*

By Stewart Taylor

ISBN 0-9717861-3-5

The lead developer of the Intel® Integrated Performance
Primitives (Intel® IPP) explains how this library gives you
access to advanced processor features without having to
write processor-specific code. This introduction to Intel IPP
explores the range of possible applications, from audio processing to graphics and video. Extensive examples written in
C++ show you how to solve common imaging, audio/video,
and graphics problems.

*66 Filled with
comprehensive
real-world
examples...99*

Davis W. Frank,
Software Program Manager,
palmOne, Inc.

The Software Vectorization Handbook

*Applying Multimedia Extensions
for Maximum Performance*

By Aart J.C. Bik

ISBN 0-9743649-2-4

This book provides a detailed overview of compiler optimizations that convert sequential code into a form that exploits
multimedia extensions. The primary focus is on the C programming language and multimedia extensions to the Intel®
architecture, although most conversion methods are easily
generalized to other imperative programming languages and
multimedia instruction sets.

*66 Rarely have I
seen a book of such
a great value to
compiler writers
and application
developers alike...99*

Robert van Engelen,
Professor,
Florida State University

Special Deals, Special Prices!

To ensure you have all the latest books
and enjoy aggressively priced discounts,
please go to this Web site:

www.intel.com/intelpress/bookbundles.htm

Bundles of our books are available,
selected especially to address the needs
of the developer. The bundles place
important complementary topics at
your fingertips, and the price for a
bundle is substantially less than
buying all the books individually.

About Intel Press

Intel Press is the authoritative source of timely, technical books
to help software and hardware developers speed up their development
process. We collaborate only with leading industry experts to deliver
reliable, first-to-market information about the latest
technologies, processes, and strategies.

Our products are planned with the help of many people in the developer
community and we encourage you to consider becoming a customer advisor.
If you would like to help us and gain additional advance insight to the latest
technologies, we encourage you to consider the Intel Press Customer
Advisor Program. You can register here:

www.intel.com/intelpress/register.htm

For information about bulk orders or corporate sales, please send e-mail to
bulkbooksales@intel.com

Other Developer Resources from Intel

At these Web sites you can also find valuable technical information
and resources for developers:

developer.intel.com	general information for developers
www.intel.com/software	content, tools, training, and the Intel® Early Access Program for software developers
www.intel.com/software/products	programming tools to help you develop high-performance applications
www.intel.com/netcomms	solutions and resources for networking and communications
www.intel.com/technology/itj	Intel Technology Journal
www.intel.com/idf	worldwide technical conference, the Intel Developer Forum

Intel
PRESS

About the Authors

Shameem Akhter is a platform architect at Intel, focusing on single socket multi-core architecture and performance analysis. He has also worked as a senior software engineer with the Intel Software and Solutions Group, designing application optimizations for desktop and server platforms. Shameem holds a patent on a threading interface for constraint programming, developed as a part of his master's thesis in computer science.

Jason Roberts is a senior software engineer at Intel Corporation. Over the past 10 years, Jason has worked on a number of different multi-threaded software products that span a wide range of applications targeting desktop, handheld, and embedded DSP platforms.

Major Contributors

James Reinders is a senior engineer who joined Intel in 1989 and has contributed to projects including the world's first TeraFLOP supercomputer, as well as compilers and architecture work for Intel processors. He is currently director of business development and marketing for Intel's Software Development Products group and serves as the chief evangelist and spokesperson. James is also the author of the book *VTune™ Performance Analyzer Essentials*.

Arch D. Robison has been a Principle Engineer at Intel since 2000. Arch received his Ph.D. in computer science from the University of Illinois. Prior to his work at Intel, Arch worked at Shell on massively parallel programs for seismic imaging. He was lead developer for the KAI C++ compiler and holds five patents on compiler optimization.

Xinmin Tian holds a Ph.D. in computer science and leads an Intel development group working on exploiting thread-level parallelism in high-performance Intel C++ and Fortran compilers for Intel Itanium, IA-32, Intel EM64T, and multi-core architectures. Xinmin is a co-author of *The Software Optimization Cookbook, 2nd Edition*.

Sergey Zheltov is a project manager and senior software engineer at the Advanced Computer Center of Intel's Software Solutions Group. He holds an M.S. degree in theoretical and mathematical physics. Sergey's research includes parallel software and platform architecture, operating systems, media compression and processing, signal processing, and high-order spectra.

IMPORTANT

You can access the companion Web site for this book
on the Internet at:

www.intel.com/intelpress/mcp

Use the serial number located in the upper-right hand
corner of this page to register your book and access
additional material, including all code examples and
pointers to development resources.